Critical Essays on
WILLIAM SAROYAN

CRITICAL ESSAYS
ON
AMERICAN LITERATURE

James Nagel, General Editor
University of Georgia, Athens

Critical Essays on

WILLIAM SAROYAN

edited by

HARRY KEYISHIAN

G. K. Hall & Co.
An Imprint of Simon & Schuster Macmillan
New York

Prentice Hall International
London   Mexico City   New Delhi   Singapore   Sydney   Toronto

G. K. Hall & Co.
An Imprint of Simon & Schuster Macmillan
866 Third Avenue
New York, New York 10022

Library of Congress Cataloging-in-Publication Data

Critical essays on William Saroyan / edited by Harry Keyishian.
    p. cm.—(Critical essays on American literature)
  Includes bibliographical references and index.
  ISBN 0-7838-0018-5
  1. Saroyan, William, 1908– —Criticism and interpretation.
I. Keyishian, Harry. II. Series.
PS3537.A826Z626 1995
818'.5209—dc20   94-48129
                                                      CIP

10   9   8   7   6   5   4   3   2   1

Printed in the United States of America

Contents

◆

ARTICLES

General Editor's Note

◆

This series seeks to anthologize the most important criticism on a wide variety of topics and writers in American literature. Our readers will find in various volumes not only a generous selection of reprinted articles and reviews but original essays, bibliographies, manuscript sections, and other materials brought to public attention for the first time. This volume, *Critical Essays on William Saroyan*, is the most comprehensive collection of essays ever published on one of the most important modern writers in the United States. It contains both a sizable gathering of early reviews and a broad selection of more recent scholarship as well. Among the authors of reprinted articles and reviews are Stark Young, Edmund Wilson, James H. Justus, Lorne Shirinian, and Thelma J. Shinn. In addition to a preface by Harry Keyishian and a substantial introduction by Alice K. Barter, there are also four original essays commissioned specifically for publication in this volume—new studies by Dickran Kouymjian on Whitman and Saroyan, Edward Halsey Foster on the influence of Gertrude Stein, Walter Cummins on the challenges facing Saroyan's characters, and Walter Shear on the theme of death in Saroyan's works. We are confident that this book will make a permanent and significant contribution to the study of American literature.

JAMES NAGEL
University of Georgia, Athens

Publisher's Note

◆

Producing a volume that contains both newly commissioned and reprinted material presents the publisher with the challenge of balancing the desire to achieve stylistic consistency with the need to preserve the integrity of works first published elsewhere. In the Critical Essays series, essays commissioned especially for a particular volume are edited to be consistent with G. K. Hall's house style; reprinted essays appear in the style in which they were first published, with only typographical errors corrected. Consequently, shifts in style from one essay to another are the result of our efforts to be faithful to each text as it was originally published.

Preface

HARRY KEYISHIAN

In the edition of the journal *Stamps* for 11 May 1991, it was reported that millions of William Saroyan stamps—featuring the author in middle age, with flowing mustache and laureate locks—had to be destroyed because the faulty machine that produced them did not "allow the perforation holes to meet evenly at the intersections."[1] At the celestial writing desk where he now sits, doing his daily timed typing, Saroyan must have enjoyed a good laugh over this incident. "See? They couldn't keep me within bounds when I was alive, and they still can't," he might have said.

His pride would be justified in part. The clamorous subjectivity and spontaneity that gained him a permanent place in American letters also had their negative side effects of self-absorption and lack of focus, which ultimately separated him from the literary mainstream and left him only his own, increasingly isolated corner in which to operate. That he endured as an artist, and persevered as a writer day-by-day, testifies to his phenomenal creative energies.

Certainly the force of his originality should not be underestimated. When he struck fire, in his own mode, there was no one to match him. Many have tried to be "Saroyanesque," thinking it easy and "natural," and come off lamely; only the real guy could do the real thing. Saroyan seems to be one of those writers whom readers find and cherish spontaneously, without coaching from the literary or academic establishments. Some will discover him when young and then pass on to different fare as they grow; others will come upon him in their maturity and perceive a fresh and welcome voice missing from the spectrum of their reading experience. Always, they will know that there is no one quite like him.

It is customary to say that William Saroyan burst upon the American literary scene with the publication of his short story "The Daring Young

Man on the Flying Trapeze" in *Story* magazine in 1934. That certainly was a spectacular start, but it put a lot of pressure on the young author to top himself and was followed by predictions that such an undisciplined character could not sustain his success. It is therefore fascinating to watch him move restlessly from subject to subject, and from form to form, finding ways not only to endure as an artist, but to confound those who prematurely declared his career finished. Winning the Pulitzer Prize for *The Time of Your Life* was one such victory (though he rejected the award, and the $1,000 that went with it, on the grounds that commerce should not subsidize art and that he already had $1,000); producing the delightful *My Name is Aram* was another. Both triumphs took place in 1940, a year that I think marks the high point of his achievement. But though the war and the challenges of artistic maturity broke him as a serious writer of fiction or drama—*The Adventures of Wesley Jackson* (1946) was a catastrophic failure on both artistic and moral grounds— he found the resources to continue producing work of value in the personal writing styles he adopted later in his life.

This collection of essays aims to shed light on Saroyan's achievement by suggesting the rich variety of responses his work has elicited. The postmodern sensibility no longer expects literary texts to sit still so they can be definitively categorized and objectively interpreted and instead prizes them for their openness, their capacity to engage a range of readerly needs and receptive strategies. It has become less important to discover the "real" identities of authors or the "true" meaning of their texts than to find out who we as readers become when we encounter them. To this end, I have deliberately included multiple and conflicting essays on some of Saroyan's key works in order to emphasize their capacity to generate varieties of responses.

With those interests in mind, and in keeping with the aims of this series, I was determined to exclude biographical accounts of Saroyan and to select and solicit essays that focused on his writing rather than his life. Though biography can be interesting and important—a literary voice like Saroyan's is cherished because it articulates experience, and the sources of that experience are fair game for analysis—biography is irrelevant when deciding whether an author is worth reading or when identifying the salient qualities of his or her writing.

The flaw in my plan, evident to anyone who has read Saroyan, is that he refuses the distinction between art and life. Only rarely, and then in uncharacteristic and usually less interesting productions, does he refrain from identifying his historical, material being with his literary voice. This voice does not seem to me the same as the narrative personae of, say, Fielding or Dickens—those invented identities through which the writing person addresses the reader—but rather represents an attempt, and a need, to be humanly, historically present in the writing. In the autobiographical books that largely occupied the last twenty years of Saroyan's productive life he allowed only that voice to be heard, and only his own experience to be evoked; pretty much the same must be said of the many conversational plays he wrote during the same period. Whether this strategy represented the last desperate shift of a depleted writer or the happy recuperation of his authentic talent is a question in part answered by some of the essays that follow. He was a man in whom forces of idealism and pragmatism, hope and despair, unity and chaos, and—yes—love and hate continually collided, and this collision, as Stephen Calonne has ably shown in his study of Saroyan,[2] provided the energies of his productions.

I regret that more could not be done with Saroyan's correspondence, an important aspect of his writing that has been virtually ignored. Leo Hamalian had, at my request, contributed a short piece on the letters, but because the Saroyan Foundation has made it difficult to quote directly from the letters, he could not really do them justice, and in the end we had to exclude the piece. As the fortunate recipient of a number of letters from Saroyan, I regret that we could not convey here their special qualities. When writing letters at large, for publication—even in a vigorous work like *Letters from 74 rue Taitbout* (1969)—he could get somewhat grandiose and dissipate his energies. When addressing a specific reader's questions, problems, comments, or opinions, he was, while still recognizably the Saroyan of his public writing, always on target, responsive, encouraging, and pragmatic. I do not say that his letters reveal, at last, the "true" Saroyan—nor, as I said above, would that matter for my purposes here—but they do occupy an underappreciated place in the spectrum of his work, and, properly understood, might influence the way we perceive the rest. Readers can glimpse something of this aspect of Saroyan's writings in the samplings of correspondence to be found in the September 1981 issue of the *Armenian Review* (The Saroyan Memorial Issue) and in the Spring 1984 issue of *Ararat*, which also contains an insightful account of Saroyan's correspondence by author Jules Archer.[3]

A word should be said about Saroyan and ethnicity. He frequently reminds the reader of his Armenian descent; it is certainly important to consider his ethnic identity when assessing him as a writer. The danger is that this aspect of his talent, overly stressed, may have the effect of further isolating him from the wider context of American literature and culture. It would be a shame if he became the cherished object of attention only of those of Armenian heritage, for his appeal was always greater than that; through his ethnicity he sought and preached a universalism that we need more than ever in a world of continuing regional and ethnic violence. Being Armenian was the beginning, but hardly the end, of his human identity and his artistic vision.

Normally the editor of a volume in the *Critical Essays* series is required to produce an introductory essay outlining the history of reception and criticism on his or her subject. I was spared that duty when I learned of Alice Barter's survey of Saroyan criticism, which she generously permitted me to use here. She has covered an enormous amount of ground in detailing the history of Saroyan's literary fortunes and reception.

Also requiring explanation is the absence from this volume of any contribution from Nona Balakian, an insightful and perceptive critic of his work during her many years at the *New York Times Book Review*. Her own study of Saroyan, almost completed at her death in 1990, will be published in the near future, and she did not want to have any of her work excerpted before its appearance in book form. I did consider using one of her published essays, "The World of William Saroyan," written in the late 1970s, but that was recently reprinted in Edward Halsey Foster's *William Saroyan: A Study of the Short Fiction*, a volume in Twayne's *Studies in Short Fiction* series whose contents I have avoided duplicating here. Rather than omit her voice completely, I would like to recapitulate briefly her acute contributions to the study of Saroyan's work over the years.

Even when critical of Saroyan's writing, Balakian stressed its positive elements and tendencies, thereby filling the role of coach as well as commentator. Discussing the text of Saroyan's play *Get Away Old Man* in the edition of the *New York Times Book Review* for 30 July 1944, perhaps her first published comments on the author, she acknowledges the faults of this failed dramatic assault on Hollywood's corruption of the artist—a work "with a mere indication of a plot, too much talk and characters with nowhere to go"—but offers the hope that the play might mark a transition in Saroyan's playwriting career towards a more uncompromising, critical view of experience. Though she expresses admiration for the spirit of the earlier *My Heart's in the Highlands*, she also criticizes its confused symbolism and its author's seemingly deliberate effort "always to get away from the definite, the particular." By contrast, *Get Away Old Man* "suggests a new Saroyan come down to earth. If only," she wishes, "he can hold on at the same time to the old poetry and magic, he and the theatre should get along better than before."[4]

Discussing several Saroyan works in the 5 August 1950 *New Republic*, Balakian is very critical of *The Twin Adventures* (consisting of the combined texts of his war novel *The Adventures of Wesley Jackson* and the diary Saroyan kept while writing it). Finding the diary "colorless," she remarks upon the failure of Saroyan's persistent but ineffectual efforts to make himself understood there: "The more he has tried to explain his work, the more he has revealed his lack of self-awareness as a writer." Nevertheless, she found the other books under review, *The Assyrian and Other Stories* and *Don't Go Away Mad and Other Plays*, much more satisfactory; in both "the real Saroyan comes through far more clearly." Specifically, she picks up on Saroyan's remark that "[e]verything I write, everything I have ever written, is allegorical," finding in it a challenge to "the two most frequent objections of his critics: his childlike denial of evil and his totally unrealistic approach to characterization."

Applying this insight, she seeks a better understanding of Saroyan's artistic vision. She notes that allegory does not pretend to show all of reality "but only to illumine one aspect of it"—in Saroyan's case, the human capacity for good. Allegory also vindicates Saroyan's supposedly faulty mode of characterization, for it does not aim to draw rounded characters, but only "to present various facets of humanity."

These problems afflict his plays more than his stories, in which he displays "a new desperate awareness of human loneliness and impotence." In *The Assyrian and Other Stories*, Saroyan's "beautiful people" are "no longer talking poetry and singing hymns of joy; they are more knowing, more 'adult,' the magic all drawn out of them by success or failure and an urban-induced isolation." As a result, Saroyan's concept of goodness, "once synonymous with love and gratitude, has become linked with man's tenacity, his will to live."[5]

Balakian takes up Saroyan again in the pamphlet *A New Accent in American Fiction: The Armenian-American Writer* (1958). Again seeking to address both his failings and his strengths, she notes Saroyan's "anxiety to discover himself as a writer," dating from his earliest days, and concludes that "he never fully developed a style that could convey the more enduring things he had to say—what one might call the essential Saroyan."[6] He was most successful, Balakian feels, when writing about children, the kind "only Saroyan knows how to write—children so completely childlike they can take or leave reality at will." Indeed, she describes him as "the writer par excellence of childhood" (11).

His other great contribution to literature, she writes, is as "a playwright whose daring experiments in the theatre give promise of still greater achievements to come" (11). These experiments, she feels, are indebted to the allegorical morality plays of medieval Europe, from which they borrow an "indifference to realistic, logical action." In Saroyan, "A character is never himself alone but an aspect of humanity, not an individual with a particular destiny but the essence of a human being with only one possible destiny—living and dying" (12). By the same token, "a situation is never simply happening . . . but a symbolic representation of ultimate human relationships" (12). Unless we understand this aspect of Saroyan's dramatic art, the plays "seem pretty ridiculous and meaningless" (12). The problem with *The Time of Your Life*, she writes, is too much individualization in his characterizations.

In her essay "The World of William Saroyan" (1978), Balakian praises the longevity and achievement of Saroyan's career. In his current mood, she finds him "a new kind of mystic, a free spirit who knows life's true worth and has retained his zest for doing what he can to cause it to be revealed."[7] Still stressing his success in conveying childhood states and the role of allegory in his work, she notes the essential humanism of his writing and the close relationship between his life and his work. He wanted to change the world, she said, not through politics but through his writing, by reminding his readers of their humanity. She concludes that, "[i]n William

Saroyan's world, the fact and the fiction have merged. His own truest convert, he earnestly—and joyously—continues to make it *a place which can be inhabited*" (176).

Her conclusion was anticipated by the distinguished critic Alfred Kazin, who, reviewing *The Human Comedy* in the 1 March 1943 issue of the *New Republic*, compared William Saroyan to a Hungarian cymbalon. Kazin reports that he had, not long before, heard "a wonderful man who played wonderfully" on that zitherlike musical instrument at a café in New York, and to him the experience suggested Saroyan's place in American literature: "The cymbalon is never admitted into the orchestra, but when people are together late at night, and there is a feeling of peace in the air, it can sing very powerfully to the human ear." It is "no doubt an inferior instrument, too exclusively personal," he concedes, but "it has remarkable characteristics— it plays heart throbs. Its tremolo is fantastic; the air shivers with it." And when the cymbalon player sings of love, "[a]t that moment, he means it, with the cymbalon throbbing before him. At that moment he really means it."[8] If Saroyan is the laureate of evanescent moods, so be it; even if he never gets into the orchestra, he has a lovely solo career and continues to find readers and audiences who will cherish his special qualities.

When selecting material for this volume I sought reviews and essays that applied a range of critical methodologies to Saroyan's work. As the selection reprinted here shows, reviewers seemed unusually concerned about making sure that he did not squander his gifts. It is as if they recognized a special but vulnerable talent in him toward which they felt protective. The selection begins with an introduction in which Alice K. Barter organizes critical responses to Saroyan into useful categories and provides a sense of his shifting fortunes over time. Margaret Bedrosian brings the influence of geography and culture to bear on the understanding of Saroyan's fiction, with particular focus on the early stories. James H. Justus, countering the attacks made on Saroyan for his lack of political engagement, takes note of the broader contributions the author made in affirming the human spirit. Dickran Kouymjian, Saroyan's friend, editor, expositor, and champion, draws parallels between Saroyan and his spiritual predecessor, Walt Whitman. Supplementing his earlier study of Saroyan's short fiction,[9] Edward Halsey Foster comments on Saroyan's connections both to Whitman and to Gertrude Stein. Also focusing on the early fiction, Walter Shear, in the first of two contributions to this collection, argues that Saroyan is "essentially a modernist in that he regards his fictional reality as multifaceted and that his awareness of the claims of the ethnic community pushed him in this direction."

Thelma Shinn's 1972 essay contributes valuably to the understanding of Saroyan by dealing with the element of paradox, both as it appears in his plays, which are her main focus, and as it effects our responses, as readers and audiences, to all his work. Kenneth W. Rhoads's essay argues that understanding the character Joe in *The Time of Your Life* as a figure for Christ best resolves the play's seeming ambiguities, and provides a good example of close reading in the service of discovering a text's symbolic foundations. To Robert Everding, too, the play has a messianic aspect, but it lies less in Joe (whom he sees more as a learner than a teacher) and more in Saroyan's wish to "force mankind to recognize the dangers of its present behavior," using theatrical conventions to put the audience in touch with reality. Challenging Rhoads directly, John A. Mills asks us to see Saroyan's play—and a number of his other works—as existentialist documents, reflecting "the absurd sense of life" of Camus's philosophy in Joe's "mission of self-discovery."

Lorne Shirinian applies Wolfgang Iser's reader-response theories and R. D. Laing's views on identity-formation to the analysis of Saroyan's *Obituaries*. Focusing on *An Armenian Trilogy*, Harold Aram Veeser invokes Edward Said (on Orientalism) and Harold Bloom (on the anxiety of influence) in dealing with Saroyan's relationship to Armenian history. Walter Cummins, editor of the *Literary Review* and a prolific fiction writer himself, spots a fresh motif in Saroyan's work, the competitive nonconformist who masters life by breaking rules, and in the process affirms new values. Dealing with Saroyan's memoirs, Walter Shear examines his confrontation with death and the paradoxes it evoked.

Although I am generally pleased with the way this volume turned out, I owe apologies to William Saroyan for again taking too long with a project connected to him. In the late 1970s I edited an issue of the *Literary Review* that commemorated the literary legacy of the Great Depression. I asked Saroyan to contribute a piece, and he responded quickly with a lovely memoir about the paradox of coming of age and gaining success in the midst of economic hard times.[10] He wrote often and eagerly, wanting to know when the piece would appear, but my other contributors took much longer. I had to put him off with excuses and explanations, and the issue did not come together until after his death. Recently I was shown a copy of an unpublished piece Saroyan had written at the time, complaining, understandably, about the delay and about me. I am sad that he died thinking hard thoughts of me; but then, he had no business dying so early.

Thanks to Leo Hamalian, a supportive and knowledgeable friend to me and many others, for his advice and help in putting this volume together; to Jim Nagel, series editor, for insisting it be better; to Melissa Solomon of G. K. Hall for patience and help; to Priyanka Kapoor and Emily Keyishian, for assistance in hunting down obscure materials. And, of course, to Marge.

Notes

1. "USPS Destroys Millions of New Stamps," *Stamps*, 11 May 1991; 219.

2. *William Saroyan: My Real Work is Being* (Chapel Hill, NC: University of North Carolina Press, 1983).

3. *Armenian Review* 34 (September 1981): 249–340 contains 104 previously unpublished letters Saroyan wrote from the 1930s to the 1970s to the editors of various publications of the Hairenik Foundation. *Ararat* 25:2 (Spring 1984): 106–23 contain thirty-seven letters, mostly of later vintage, and a charming piece by Jules Archer (124–28) on the experience of corresponding with Saroyan.

4. "Dramatic Progress of William Saroyan," *New York Times Book Review*, 30 July 1944, 21.

5. "So Many Saroyans," *New Republic*, 5 August 1950, 20.

6. *A New Accent in American Fiction: The Armenian-American Writer* (New York: The Armenian General Benevolent Union, 1958), 9.

7. Nona Balakian, *Critical Encounters: Critical Views and Reviews, 1953–1977* (New York: Bobbs-Merrill, 1978), 165.

8. "The Cymbalon," *New Republic*, 1 March 1943, 291.

9. *William Saroyan: A Study of the Short Fiction* (New York: Twayne Publishers, 1991).

10. William Saroyan, "Memories of the Uppression," *Literary Review* 27:1 (Fall 1983): 9–11.

Introduction:
Saroyan and His Critics

◆

ALICE K. BARTER

I

When William Saroyan died on 18 May 1981, Armenian-Americans lost their most gifted writer, a man who in his lifetime had inspired controversy and disparagement almost as much as he had symbolized man's capacity for hope and affection. These opposing feelings and attitudes were elicited as much by the personality he projected to the public as by his words, in the many forms they took, whether song, story, play, essay or interview.

Quite early in his literary career, which began in 1934 with the publication of his short story, "The Daring Young Man on the Flying Trapeze" (and, later that year, an eponymous collection of stories), Saroyan's output was so voluminous that critics poured out judgments about his growth as an artist, or lack thereof; they traced the influences of or found similarities to earlier writers, placed him in the larger context of American literature and its traditions, and identified typical characteristics of his style and thought. The most persistent concern in this body of criticism was that Saroyan, for all his promise, would waste his considerable talents because of his own lack of critical insight and restraint.

These anxious messages of admonition and dissatisfaction grew vehement in the postwar years. Although the average reader continued to remember Saroyan with affection and pleasure, by 1960 it was clear to him and his critics that he had "missed" it. There was a derisive tone in the allusive titles that critics bestowed upon him over the years and, fair or foul, deserved or not, these epithets did capture some recognizable attributes of the writer. They are mentioned here for their metaphorical language and the range of associations they provoke: "the Fresno Bernadette" (George Jean Nathan); "the kiddie Tolstoi" (Clifton Fadiman); "the whirling dervish of Fresno" (George Jean Nathan); "the Armenian Wunderkind" (G. T. Hellman); "the Pied Piper in person" (*Theatre Arts*); "Peter Pan" (Grenville Vernon); "Captain of Nothing" (the *New Yorker*); "the Armenian Orson Welles" (the *New Yorker*); "William the whim" (Joe Dever); "champion of the misfit" and "chronicler of the bum" (Elizabeth Bowen); "the well-known Armenian cornucopia" (the *New Yorker*); "the long-winded poet-laureate of waifdom" (*Time*); "Wild Bill" (David Burnham); "the aging boy wonder" (*Saturday Review*); and "the Douglas Fairbanks of conversation" (Elizabeth Valentine).

In addition to these pejorative titles, a disparaging attitude was evident in the parodies he inspired very early in his career, such as E. Beloin's "Saroyanesque"[1] in 1934 and Clifton Fadiman's "The Wolf and Saroyan" in 1936. Fadiman complained, "when Saroyan is being most himself and telling us all about the World and Life and Time and Death, I don't understand him. . . . 438 pages of spontaneity are too much for this dusty, academic mind."[2] In 1945 M. M. Flood, in the *Saturday Review*, composed a satiric dialogue between Walt Whitman and William Saroyan consisting of bombastic, drunken gibberish laced with quotations from their own works or interviews. While both authors are portrayed as calculating phonies, Whitman holds his posture of brotherhood to the end, while Saroyan sobers up enough to see that, for all their talk, nothing was being said; turning critical, practical, and petty, he ends up running away from Whitman.[3]

Although many critics viewed Saroyan as an anomaly, some tried to relate him to other writers, groups, or trends. Joseph Remenyi concluded that Saroyan was an overrated romanticist whose talents were more quantitative than qualitative.[4] Taking a regional view, West Coast critic Frederic I. Carpenter saw in Saroyan elements of the "new Transcendentalism" of the California writers. Standing somewhere between the idolaters and the brick-throwers, he stated, "Of all American authors who have achieved fame since 1930, William Saroyan is perhaps the most original, the most versatile, and closest to the mood of the common people."[5] Though he recognized that there was much to criticize in Saroyan's work, which was sometimes "amorphous," "bumptious," and "third-rate," Carpenter concluded that while his faults and virtues suggest comparison with Whitman, in philosophy he resembles Emerson and other American transcendentalists. Because of his "colloquial, instinctive, and unliterary" style, Saroyan "remains an American natural, whose similarities to writers living or dead are entirely coincidental" (94).

Asserting that Saroyan's writing resembled nothing else in American literature, Howard Floan, who was to write the first full-length critical study of the author, compared him to Cervantes: going back to *Don Quixote*, Floan thought, would help us understand "Saroyan's delineation of character, his quality of humor, and his evaluation of human suffering." Like Cervantes, Floan said, Saroyan had the "ability to focus simultaneously on both the tragic and comic aspects of man's inability to realize his dreams. It is a double vision that reveals itself most successfully in the whimsical way in which some of his characters, suggestive of Don Quixote, overestimate their own powers and misjudge the situation in which they find themselves.

Furthermore these misjudgments, by their naïveté, often imply a criticism of an insensitive, opportunistic world in which idealism appears incongruous."[6] Several drama critics have taken note of Saroyan's admiration for George Bernard Shaw and Shaw's influence on Saroyan as a playwright. In 1941 Elizabeth Valentine wrote: "Some people think he is the modern Shaw, with less dialectic and more Freud; others that he is just an ego getting away with murder. But one thing he certainly is—that is, a great reporter, who reports what he feels as well as what he sees and hears. And nearly everyone agrees that he has given the New York Theatre a shot in the arm."[7] Stark Young, on the other hand, said that what Saroyan shared with Shaw was a lack of artistic understanding; he found "a certain blind willfulness in his work."[8] (Saroyan's dramatic ideal was somewhat tarnished when he learned that Shaw despised Armenians.)[9]

Because one of Saroyan's favorite subjects was childhood's faith and goodness, as contrasted with adult disillusionment and corruption, Howard Floan noted his similarity to Mark Twain.[10] The same connection was made by Henry Seidel Canby, who described *My Name Is Aram* as both "an Armenian book . . . written with the naive blend of spirituality and realistic cynicism that one finds in Arabic popular literature," and "at the same time intensely American," brother to *The Story of a Bad Boy*, *Tom Sawyer*, *Huckleberry Finn* and *Penrod*. "Mark Twain stuffed the prejudices, the folk lore, the freedom, and the ideals of the Mississippi valley into his books; Saroyan has depicted the pioneer generation of the native born of foreign stock, adjusting themselves to America with rude aggressiveness, and complex imaginations and immense energies. . . . I should vote, indeed, for this story of an Armenian boyhood as the most truly American book of the year."[11] Not surprisingly, Saroyan was also likened to Charles Dickens for his belief in the basic human virtues, his characterizations, and his romanticism. But while perceiving similarities in the two writers, Grenville Vernon criticized Saroyan's indifference to form and unwarranted optimism. Noting that "[w]ithout form there can be no concentration of effect," Vernon said "Mr. Saroyan has great talent, perhaps even genius, but the arts must not be always like truant boys, all play and no work. The intellect, the will, the critical sense, have their place even in the romantic; a writer can not forever be Peter Pan. There *is* ugliness and deviltry in the world."[12] The complaint that Saroyan, unlike Dickens, was blind to the evil in this world was repeated throughout the late thirties and early forties, as was the accusation that his work was prolix and lacked focus. Clifton Fadiman complained: "Give Mr. Saroyan a word, a memory, and a whole battery of differentiated and spontaneous emotions is called into play. The slightest collision with an idea, and he is off like the wind. He is the greatest hit-and-run writer in the history of American letters" (Fadiman, 67). Horace Gregory thought that Saroyan, like Thomas Wolfe, had equated vitality with facility and, as a result, was repeating himself. Though he found "a touch of pathos running through Saroyan's evident plea for immortality," he conceded that Saroyan "will gain, I think, immortality of a specific kind."[13] Reviewing *The Daring Young Man on the Flying Trapeze*, William R. Benét remarked that Saroyan's writing had the same effect on him as Sherwood Anderson's; at times moving him intensely with profound observations about life, but at other times rambling so pointlessly that he lost interest. "He listens to life as a man in one of his stories listens to a phonograph record."[14]

Saroyan did not escape the tendency of American critics to discover the influence of Hemingway upon his contemporaries and successors, though Edmund Wilson in 1940 argued that Saroyan was different from the others in that he was not "hard-boiled" and was original in creating "the good drunk," as opposed to the bad drunk of the Hemingway school. While Wilson credited Saroyan with having "an instinctive sense of form," he also warned that he would lose his audience as well as his gift if he continued to write like a columnist.[15]

A quarter of a century after Wilson's "The Boys in the Back Room," Howard Floan located Hemingway's influence on Saroyan in the interval between the publication of *The Daring Man on the Flying Trapeze* and *My Name Is Aram*. "During this period of prolific effort—by his own estimate he wrote more than five hundred tales in these years—he learned to get into his story immediately; to fit character, setting, and mood to the action; to express with colloquial vigor what his people were capable of saying, and to imply much about what they were able to feel. His style grew lean, partly because of the influence of Hemingway and partly because of his own reaction to the criticism that he tended to talk too much" (Floan, *William Saroyan* 90). Floan also notes Saroyan's move at this period to dispense with description and "rely on simple statement." "He began to do little more than to assign names to his people and to start them talking. Because of his mastery of colloquial speech, these sketches often appeared vital and significant when they were at times no more than incomplete exercises in dramatic composition. But, at their best, they achieved moments of genuine recognition; and at such times the economy of drama became an important virtue of his story form" (Floan, *William Saroyan* 90). Saroyan the playwright was soon to be born.

Commenting on Saroyan's first novel, *The Human Comedy*, critic Philip Rahv stated scornfully that it had "the structure of a kindergarten primer" and that it employed an elementary language derived from Gertrude Stein, Ernest Hemingway and Sherwood Anderson. Its view of life, he added, was "a mishmash of Whitmanesque pantheism, romantic rapture, and literary bohemianism thickly flavored with the famous Saroyan cuteness. This novel, ostensibly a picture of American boyhood, has more in common with Louisa Alcott's *Little Women* than with Mark Twain's *Huckleberry Finn*."[16] Many years later, Jack Kroll, writing about the 1969 revival of *Time of Your Life*, revived the Whitman connection: "Saroyan really was a son or an Armenianblooded godson of Walt Whitman; he really squared off against the world (which he saw clearly as a brute and a scoundrel) with a free-swinging, yes, a cocky, melodious, hat-over-the-eye song and dance that shook a manly sweetness out over the scared euphoric temper of an America wrenching itself out of depression and into war."[17] Yet in spite of his admiration for the "valor" of this vision, Kroll agreed with other critics that there was something immature in Saroyan's view of the world, a complaint that would become the most persistent criticism of his work.

Still, some critics looked more favorably upon this quality of "immaturity." In his review of *The Assyrian and Other Stories* William Peden described Saroyan's considerable contribution to the short story and remarked that "he brought to the American literary scene freshness of vision, simplicity, spontaneity, and gaiety." "He possessed a sympathetic understanding of little people, a distinctly personal literary style, and a contagious sense of humor. He exerted a beneficial influence against the pretentious, the overwritten, the too-fancily-plotted short story. Like Mark Twain, he opened the windows and aired the room at a time when fresh air was badly needed." In the sections following, I will describe the evolution of Saroyan criticism in the period before, during, and after World War II.

II
CRITICISM, 1934–1945

During his first ten years as a published writer, critics generally agreed that, while Saroyan had great promise and native abilities, he had much to learn about his craft. They tried to point out his excesses in taste and form and to convey both their resentment of what seemed empty postures of sentiment or philosophy and their fervent hope that he would, in fact, fulfill his promise as he matured. As it turned out, this period was to be the "high time" of Saroyan's life, when he wrote his best remembered work and achieved his greatest popularity. His faith in his own invulnerability and infallibility was at its peak; he could even believe in his own immortality. This buoyancy of spirit in both the man and his work gave hope and confidence to Americans worn down by the hardships of the Great Depression and the uncertainties of the Second World War. Indeed, it seemed that nothing could go wrong for him.

At the end of this period, Saroyan's critics were not nearly so receptive. By 1945 Saroyan was being accused of shortchanging his audience by publishing imitations of his earlier work and using the techniques of writers he had once professed to despise. It was hinted that he was a failure or, worse yet, an anachronism. Paradoxically, it was during this period that critics made their most astute efforts to recognize and appreciate the distinctive qualities of his work, whether published or performed, and to try to find the proper place for it in the larger body of American literature. In covering this period of criticism, I will proceed as much as possible from more to less favorable.

From the beginning, the "naturalness" of Saroyan's style was commended by many critics. William R. Benét forgave Saroyan's tendency to ramble because he admired the tendency in Saroyan's stories to reject "fake drama" and "concocted plot" (Benét 221), while T. S. Matthews declared that for those who understood him "there is something in Saroyan's cockeyed flamboyance that sounds more refreshingly natural than all the sound sense and artistry they have blinked at in half a lifetime."[18] Though objecting to the exhibitionism he perceived in *Inhale and Exhale* (1936), Matthews added that the book was well named, for "[i]t is not so much a book of short stories as a book of breathing" (173). Burton Rascoe, after recalling the literary feud between Hemingway and Saroyan, stated that Saroyan made "the imitators of Hemingway seem like a nice little bunch of schoolboy scalawags with each a piece of chalk" (Rascoe, 36). George Jean Nathan, writing about the flawed New Haven production of *The Time of Your Life*, was moved to say that notwithstanding its faults the play brought to American drama "a new and noteworthy originality, life, force, freshness and humor. In its very lack of discipline and in its airy rejection of the tried and true and easy dramatic formulae lie its paradoxical strength and vigor."[19] Stark Young wrote that *The Time of Your Life* illustrated the difference between the mere craftsman and the artist: "Which is to say that the basic, underlying, fecundating and generalizing principle of life is there in him, in his theatre writing."[20] Edmund Wilson praised Saroyan both for being an "engaging fellow" and for having a "natural felicity . . . and an instinctive sense of form" (Wilson, 967). Stark Young thought Saroyan's unique style defied analysis and felt that *The Beautiful People* was more deserving of the 1941 Drama Critics' Circle Award than the winner, Lillian Hellman's *Watch on the Rhine*.[21] Though critical of the play's form, he admired its imaginativeness. "As to what the final virtue of *The Beautiful People* is, *we know*, as St. Augustine said of God, if you don't ask us."[22] In another review a year later, Young wrote: "For the truth is that Mr. Saroyan's theatre writing in general is a challenge to our stage and its acting and producing methods."[23] Calling Saroyan "the Pied Piper in person," who "would charm even the tiger out of its nature," a reviewer for *Theatre Arts* concluded that his plays are impossible to analyze because they are conceived in terms of mood rather than structure and expressed in symbolic forms, both visual and oral. "They are in a sense dream-plays speaking directly to the unconscious through concepts relating to the lost and longed-for childworld of security and affection. His plays are not only shot through with music; they are themselves music, haunting, nostalgic, steeped in the pathos of half-forgotten." The reviewer added, "In spite of his robust humor . . . loneliness is the predominant mood of his writing, loneliness which only brotherly love, the love of all living creatures for each other, can cure."[24]

Saroyan was frequently classified as a romantic because of his optimistic view of human nature and his voice of affirmation, characteristics that were the objects of both enthusiastic commendation and scourging ridicule. Many critics were impatient with a writer who persistently presented a closed dreamworld in which evil, when it did arise, was invariably overcome. Part of the problem was Saroyan's trick of pretending to mean more than either he or his audience could understand through reason alone. He made it seem necessary to set analysis aside so that the drama or narrative could play on readers' or spectators' emotions, making them feel uplifted and convincing them, at least momentarily, that all was well.

Describing Saroyan as a "prolific writer of bewildering short stories that never take him more than three hours to knock out," W. A. H. Birnie called him neither a surrealist nor one of the "crazies," but a "high pressure salesman of youthful dreams and flesh-and-blood proof that they can be made to come true."[25] Another reviewer referred to Saroyan's romantic attitude in "Love's Old Sweet Song" as "that cheerful lunacy which is the essence of [his] gift."[26] Joseph Wood Krutch defended these romantic tendencies, saying: "He accepts the universe, believes in the goodness of the human heart, and holds that God is love. He distrusts the respectable, rejoices in the variety of the world, believes in the unique individual, and assumes as self-evident that Beauty is Truth. Above all, he is convinced that the secret of success in both life and art is to let oneself go—as completely and unthinkingly as possible."[27] Calling Saroyan a "romanticist . . . impressed with his own histrionic emotionalism," Joseph Remenyi noted that he is "also an uplifter, a moralist who does not dare to preach. He rationalizes the chill of life with a deceiving tenderness; it is like introducing an oriental lantern into an occidental darkness." He found in Saroyan "a communicative emotional heat . . . coupled with a confusing irony—his most important gun against a conventional world" (Remenyi, 96). The corollary to this perception was the understanding that loneliness was at the heart of his writing. Reviewing *Razzle-Dazzle* (1945), a critic took note of Saroyan's sensitivity not only to "the terrible, beautiful hunger of the body" but, more significantly, to "the yet more terrible, more beautiful hunger of the humble spirit for comprehension."[28] Howard Floan was later to say of this aspect of his work: "Saroyan's best writing is about those who can live happily only in their private world of mind, a theme that is especially appropriate to American life when he combines with it his awareness of the loneliness and sense of not belonging which have haunted the immigrant" (Floan, "Cervantes" 86–87). Some critics, at least, perceived the deeper sources of Saroyan's dismissal of conventional realism.

Saroyan's imagination, originality, and humor were recognized in the early criticism. About the last quality, Nathan wrote: "In Saroyan the American theater has found the freshest, most imaginatively audacious, and the most genuine humorous talent that has tickled it in a round of many moons."[29] Krutch argued that those who dismissed Saroyan's plays as inconsequential were blind to the "freshness of fancy, a gaiety of humor, and a sincerity of sentiment which make them, in my opinion, unique" (Krutch, 537). After seeing *Hello Out There*, Wolcott Gibbs, who had previously been severely critical of Saroyan, expressed the view that he "shows that bite of true perception which is one of his most valuable gifts as a writer."[30] Brooks Atkinson called this play "a perfect creation."[31] Valentine, too, had observed Saroyan's "intuitive understanding of people." She noted, "He listens intently, as if he were fine-tuning a piano. He is an author in search of not one but a thousand characters" (Valentine, 29).

Saroyan's way with language was both praised and condemned. Valentine thought his choice of words, both simple and uncommon, fit his meaning exceptionally well; she called him "the Douglas Fairbanks of conversation" because of his ability "to stand off six people at once" (Valentine, 29). For Philip Rahv, on the other hand, Saroyan's language had been tainted too much by the influences of Stein, Anderson, and Hemingway (Rahv, 372). James Thurber, who had a strong distaste for Saroyan, thought he ought not to be excused for the sloppiness and mushiness in his writing simply because he was a "proletarian writer."[32]

Throughout this decade one attitude shared by many critics was that Saroyan showed the promise of being a very fine writer and would become one if he would follow their advice. What was wrong with Saroyan? Edwin B. Burgum asserted that most of his plays were failures, empty of even allegorical or surreal meaning. Although his novel *The Human Comedy* (1943) exhibited a sense of form absent from the plays, it was a disappointment because it cushioned the reality of war and provided an escape from the responsibilities of maturity.[33] Probably the most frequently expressed reaction to Saroyan was that he was an egocentric, pretentious poseur. Lewis Gannett put it succinctly when he said, "Mr. Saroyan is a writer. He is also an act."[34] Vernon quoted Kipling's comment about a gorilla—"he had too much ego in his cosmos"—and considered Saroyan's "version of a modern honky-tonk Camille" in *The Time of Your Life* (1941) to be artificial and ridiculous. Yet he added, "Even now for what he is he is very good indeed."[35] Wolcott Gibbs, while admitting that Saroyan was "a man of considerable talent and high Christian feeling," also called him "the author of some of the most vacant and pretentious nonsense written in our time."[36] Brooks Atkinson decried *Across the Board on Tomorrow Morning* for dealing with "metaphysical matters that Mr. Saroyan does not understand but cannot get out of his head."[37] Philip Rahv thought *The Human Comedy* contained only one realized character, Byfield, and that all the rest were "so many versions of Saroyan in his corn-

iest public role: that of the supremely devoted lover of mankind"
(Rahv, 375–76).

The Adventures of Wesley Jackson (1946), Saroyan's badly received war
novel, was deplored for its narcissism by Harrison Smith.[38] Another critic,
finding in *The Beautiful People* equal portions of "genius" and "junk," sur-
mised that in his childhood Saroyan had become infatuated with his ideal
hero, "composed of his real self and his would-be self," and that this was
the hero he repeatedly created.[39] In Rahv's opinion Saroyan tediously and
perpetually imitated himself in his stories. Rahv blamed drama critics for
hailing Saroyan as a writer with ideas when, in his opinion, all Saroyan had
done was to revamp his original posture as a literary rebel and fit it to a
different audience. Rahv objected to Saroyan's egotistical revelations about
the secret of his success and suspected that behind "the formula of innocence
there lurks an uncanny old-world cynicism" (Rahv, 375–76).

Almost as frequently as they complained about his postures and vanity,
critics were disturbed by the unconventional form of his stories and the lack
of discipline and critical judgment that they perceived in his torrent of
words. Benét said that his stories "seem to have no particular beginning,
middle, or ending. They roam around until they complete some sort of
evolution at the end. Some of them are hardly stories at all" (Benét, 221).
Wilson warned Saroyan not to follow the path of mediocrity that led "to
Eddie Guest, William Lyon Phelps and Dr. Frank Crane" (Wilson, 697).
Nathan feared that Saroyan was deceiving himself "into mistaking squirrelish
activity for versatility."[40] While Nathan deplored Saroyan's lack of organization, his carelessness, his impatience to get before his audience, Rahv declared
that Saroyan's career exemplified the deterioration of the "national literature"
(Rahv, 373). From these and others came the charge that Saroyan had lost
his inventiveness and was repeating himself.

III

CRITICISM, 1945–1981

From 1945 to 1981 Saroyan's pace of publication was fairly constant, providing critics in a carnivorous mood with much to dissect. During the period
following his military service, most expressed disappointment with him for
not having achieved his earlier promise; some even dismissed him as a has-
been. Though a few still saw him as a genius "of sorts," no serious critic
regarded Saroyan any longer as "a major prophet," Harrison Smith asserted.
When Saroyan lit up the literary horizon, the time was right for his kind
of humor, his Armenian folktales, and "his naive emotionalism," Smith
wrote, but he had failed because the war and the events that followed made
him an anachronism (Smith, 7).

In 1950, Nona Balakian, reviewing *Twin Adventures* (which contains both *The Adventures of Wesley Jackson* and *The Adventures of William Saroyan*), *The Assyrian and Other Stories* and *Don't Go Away Mad and Other Plays*, declared that Saroyan did not yet understand himself as a writer. He was still master of the fablelike tale, she said, and was at his best creating, not children, "but the child-mood, the child-experience."[41] She also noticed, however, that Saroyan's concept of goodness had deepened, so that failure and irony were now present in these works.

John Brooks said *Rock Wagram* (1952) was so full of sloppy writing that it couldn't possibly have been written by anybody other than Saroyan.[42] Oscar Handlin deplored a lack of continuity in *The Bicycle Rider in Beverly Hills* (1953).[43] While conceding that Saroyan had probably done more for the short story than any writer since O. Henry, Elizabeth Bowen called *The Laughing Matter* (1953) a dreadful book containing inane dialogue and a plot that grew too violent too soon, a book redeemed only by its irony.[44]

Twenty-one years after Saroyan had first caught the public's fancy and the attention of critics, William Fisher found in his "amazing success and rapid decline . . . a history of American optimism": "Saroyan rose in mid-Depression as a bard of the beautiful life, a restorer of faith in man's boundless capacities; he has declined as a troubled pseudo-philosopher, forced to acknowledge man's limitations, yet uncomfortable in the climate of Evil."[45] While it is true that Saroyan "has followed the tradition of American transcendentalism," "it need hardly be said that Saroyan is no Emerson, either by temperament or by talent. The extent to which his later work has failed reflects, in one sense, the inadequacy of his equipment for the task he set himself. Yet it is also true that Saroyan is the representative American of the mid-twentieth-century, a man baffled at the failure of the Dream but unwilling to give it up; incapable of facing his dilemma frankly or of articulating it meaningfully" (Fisher, 339). Fisher wrote that while Saroyan's early work, with its themes of individualism and affirmation, served a purpose in countering the hopeless mood of the times, his writing lost its "buoyancy" in the 1940s and became weighted down by "sermons on virtue," oozing sentimental muck. Fisher saw Saroyan's disastrous experiences on Broadway just before he was drafted as the turning point in his career and believed that the work produced from that time suffered from pseudo-philosophical posing and a loss of exuberance and failed to deal with adult problems from an adult point of view (339–40).

On the other hand Thomas Curley, reviewing *Mama, I Love You* (1956), marveled that "despite years of abuse Saroyan's gifts have not deserted him. . . . This is not faint praise, it is blame. He could not write like the telephone company if he tried." He did acknowledge that Saroyan's work had deteriorated, and attributed the decline to the fact that "there are no Armenians around" in this book and to the author's temperament. Saroyan seemed to have discovered that, as the character Aram says in one of the stories, the easiest thing in the world is to pretend to believe everything and to stop trying to understand or analyze anything.[46]

Saroyan returned to Broadway with the 1957 production of *The Cave Dwellers*, which received mainly negative notices. Although Henry Hewes thought that with this play Saroyan had "refound himself as an artist,"[47] few agreed with his judgment. Wolcott Gibbs criticized it harshly;[48] another critic found it gaseously euphoric and lacking in substance.[49] The critic for *Time* wrote that with this first play in fourteen years Saroyan was back "at the same old stand, making the same old pitch—but without his onetime showmanship." He had become "the long-winded poet-laureate of waifdom," reducing everything to love, even hate.[50] Patrick Dennis wrote that he hadn't missed Saroyan a bit in the years he had been absent from the theater and commended the actors and the director for making their way through "the mawkish morass of Saroyan silliness with no fatalities."[51]

From reading Saroyan's critics, one might assume that once his fame was established his development stopped. Stanley Kauffmann, for example, saw Saroyan as a case of arrested development. Reviewing *Places Where I've Done Time* (1972), Saroyan's fifth book of memoirs, he wrote that while Saroyan's tone showed him to be more aware of his shortcomings, he continued to remain a child, whether his view was from Paris or Oakland; for Saroyan to grow up now would be a surprise. "In the long view, it's a sad career. How much he poured out and how little sticks. What a fresh, unique, welcome voice he had when he started—those early stories, those first carefree plays. . . . The voice is still unique; he has no memorable disciples or even imitators. But mostly it has kept saying the same things, most of which it had already said better."[52] Nevertheless, the more discerning of his readers and professional critics detected significant changes in content and style, such as his shifting the setting for his stories from the San Francisco of "The Daring Young Man" to Fresno, which was to become the wellspring of his most memorable tales. Floan, for whom this shift represented artistic growth, saw the San Francisco stories as merely self-conscious projections of the author's personality, whereas those set in Fresno truly dealt with other people.

> *Little Children* and *My Name Is Aram* are not about Saroyan's childhood, nor really about childhood at all. They are about the immigrants of Fresno and the San Joaquin Valley, the people recalled from his boyhood days whose images gave him the impetus to extend himself beyond the lyricism of his early tales to the more dramatic later ones. The uncles, cousins, and neighbors of Aram, while containing enough of the author to possess vitality and immediacy, are distinct in themselves. If Saroyan had not discovered the literary use of Fresno and the valley, he could not have given us the best of his short stories—nor his plays. (Floan, *William Saroyan*, 92)

Related to this shift in setting is Saroyan's search for self-identity. Floan cited the monologue "Myself Upon the Earth" (from *The Daring Young Man*) as a clear indication of Saroyan's desire "to discover his own identity in terms of its full Armenian-American duality." According to Floan, the portrait he paints there of his father anticipates "what was to become one of Saroyan's finest themes: the profound spiritual uprootedness of the immigrant" (Floan, *William Saroyan*, 62). Floan considered *My Name Is Aram* the book most likely to prove representative of his short fiction. "By this time he had evolved a style of swiftness and simplicity, an ability to select images both strikingly concrete and richly suggestive, and to create sharply visualized scenes without retarding the forward movement of his stories" (Floan, *William Saroyan*, 81). In Floan's opinion, it was also the first book in which the braggart writer acknowledged his debts to others. Even more significantly, with this book Saroyan had found "his truest subject," the spirit of his people. "To read his books in sequence from *The Daring Young Man on the Flying Trapeze* to *My Name Is Aram* is to see how gradually but inevitably Saroyan found his way into this subject" (Floan, *William Saroyan*, 83). Three years after the publication of his book on Saroyan, Floan was to reiterate this judgment in his review of *Letters from 74 Rue Taitbout*, a book written during the years of Saroyan's exile abroad due to his difficulties with the IRS. It consisted of a series of "letters" addressed to friends, writers, and public figures, most now dead, who had touched the author's life in some way. Floan felt that it was not a very good book, but that it would be appreciated by those who had followed Saroyan's career, "from his meteoric rise to fame in the thirties, through the shattering effect of the war on his creative sensibilities, to his dogged but on the whole successful struggle to reshape his art during the years that followed."[53] If success didn't change Saroyan, war, marriage, rejection, and failure did.

Through most of his career Saroyan was treated as a stepchild or an impostor by the more elite of the fraternity of critics. Floan attributed this to two factors: Saroyan's own inherited attitudes and tastes and his refusal "to accept the prevailing ideals of composition and the predominant pessimism of Naturalism." He noted, "Rarely has his fiction received careful consideration beyond the initial reviews. The occasional references one finds in scholarly journals often imply a note of regret that his extraordinary gifts have not been more fully developed" (Floan, *William Saroyan*, 155). Floan blamed his fellow critics for not recognizing the difference between the "I" in Saroyan's tales and Saroyan the person (*William Saroyan*, 73). He believed their comments had hurt Saroyan enough to make him go against his own best judgment. Floan also considered Saroyan's reply to Eric Bentley's criticism of his sloppy writing—"One cannot expect an Armenian to be an Englishman"—a just rejoinder inasmuch as American criticism, for the most part, was based on aesthetic standards that reflected Anglo-Saxon rather than Middle Eastern or Oriental culture (*William Saroyan*, 153).

In a 1960 *Esquire* article, Budd Schulberg, having the advantage of a long and intimate acquaintanceship with the author, gave a fascinating firsthand account of Saroyan and his development. When he had read "The Assyrian" in *Story* magazine while on his way to Dartmouth in 1934, Schulberg instantly recognized a new and unique voice. After reading more Saroyan and growing curious about him, Schulberg went to San Francisco to inquire about him. Saroyan—who was well known among writers and bartenders— was easily found, very accessible, and, despite his reckless egotism, utterly charming. "Every word he put down was a holy miracle to him, the son of an immigrant Armenian grape-grower who could not only talk the adopted language but use these words to make beautiful American sentences!"[54] Their friendship continued in the Stanley Rose Book Shop, a hangout for writers and artists, during the time when Schulberg's father was a well-known producer at Paramount Studios.

When Saroyan decided to become a playwright, he laughed at Schulberg's cautionary remarks about the difficulties of mastering drama. At the time, Schulberg predicted failure, but later admitted how wrong he had been. "In Boston I watched with wonder as *The Time of Your Life* unfolded with grace and humor and warmth and the miracle of dramatic unity. . . . In that fool's gold peaceful October of 1939, William Saroyan had grabbed the gold ring that only America holds forth to its artists. . . . With that golden ring on the merry-go-round Bill had been given a free ride on everything that was swinging and whipping in the whole amusement park and I watched him, in fact cheered him on" (Schulberg, 89–90). And indeed, it was a perilous ride. Schulberg portrayed Saroyan at fifty as a disillusioned man, broke and broken, retreating into himself. The pathos and irony of an artist's surviving to witness his own decline were evident to Schulberg. He chose to remain among the loving faithful.

It was at that age that Saroyan, in his own defense, explained during an interview (before departing for Yugoslavia to create a movie for Tito) why TV producers wouldn't buy his material. "What I write is of a different dimension. TV wants literal stuff, lumber. My approach is that of a poet."[55] It was the same attitude he had displayed a quarter of a century earlier when he had rejected the formulas of the conventional short story and the well-made play.

In the fifties, Harold Clurman had not always been generous in his praise of Saroyan, but in 1969 he commented favorably upon a revival of *Time of Your Life*. "Saroyan, it has never been sufficiently realized, writes beautifully, without any trace of affectation. His language is robust, juicy, colorful—true Americana with no vulgarity or recourse to current smart talk. It is lightened by warm laughter. It is loose but not limp."[56] *Time* also offered insight on hindsight about the same production. In retrospect, the reviewer saw that Saroyan had really been, in the thirties and forties, a harbinger of the mood and events of the fifties and sixties, "the U. S. father of the unmade play": "It is a combination of mood music and action painting. In 1939 this was as disconcerting and puzzling to playgoers as Harold

Pinter's plays have proved to be to more recent theater audiences . . . To the audience of today, these characters seem like a commune of drop-outs, and Saroyan qualifies as the first articulate hippie. . . . In 1939 Saroyan was known as the 'crazy man' of the theater. Now it seems he had the intuitive sanity of a seer."[57] Responding to the same revival, Stanley Kauffmann wrote of discovering in *The Time of Your Life* that "[u]nderneath the boozy friendliness, its basic view is rigidly moralistic." "What makes the play especially interesting to see again is that this tension, between superficial humanism and underlying puritanism, is more apparent than before. But also, to be sure, Saroyan's gift for cutting, disrespectfully, right to the core of every new situation is as humorous as ever, and some of his fancies still glisten untarnished."[58] Jack Kroll also found reason to praise *The Time of Your Life*: "There are moments in this play that may look small or sentimental, but they are the work of a writer who had an incandescent moment in our literature, and they are effects possible only to one who was himself touched with a kind of grace" (Kroll, 139). While agreeing with other critics that there was something immature about Saroyan's view of the world, Kroll preferred Saroyan's brand of "lyric populism" to the "plastically poetic, brooding libertarianism of such plays as Maxwell Anderson's *Winterset*" (Kroll, 139). Jack Richardson thought that Saroyan's "impregnable" innocence, which the playwright would neither apologize for nor embellish with literary symbols, accounted for this play's becoming "a small, but sturdy American classic."[59]

Jack Richardson, Howard Clurman, and Howard Floan were among those latter-day critics who found a link between Saroyan's work and other American literature. Richardson, discussing the 1970 revival of *Time of Your Life*, compared it to other "visions of purity" such as Tennessee Williams' *Camino Real* (1953) and Thornton Wilder's *Our Town* (1938). These playwrights, he observed, were considered mavericks in their time because they experimented with the distance between the audience and the stage, and with narrative and dramatic structure. Like Wilder's small town and Williams's Kilroy, Saroyan's saloon, he said, was a "very American symbol" that held the play together (Richardson, 20). Clurman stated unequivocally that *Time of Your Life* was surely one of the best plays the American theater had produced, a folktale which had caught "something permanently benevolent, gusty, zestful in the American ethos" and was "as native as *Huckleberry Finn*, with greater relevance" (Clurman, 22).

Although interest in Saroyan's work had diminished by the last decade before his death, useful articles on various aspects of his life or work continued to appear. In 1972, Thelma J. Shinn remarked on the paradoxes that she feels have confused Saroyan's critics. Warning, wisely, that "we should avoid placing only one interpretation on Saroyan's symbols,"[60] she saw Saroyan as a writer who has recognized and accepted the conditions of life and is "trying to find for himself some meaning in this absurd universe—and the meaning, if any, appears to be within himself. In this sense, at least, the existential theme is precisely what concerns Saroyan" (186). She observed that though the ingredients of *The Time of Your Life* are romantic, the play reflects a "realistic pessimism" (193) and reveals "an undercurrent of resentment . . . of the artist who was criticized for appealing to the heart" (193).

In 1976 Kenneth W. Rhoads offered to correct the prevailing view that the protagonist of *The Time of Your Life* is an alcoholic by arguing that nothing in the script suggests Joe lacks control of himself. Indeed, "[a] careful reading shows that Joe may be seen as a . . . type of Christ, essentially realistic and certainly very human—whose nature and behavior are completely consonant and who takes on stature as heroic protagonist within such a mode."[61] Whether Saroyan did this consciously is immaterial, Rhoads claimed; such a character emerges in the text through intentional ambiguity, allusion, indirect revelation, implicit scriptural parallels in Joe's motivations and the shape of his life, and by specific episodes whose relevance to the meaning of the play is conveyed by their symbolic content. Calling *The Time of Your Life* "a play of intense romanticism and unabashed sentimentality," Rhoads concluded that "Saroyan is not for the cynic or the iconoclastic realist" (242).

In "Mr. Saroyan's Thoroughly American Movie" Patrick McGilligan described Saroyan's encounters with the movie industry in connection with the film and subsequent novel of *The Human Comedy*, both of which he characterized as "timeworn bits of Americana, contrived, somewhat dated, albeit effusive in good will and idiosyncratic humor." Remarking that "much of what survives on the screen is distinctly Saroyanesque, coated with MGM gloss," he called Saroyan "a rambling, vernacular, wistful, hyperbolic, garrulous sort of writer, who excels with mood and theme, and soars buoyantly with character sketches," and who is not very interested in plot. "Saroyan is more fascinated by the road than the route."[62] McGilligan noted that for Saroyan, reacting to his loss of control over the film's production, "the screen became an obsessive subject of many essays," as well as of an unsuccessful stage play about his experiences in the film colony, *Get Away Old Man* (167). But in the end, he said Saroyan had his revenge when he refused to accept MGM's offer for *The Time of Your Life*, selling it to Cagney Productions instead for 75,000 dollars less than MGM's offer.

In his article "Michael Arlen and William Saroyan: Armenian Ethnicity and the Writer," also published in the seventies, Harry Keyishian compared Saroyan with the commercially successful Anglo-Armenian author who flourished in the twenties, contrasting their choice of setting and characters (fashionable Mayfair vs. rural Fresno; the British upper classes vs. the immigrant poor) and their style (cultivated cerebral comedy vs. a direct appeal to the senses).[63] Despite these differences, Keyishian observed that in each author's most successful work (Arlen's novel *The Green Hat* and Saroyan's play *The Time of Your Life*) the major character is a social outcast who embodies virtues and special insights lacking in conventional society (199).

Saroyan's last three books, *Chance Meetings* (1978), *Obituaries* (1979), and *Births* (published posthumously), fall somewhere between memoirs that resemble timed exercises in writing and the last utterances of a once-famous author. Their style might be characterized as indiscriminate, incoherent, digressive, delirious, unrestrained, angry, or ironic, but rarely sentimental. The most interesting and longest of these three, *Obituaries*, is mentioned in Herbert Gold's "A Twenty Year Talk with Saroyan." Gold, who had known Saroyan during his years of fame, was saddened by the loneliness and melancholia the author displayed at their last meeting in the spring of 1979. Complaining about editors who tried to get him to revise his work, Saroyan had ridiculed their cut-and-paste mentality; he said that he had tried to apply this method with *Obituaries*, but on rereading the manuscript decided it was right as it was. Gold, though a staunch advocate of revision, observed, "I think he knows his proper business. Some (myself included) might want to edit, cut, collect, organize the tides of his voice. We can pick out the funny, the insightful, the astonishing stabs of knowledge, the griefs within the celebrations; deep matters astonish us, hidden in the charm and ebullience."[64] But, he said, reading *Obituaries* reminded him of an American Indian peyote ritual, in which participants know they will always find something of value, but will never reach an end, for "it is forever" (51).

Reviewing Aram Saroyan's memoir, *Last Rites*, published the year after his father William's death, Mark Harris called *Obituaries* "misanthropic," and wondered how the father described in *Last Rites* could be the same man the public had known for forty years or more. In Harris' judgment, William was a tragic figure: "He was a meteor. His innocence was all too real. He squandered his fame and descended into cynicism. The man outlived his work."[65] Richard Lingeman, in the *Nation*, characterized *Obituaries* as "a kind of prose six-day bicycle race against death, by a man who knows that on the seventh day God, six-day bicyclists and all of us will rest."[66] The reviewer in *Forbes* regretted that the book didn't have an editor, saying that it was filled with "repetitive, meandering musings" so that in spite of some "bright spots," getting through the 354 pages was a chore.[67] On the other hand, *Publisher's Weekly* described it as a "solemn, beautiful, hilarious, raunchy, heartbreakingly sad and funny testament and one of Saroyan's best books."[68]

Obituaries should be of special interest to future students of Saroyan for its revelations. In this book he disclosed a facet of his personality that conflicted with his carefully cultivated public image. The portrait drawn there was of a recluse who withdraws into his own world and shuts out others, a man who distrusted the world of people, including himself. How deeply he had been hurt by the critics can be seen again and again as these painful memories intrude no matter what subject is at hand. Here is an example of the intensity with which he defends himself against one of the persistent criticisms of his work. "Don't tell me I'm sentimental, you sons of bitches. You are contemptible, your dishonesty is contemptible, your careful plodding with words, to keep them safely captured inside your silly little theories are contemptible, but I don't hate you because each of you is a sad little pompous son of a bitch, with a chair at a university, and you are fighting bravely to be somebody."[69] In an essay near the end of the book, in dwelling disproportionately on "a snide belittling reference" he had read the previous evening, his outrage seems to express the culmination of years of repressed resentment. "Dear lady, reader, dear gentleman, reader, that's not right . . . to put down this writer on his writing. . . . And I'll tell you why, too: it hurts, that's why. . . . Dirty remarks passed by dirty dirty but damned nicely educated and very highly-paid ladies and gentlemen have the effect of killing writers" (345–46). Perhaps he would agree that he had written his own literary obituary more objectively in *After Thirty Years*. "There was one small doubt or anxiety in my mind, however, and there was something slightly contradictory and therefore to me comic about it. . . . I wondered if it wouldn't have been better in the long run for me to have worked much slower and over a much longer period of time before having my writing accepted and published. . . . Still, I now and then felt, 'Hell, you've made a beginning, but you have put forward a bragging character, and that may not be a good thing. It may be something you will have to live down.' "[70] He was a shrewd observer and well understood the advantages and disadvantages of his public image.

IV
CRITICISM, 1981–1991

Several critics of the eighties and nineties, finding *Chance Meetings* and *Obituaries* to be among Saroyan's most significant works, have expressed the feeling that his place in American and world literature has been undervalued. Several noteworthy book-length biographies and studies that have appeared since 1981 will be discussed in the remainder of this essay, briefly and in chronological order.

Shortly after his father's death Aram Saroyan published *Last Rites* (1982), the contents of a journal he had kept during the last month of his father's life, which reveals many facets of his own personality as well as his father's. He followed this with *William Saroyan* (1983), a more formal study of his father's literary career and works. These two books prove the son to be one of his father's more discerning and appreciative critics, though stronger when not leaning on psychoanalytic theory.

The difference between his father's public image and private self is the recurring theme and unifying element in *Last Rites*. Despite a four-year lapse in their communication and many standing grievances against him, Aram feels he can love his father again when his death is imminent, and can appreciate him as a "good writer, at his best a wonderful, true writer."[71] "What a supple style he had! What a marvel of ease, at it best something very close to breathing itself . . . a style he had that used only the oldest and simplest and truest words and that made those words into song" (44–45). For Aram, his father's style was inseparable from his youth; he compares *The Time of Your Life* to "a jazz dance, in which the words themselves are part of an overall choreography . . . that infects one with the same *physical* sense of pleasure that is usually the unique domain of music. . . . He wrote with a purity and profundity from the depths of his own nervous system, celebrating less in narrative than in sustained jazzlike song what it was like to be young" (62). Like the cluttered collections of junk mingled with treasured memorabilia that filled William's Fresno houses, Aram saw his father's books of the past twenty years as "collections" of memories, "ways of telling himself that he has continued to stay alive, that he is still, up to that moment, 'not dying' " (78). Aram also thinks of them as a gift from his father to us, "a kind of enormous mixed-media self-portrait, perhaps the major work of his lifetime—his last will and testament, his final and deepest claim to immortality itself—and the one by which . . . he intends to freeze his assets beyond the grave itself" (78). In *William Saroyan*, Aram remarked that in his father's work there is only one voice and one character, Saroyan himself, all else being variations of the same entity. He also noted the lack of realism in his father's work. "There is something abstracted and dreamlike about almost all of Saroyan's figures and their central relationships. What fascinates rather is the *movement* from character to character." Aram compared these movements to the interactions among superego (the parent figure), ego (the adult), and id (the child).[72]

Aram saw a connection between his grandfather, described as a weak and impractical man by his relatives, and William Saroyan's older characters, who are "dreamers, human castoffs"; he said that these characters "lend a poetic dimension to the writings in which they appear that is essential to the charm of Saroyan's work" (21). In his search for the lost father, Aram suggested, William Saroyan became his own father by becoming a writer (21–22).

Aram called attention to the way Saroyan's preoccupation with "speed and mechanical mobility" evolved into "a prose style that was, in its own way, an example of the American genius for invention. He learned to write . . . with an easy-natured clarity and economy of means—like the 'clean lines' of the new American cars or skyscrapers" (28). Later, he experimented with stream-of-consciousness, then economy of means, via Hemingwayesque prose and point of view, until he arrived at "his own American-style amalgam; a streamlined, economy-sized, and immediately popular version of the best of innovative modern literature" (32).

As he had in *Last Rites*, Aram suggested that William's emotional development was crippled by a "psychic freeze" that resulted from his being sent to an orphanage for five years after the death of his father (4). Although this experience made him an artist, it limited his achievement. Aram described his father as motivated by the desire to please and entertain, rather than to confront the implications of what he wrote. Like the entertainer, "he had his stock of tried and true effects, his perennial bag of tricks" and knew how to use them to manipulate his audience (35). And for such a shy man, he noted, his father really had a gift for publicizing himself. After criticizing *The Assyrian* and *Rock Wagram* for "the insistent opacity of the major figure in each" (which he perceived as extensions of his father), Aram stated that these limited characterizations give the impression that "staying in *motion*" is the "real heroism in human affairs," which is akin to equating youthful exuberance with talent (101). In discussing the last phase of his father's writing, Aram noted that though the memoirs, like the mediocre autobiographical novels that preceded them, are less accomplished than his best work, they have their moments of excellence. From this group, Aram chose *Not Dying* as the finest and most psychologically representative work.

Aram blamed his father's success for making it impossible for him to return to the dreary times of his early writing and for his subsequent choice of subject matter. He may have been right. In an essay published posthumously, entitled "Memories of the Uppression," Saroyan recalls the Depression, his bus trip to New York in search of fame, his homesickness, his being a literary misfit, the meaninglessness of the Depression and stock market crash to him—a penniless writer—and his feeling of awe when he saw his first book in print and knew he had made his mark. Thus, Saroyan could say, "this Depression was the best time of my life in a certain sense."[73]

In her essay "William Saroyan and the Family Matter," Margaret Bedrosian discussed the importance of family and ethnicity to both the man and his work, especially *The Assyrian*, *Rock Wagram*, and *The Laughing Matter*. Emphasizing the difference between the author's expressions of affinity with his people and his inability to relate to anyone outside of himself, she commented, "there isn't much that is particularly Armenian or Assyrian or halfway ethnic about the characters in any of these stories, if by those terms we mean a detailed and accurate delineation of a specific people. They are merely props for the central character's introspective battles, bearing foreign-sounding names, sometimes suspicious of outsiders or quaint in speech, patient with whatever fate brings, but leaving us hard-pressed to identify them as Armenian, Assyrian or whatnot."[74] Drawing upon Aram Saroyan's comments about his father's life and writing, she noted ironically that "the poet of the family was himself totally inadequate to the demands of family life" (22).

In his introduction to the posthumously published *Births*, the poet David Kherdian, who had earlier compiled a bibliography of Saroyan's works from 1934–64, called him "the poet of childhood" and "my mentor." He declared that the young of his time found themselves in reading him, and though today the world of the young has changed dramatically, Saroyan still "belongs to youth."[75] To Harry Keyishian, however, *Births* "suffers from the generalizing, wheel-spinning, churning mode that Saroyan sometimes fell into in his later books like *Obituaries*."[76] Joel Oppenheimer's review of *Births* described it as an incomplete work "forced from age," rather than the spontaneous flow of the writer's youth.[77] Though the book is made up of fragments, the reviewer is reminded too that Saroyan once defined the function of the writer as "to gather together again the fragments of a man" (21).

My Name is Saroyan, a collection of Saroyan's contributions to the publications of the Hairenik (Fatherland) Association of Boston from 1933–63, contains a lengthy preface by James H. Tashjian, former editor of the *Armenian Review*, introducing selections from the ninety-seven stories, four plays, five poems, and other works that appeared in *Hairenik Daily*, *Hairenik Weekly*, and *The Armenian Review*. Among them are some of Saroyan's best works. Stressing the many ways in which *Hairenik* publications encouraged and developed Saroyan's career, Tashjian conjectured that Saroyan found in Dr. Reuben Darbinian, their editor-in-chief, a living surrogate father (34).

Reviewing this anthology, Joel Oppenheimer wrote, "The work is a valuable as well as lovely addition to the body of Saroyan's work." Considering the rise and fall of Saroyan's career, he observed that although academics in search of "something more arcane to demonstrate their tastes" tended to dismiss Saroyan's fiction, his stories "still have the power to move the reader. . . . It is fifty years later, times and places and paraphernalia have changed, but Saroyan's vision of the needs of the human being is still pertinent and stirring." His only reservation is that Saroyan might be "too sweet" for today's world.[78]

One of the most thoroughgoing recent studies of Saroyan's work is David S. Calonne's 1983 volume, *William Saroyan: My Real Work is Being*,[79] for which Dickran Kouymjian, who later edited *An Armenian Trilogy*, provided the preface. Kouymjian stated that Calonne had provided "the criterion by which Saroyan's place in twentieth literature can be judged" by relating his "style" and "temperament" either to those writers who influenced Saroyan (i. e., Whitman, Anderson, Shaw) or to those with whose view of life and / or temperament he could identify (Wolfe, Miller, Beckett). Kouymjian described this book as a "meditation on Saroyan firmly anchored in the works themselves" and thought that it initiated a long-overdue understanding and respect for his work (xi).

In his introduction, Calonne attributed Saroyan's fall from favor to the influence of the New Critics on the teaching and evaluation of American literature. In addition, he thought that academics may have taken umbrage at Saroyan's irreverent and often unflattering remarks about them. Noting that "The angst of the twentieth century pervades his work," Calonne asserted that "This darker, existential side of Saroyan's work has been almost completely ignored by commentators." Saroyan, conscious that he was a self divided, was obsessed by the theme of "madness." (His compulsion to write daily might have been his way of unifying segments of himself, Calonne suggested.) Saroyan believed the world needed to change, to be cured and psychically regenerated through art, and for Calonne his sense of the "essential" loneliness of man links him with the philosophy and writers of our time (8–11).

Calonne identified five themes in Saroyan's work: the relation of art to reality, love and loneliness, the exile in search of home, the world of childhood and the family, and the autobiographical quest. He felt that although Saroyan saw both the world and the self as chaotic and full of conflict, he also found that "it is this dialectical tension between despair and joy which gives his work its strength and lasting worth" (11). Saroyan's symbolic use of the trapeze artist in the story that first brought him fame suggests "the perilous nature of humanity's search for meaning and the essential tenuousness of life itself" as well as "the continual oscillation between faith and despair which occurs throughout [Saroyan's] work" (15). In the rush and accumulated detail of Saroyan's style Calonne saw his wish "to show the oneness of all things through multiplicity" (16).

It was Calonne's view that the twenty-six stories in *The Daring Young Man on the Flying Trapeze* contain within them the major themes to be found throughout Saroyan's work (205). Of *My Heart's in the Highlands* he remarked that "one of the greatest messages of Saroyan's drama is first sounded here: that we are not at home on Earth." Remarking that "Death pervades the play" (78), he concluded that "Like so many works of modern literature, *The Time Of Your Life* leaves its hero suspended between two worlds: one dying and the other powerless to be born" (97).

Citing Saroyan's own statement that all his work is allegorical, Calonne stressed his insightful portrayal of human alienation (118). Discussing *The Cave Dwellers* and Saroyan's other postwar plays, Calonne concluded, "The artist's ability to allegorize humanity's estrangement and still submerged divinity through drama is his greatest claim to supremacy" (210). He described *The Human Comedy* as an allegory "full of strange encounters of the self with some deep beauty at the heart of existence" (101). In his concluding chapter, Calonne asserted that Saroyan's last phase, which contains some of his best prose, repeatedly expresses his sense of a divided self. The effort to unite the self through recollection, Calonne pointed out, is similar to the method of psychoanalysis, and Saroyan's interest in the autobiographical mode, which appeared very early, reflects his belief that the artist while alive is not only creating his art but living his life so that it becomes a work of art (142–44). Callone asserted that in his writings Saroyan consistently pursued one idea, the "nameless, awful, and beautiful mystery at the heart of life," and concluded that "his genius lay in his ability successfully to evoke and celebrate it through art" (149).

In the first of two studies of the author, *William Saroyan*[80] (1984), Edward H. Foster discussed Saroyan's search for identity, the effects on him of being an outsider, and his disengagement from twentieth-century social and political movements. More directly critical of Saroyan's work as a whole than Callone, Foster felt that while his work is entertaining, it makes few imaginative or intellectual demands (11). Nevertheless, he concluded that when Saroyan did write well, he showed "an acute and disturbing sense of the life of his time" (12). "At his best, Saroyan was often, in one way or another, writing autobiography and the final autobiographical works are logical continuations of what he had been doing from the start" (14). Since the booklet is part of a Western Writers series, Foster also points out the ways in which the provisional, transitory world Saroyan creates is characteristic of other writers of the American West. In the section entitled "Fresno," Foster stated that what Saroyan created was "a cleaned-up version" of his home town, free of the prejudice he himself had experienced. Foster criticized Saroyan for writing too much and too carelessly and for being too prone to ignore the ugly side of human experience (24).

Foster reminded us that Saroyan developed a literary voice with "a highly personal vocabulary and attitude"; it was "sentimental, generous, genial, warm, whimsical, amused and amusing," so that though critical readers may not find much of literary value, they "will still have the pleasure of listening to very good and charming talk" (29). He pointed out that ". . . a writer like Saroyan is not to be judged by conventional standards; the only appropriate standards are, in the end, the standards his work itself proposes" (31). While Saroyan failed to write a masterpiece, Foster states, the combination of Saroyan's politics, "his theories of art and his regional and ethnic identities," formed a "complex literary presence" that resulted in "an accomplished literature" (34): "Saroyan's early accomplishment is substantial both within itself and its apparent effect on subsequent writers. While he later became mostly an entertainer, his early work was a real contribution to the literature of freedom. For that and for his distinctive voice, Saroyan must be given major focus when the definitive literary history of America in the 1930's and 1940's is written" (47). In 1984 the English author Brian Darwent edited a collection bearing the subtitle "A Connoisseur's Anthology of the Writings of William Saroyan."[81] Preceded by a ten-page introductory biographical sketch, drawn primarily from Saroyan's own writing, the book consists of sixty-five selections spanning Saroyan's career. Noting that "William Saroyan once said that to write was for him simply to stay alive in an interesting way," Darwent remarked that in nearly half century of writing Saroyan continued to be a writer "in the purest sense, writing almost invariably out of himself, as he put it, in the manner of a poet," giving only superficial attention to traditional literary form but creating a simple style, capable of "depth" and "complexity" and free of cliches (xviii).

Interest in Saroyan's life continued. In 1984 journalist Lawrence Lee and novelist Barry Gifford combined oral with conventional sources to put together a compelling biography of Saroyan.[82] Drawing upon more than 100 conversations with famous people and members of the family, they created a vivid, not always complimentary, portrait of the person they knew and the time and culture they witnessed. Among the famous, actress Julie Haydon Nathan, artist Al Hirschfield, writers Budd Schulberg and Irwin Shaw, and musician Artie Shaw are quoted extensively. In *Trio*,[83] a book about his mother's friendships with Gloria Vanderbilt and Oona O'Neill, Aram Saroyan again discussed his father, this time stressing his mother's point of view.

Seven years after Kenneth W. Rhoads' article depicting the protagonist of *The Time of Your Life* as a type of Christ, John Mills responded in " 'What, What-Not': Absurdity in Saroyan's *The Time of Your Life*,"[84] arguing that Joe should be viewed "as an homme absurde" and the play "as an embodiment of the absurd sense of life, expressing in its structure and all of its parts man's confrontations with nothingness" (139). Within the traditions of absurdist literature, in which optimism and pessimism coexist, Joe's "immobility," which makes him "a still center amid the flux of quotidian activity," is actually "a counterpart of an inner, psychic immobilization" resulting from his realization of the absurdity of life (145). Mills saw this factor in Joe's other actions—e. g, his indecisive behavior—and concluded that "Joe has come to regard all tasks as Sisyphean . . . meaningless activity" (145).

Citing parallels with Beckett and Camus, Mills placed special emphasis on the arab's repeated refrain in the opening sequence: "No foundation, all the way down the line" (146). According to Mills, Joe's mission is not the salvation of his fellow man, but self-discovery. The absurdist view is expressed not only in the dialogue and actions, but also in the play's structure, which is "conspicuously non-linear, static, mirroring in its randomness and clutter that chaos which, in its absurdist view, characterizes life itself" (154). Mills considered the harmony between feeling and form as making this play the most "aesthetically satisfying" of Saroyan's works, but, he cautioned, "its surface charm ought not to blind us to the weightier metaphysical import which lies just beneath" (159).

A differing interpretation was offered by Robert Everding in his 1986 article "*The Time of Your Life*: A Figment in a Nightmare of an Idiot,"[85] where he maintained that Saroyan's purpose in the play is messianic, serving his commitment "to awaken the audience not only to the necessity for a new approach to life, but also to the absurdly theatrical nature of its own behavior" (12). In a note at the end of the essay, Everding reminded us that Saroyan declared repeatedly that Bernard Shaw had the greatest influence on him. "Both men use what Shaw called the terrible art of sharpshooting at the audience, trapping them, fencing with them, always aiming at the sorest spot in their consciences, to overthrow the audience's narrow values and thus prepare the way for the dramatist's own ideas" (21). Everding analyzed the ways plot, setting, props, and characterization (particularly of the protagonist, Joe) serve Saroyan's purpose, which is to change the audience's conception of heroism: "The spectators find in the enlightened Joe a more credible hero, one in whom they can recognize their own humanity and through whom they can understand how to live authentically in the modern world" (17). Noting that Saroyan identified the pinball machine as essential to the climax of the play, Everding discussed its role as "the central symbol for the destructiveness of the world's ethic" (18). Everding concluded that Saroyan (like Shaw) felt that once the curtain falls, "the real play begins" when the now enlightened audience departs from the "theater of illusions" to meet the challenges of real life outside the theater doors (21).

Gerald Haslam's "William Saroyan and the Critics,"[86] published in 1985, pointed to Saroyan's adversarial relationship with critics as a key factor in his being denied his rightful place in American literature. Remarking that "Few American writers have risen as fast or tumbled as dramatically as William Saroyan," Haslam cited as causes of his downfall both his "disordered output" and his personality. In fact, he said, "Saroyan's self-centered, sometimes abrasive character became more important than his writing to some. He was, during the first half of his career, as much a public figure as an artist; the confusion by him as well as the critics made it easy to ignore his literary accomplishments once his notoriety faded" (87). Still, Haslam hailed Saroyan as "an authentic, singular American genius" (87) whose "freedom from conventional literary modes of reality" marked him as a precursor of magical realism. He concluded that, owing to the volume and quality of his creative legacy, "Saroyan's position in American letters appears secure. Few twentieth century American authors have produced a richer, more diverse body of work" (88).

In his article "Saroyan's Study of Ethnicity,"[87] Walter Shear pointed out that "At one time William Saroyan was America's most famous ethnic writer" (45). Limiting his discussion to *My Name is Aram*, specifically "the relationship between the ethnic community and the mainstream culture and its examination of the social interaction within each group" (46), Shear remarked that "the personal comes to have several shades of meaning in this collection" (50). In many of these stories, "the movement around and about the official social situation creates the playfulness of a game situation. The characters involved are more apt to appreciate the ingenuity, the active intention, and the persistence of the other person. They are inevitably moved to an attempt at understanding" (53). Defending Saroyan against charges of escapism, Shear argued that "Saroyan is essentially a modernist in that he regards fictional reality as multifaceted" and identifies his awareness of the claims of the ethnic community as the quality that pushed him in this direction: "The book seems based primarily on Saroyan's recollections of people's infinite capacities for manipulating their conventions. In it he creates, through a rhythmically comic interchase of internal values and social perspectives, a version of how culture might work" (249). In these observations Shear usefully connected Saroyan's ethnic themes to the wider literary currents of which he was a part.

Perhaps the most unusual and most ethnic of the heretofore unpublished work by Saroyan are the three plays—*The Armenians* (1971), *Bitlis* (1975), and *Haratch* (1979)—collected in the volume *William Saroyan: An Armenian Trilogy*, edited by Dickran Kouymjian.[88] Kouymjian believed the collection to represent Saroyan's "non-public . . . inner" world, whose most important elements are his family (especially his father), his origins, his Armenian experience, and his selfhood—his struggle to define, understand, and accept the person he had become" (vii). Though Saroyan approached the subject indirectly, Kouymjian said, genocide "is the genesis of the two major themes in the trilogy: exile, and the survival of a dispersed nation denied the right of repatriation" (7).

Kouymjian said that in his later years Saroyan came to think of the play, rather than the short story or the essay, as his best medium, although a great number of Saroyan's late plays—he wrote fifteen in the spring and summer of 1975—have yet to be published (2–3). On Saroyan's working techniques, Kouymjian noted that he spent 20–30 minutes a day on the plays, producing a page a day, without notes, outlines, or revisions (9). *Haratch*, the "longest, densest, and most serious" (30) of the three plays, was composed in thirty days, at the same time as *Births*, Kouymjian noted, though the works bear no resemblance in style or subject. All the discussion in it evolves from the question of the meaning of Armenian identity today. Saroyan is the leading character in this play, as he is in *Bitlis*, and its dialogue seems to be modeled after the dialogues of Plato. "It is a play of ideas," Kouymjian asserted, that illustrates Saroyan's love of the paradoxical (34) and shows the effect of the loss of fatherland on his life and work. Claiming that this loss was "the source of many of his most characteristic traits and attitudes," Kouymjian remarked, "Until the internal landscape of these plays is grasped, studied, and appreciated, any biography of Saroyan will be perforce incomplete" (37). Despite the fact that the second and third plays have no stage directions at all and almost no action, Kouymjian asserted that "they are theatrical pieces intended for the stage. Like every one of his plays, they are a challenge to the skill of the most talented directors because of the problems and paradoxes they seek to unravel. Their intensity and brilliance is not defined by action or plot, but by language and idea. Their message is universal and enduring" (38). The *Library Journal*'s reviewer took a contrary view of this collection: "In these most undramatic of plays, the dialogue is rhetorical, the plot non-existent, and the subject matter narrowly focused;

they are more Socratic dialogues than dramas. They will be of interest primarily to Saroyan devotees and those of Armenian heritage."[89] Perhaps this criticism was answered in Nishan Parlakian's review of a 1975 performance of *The Armenians*. Parlakian noted that although the script alone seems difficult to stage "because it is short on plot and long on words," that sort of writing is Saroyan's strength because he wants his plays to seem as "wayward and formless as life itself": "For him plot and story telling are artifices; straight talk from characters is truth. And in "Armenians," the talk—lyrical, poignant, and transcendent—is all true and it gives us some of Saroyan's most memorable characters."[90] Leo Hamalian's collection of thirty essays, *William Saroyan: The Man and Writer Remembered*,[91] provides a variety of close-up views of Saroyan, several previously unpublished, which the editor felt "compose a picture that puts Saroyan in a new and different light, one that separates the solid accomplishments from the flashy myth" (12). He remarked that though Saroyan's work has not been properly valued by "the literary establishment," there are signs now "that readers' tastes are changing, that critical assumptions about his work may be broadening," so that with time Saroyan may be honored as the trailblazer for those writing about the immigrant experience in America (12). In support of this purpose, Hamalian also edited *Madness in the Family*,[92] a collection of sixteen short stories written in the last decade of Saroyan's career which Hamalian considered to be among his best. Noting that Saroyan initiated his career with the short story, Hamalian observed that "he remained an innovative and distinguished practitioner of the form throughout his career" (vii).

In the article "William Saroyan in California,"[93] Margaret Bedrosian related the fluctuating images of California that appear in his writing to the tensions enveloping him in his life. Observing that "The sources of these tensions cannot be separated from Saroyan's family and cultural past" (202), she drew a historical portrait of Fresno in the first two decades of this century. Describing the Armenian refugees who immigrated to the San Joaquin Valley, the hostile feelings they generated among the "Americans" there, and some of the reasons for prejudice against them, she linked those experiences to Saroyan's ambivalence about being an Armenian, as expressed in such works as *My Name is Aram*. She attributed the fact that these stories are the most popular of his works as much to "what Saroyan avoided saying in them as [to] what he actually described." For Bedrosian, "the book's Armenians and other ethnic characters belong to a fairy tale about how things ought to have been" rather than to reality, for Saroyan leaned heavily on the comic to transform the ugly (205).

In his review of *An Armenian Trilogy*,[94] Harold Aram Veeser also dwelt on the subject of ethnicity, asserting that although Saroyan "spent a lifetime evading Armenian history," he finally faced the past "squarely" during the last ten years of his life, while writing the trilogy under review (95). Calling Saroyan "a giant . . . a literary precursor with whom subsequent Armenian writers must grapple," he added, "wherever such writers begin, Saroyan precedes them" (95–96). Seeing Saroyan as progenitor of Michael J. Arlen and Peter Balakian, as well as such non-Armenian writers as Salinger, Brautigan, Kerouac, and others (105), Veeser saw this book as "a mandate to reevaluate Saroyan's earlier writings" (107) and thereby counterbalance "the patronizing, uncomprehending, and ethnocentric North American critics" who have kept this author in obscurity (107).

Edward Halsey Foster's *William Saroyan: A Study of the Short Fiction*[95] is organized into three parts: Foster's own excellent discussion of the short fiction; selections by and about Saroyan and Armenia; and critical pieces spanning the period from 1935–84 by a number of critics. Beginning with "The Daring Young Man," which he said "should be read as a parable of Armenia and its survival through centuries of oppression" (5), Foster likened Saroyan's world view to Rousseau's (9, 74–76). He also traced the influences of James Joyce, Walt Whitman, and Sherwood Anderson on Saroyan's form and style, discussed Saroyan's influence on younger writers like J. D. Salinger, Budd Schulberg, and Jack Kerouac (286), and tried to correct "misreadings" or dismissals of Saroyan's work by Marxists, conservatives, the New Critics and others. Defending Saroyan against criticism based on the standards of formalists like Percy Lubbock, for whom the author of a piece of fiction "should be invisible like the puppet master behind the screen, allowing the story to reveal itself" (17), Foster pointed out that Saroyan's work depended on "a sense of urgency, freshness, and immediacy," and that Saroyan believed that ideally "a story would try to maintain the illusion that it was spoken" (18).

Saroyan's perceptions of himself as an Armenian, said Foster, can be best understood by "comparing his stories to the gestural paintings of the Armenian-American painter Arshile Gorky," though he noted that unlike Gorky "Saroyan moved increasingly toward pure abstraction" (27). Of the story "Antranik of Armenia," for example, Foster argued that " 'Armenia' is an abstraction, like Gorky's painting of his father's farm" (28). Foster claimed that the movies "taught Saroyan how to create gently comic worlds in which real suffering never exists" (30). Perhaps, too, he speculated, Hollywood taught Saroyan about marketing (49). Of Saroyan's change by the late thirties and early forties from ardent expressionist to slick master of "verbal mannerisms and techniques," Foster commented, "Indeed, by this time the Saroyan story was itself a recognized type and Saroyan in effect had become his own best imitator" (47). Noting the paucity of short fiction published by Saroyan in the last thirty years of his life, and Saroyan's spate of autobiographical books from *Here Comes, There Goes You Know Who* in 1961 to *Births* published after his death, Foster observed, "Many of these books involve a gimmick that is little more than an excuse for writing. . . . What matters in each case is the ongoing fact of writing, and the memoir or informal essay serves much the same function as the short story had earlier" (70). In this enduring dedication to self-expression lies Saroyan's personal and artistic heroism.

CONCLUSION

There are indications that Saroyan's work will survive the caprices of time and taste. In summer 1983 the Royal Shakespeare Company staged *The Time of Your Life* in Stratford, England, where Saroyan's play shared billing with three plays by Shakespeare.[96] His wartime novel *The Human Comedy*, made into an opera by Galt MacDermot (the composer of *Hair*), was produced early in 1984 at the Joseph Papp Theater in Manhattan.[97] Jon Whitmore's *William Saroyan: A Research and Production Sourcebook*, which appeared in 1995, describes and assesses Saroyan's contribution to drama and provides critical bibliographies of his writings for and about the theater.[98] As this volume goes to press, author Jack Leggatt, assisted by the Saroyan Foundation, is completing an authorized biography of Saroyan. Nona Balakian's study of the humanist strain in Saroyan is also on its way to publication. Time and additional perspectives will reveal more about the contributions of this paradoxical man and remarkably gifted writer.

Notes

1. E. Beloin, "Saroyanesque," *New Republic*, 26 December 1934, 201.

2. Clifton Fadiman, "The Wolf and Saroyan," *New Yorker*, 22 February 1936, 67.

3. M. M. Flood, "To You, Endless Announcements: An Imaginary Conversation With Walt Whitman," *Saturday Review*, 8 September 1945, 14–15.

4. Joseph Remenyi, "William Saroyan: A Portrait," *College English* 6 (November 1944): 95–96.

5. Frederick I. Carpenter, "The Time of Saroyan's Life," *Pacific Spectator* 1 (November 1947): 88.

6. Howard Floan, "Saroyan and Cervantes' Knight," *Thought* 33 (Spring 1958): 81–82.

7. Elizabeth Valentine, "Time of His Life," *New York Times Magazine*, 20 April 1941, 29.

8. Alfred Kazin, *New Republic*, 13 December 1943, 851.

9. Ralph Allen, "Private Saroyan and the War," *New York Times Magazine*, 4 June 1944, 46.

10. Howard Floan, *William Saroyan* (New York: Twayne Publishers, 1966), 82.

11. Henry Seidel Canby, "Armenian Picaresque," *Commonweal* 34 (16 May 1934), 1.

12. Grenville Vernon, "More On Saroyan," *Commonweal* 34 (16 May 1934), 86.

13. Horace Gregory, "The Significance of Saroyan," *New York Herald Tribune*, 23 February 1936, 7.

14. William R. Benet, "A Daring Young Man," *Saturday Review*, 22 October 1934, 221.

15. Edmund Wilson, "The Boys in the Back Room," *New Republic*, 18 November 1940, 697.

16. Philip Rahv, "William Saroyan, A Minority Report," *American Mercury* 58 (September 1943): 373.

17. Jack Kroll, "The Time of Saroyan," *Newsweek*, 17 November 1969, 139.

18. T. S. Mathews, "Yea-Sayer," *New Republic*, 18 March 1936, 173.

19. George Jean Nathan, "Merit in Cocoon," *Newsweek*, 23 October 1939, 30.

20. Stark Young, *New Republic*, 29 November 1939, 169.

21. Stark Young, "Critics in a Circle," *New Republic*, 5 May 1941, 632.

22. Stark Young, "Saroyan Directing," *New Republic*, 12 May 1941, 664.

23. Stark Young, "Saroyan Theater," *New Republic*, 31 August 1942, 257.

24. *Theatre Arts* 25 (June 1941): 411.

25. W. A. H. Birnie, "Daring Young Man," *American* 129 (June 1940): 16.

26. *New Yorker*, 11 May 1940, 28.

27. Joseph W. Krutch, "God is Love, or Why Worry?" *Nation*, 3 May 1941.

28. *Commonweal* 32 (11 October 1940): 182.

29. George Jean Nathan, "Again the Fresno Kid," *Newsweek*, April 1940, 45.

30. Wolcott Gibbs, "The Good With the Bad," *New Yorker*, 10 October 1942, 30.

31. Brooks Atkinson, "Hello Out There," *New York Times*, 30 September 1942, 28.

32. Burton Bernstein, *Thurber* (New York: Dodd, Mead, 1975), 230–31.

33. Edwin B. Burgum, "The Lonesome Young Man on the Flying Trapeze," *Virginia Quarterly Review* 20 (Summer 1944): 399–403.

34. *Theatre Arts*, October 1939, 716–17.

35. *Commonweal*, 11 October 1940, 512.

36. Wolcott Gibbs, "Back Again Briefly," *New Yorker*, 29 August 1942, 28.

37. Brooks Atkinson, "Two to Show on Saroyan," *New York Times*, 21 March 1942, 13.

38. Harrison Smith, "Saroyan's War," *Saturday Review*, 1 June 1946, 7.

39. *Life*, 19 May 1941, 128–29.

40. George Jean Nathan, "Saroyan: Whirling Dervish of Fresno," *American Mercury* 51 (November 1940): 305.

41. Nona Balakian, "So Many Saroyans," *New Republic*, 7 August 1950, 19–20.

42. John Brooks, "A Man Who Hates Nobody," *Saturday Review*, 24 March 1951, 13.

43. Oscar Handlin, "Grapes and the Sea," *Saturday Review*, 11 October 1952, 27.

44. Elizabeth Bowen, "In Spite of the Words," *New Republic*, 9 March 1953, 18–19.

45. William Fisher, "Whatever Became of Saroyan," *College English* 16 (Spring 1958), 336.

46. Thomas F. Curley, "The Severe and Light-Hearted World of Saroyan," *Commonweal* 64 (22 June 1956): 302.

47. Henry Hewes, *Saturday Review*, 2 November 1957, 22.

48. Wolcott Gibbs, *New Yorker*, 2 November 1957.

49. *Commonweal* 67 (13 October 1957): 289.

50. *Time*, 28 October 1957, 90.

51. Patrick Dennis, "Waiting for Saroyan," *New Republic*, 4 November 1957.

52. Stanley Kauffmann, *New Republic*, 25 March 1972, 21.

53. Howard Floan, "I Am Still Here," *Saturday Review of Literature*, 18 January 1969, 42.

54. Budd Schulberg, "Saroyan: Ease and Unease on the Flying Trapeze," *Esquire*, October 1960, 85.

55. "Hello, Saroyan, Goodbye," *Newsweek*, 2 March 1959, 57.

56. Harold Clurman, *Nation*, 24 November 1969, 581.

57. *Time*, "The First Hippie," 24 November 1969, 57.

58. Stanley Kauffman, *New Republic*, 22 November 1969, 22.

59. Jack Richardson, "Innocence Restaged," *Commentary* 49 (March 1970): 20.

60. Thelma J. Shinn, "William Saroyan: Romantic Existentialist," *Modern Drama* 15 (September 1972): 190.

61. Kenneth W. Rhoads, "Joe as Christ-type in Saroyan's *The Time of Your Life*," *Essays in Literature* 3 (1976): 228–29.

62. Patrick McGilligan, "Mr. Saroyan's Thoroughly American Movie," in *The Modern Novel and the Movies*, ed. Gerald Peary and Roger Shotzkin (New York: Frederick Ungar, 1978), 158–59.

63. Harry Keyishian, "Michael Arlen and William Saroyan: Armenian Ethnicity and the Writer," in *The Old Century and the New: Essays in Honor of Charles Angoff*, ed. Alfred Rosa (Madison, N J: Fairleigh Dickinson University Press, 1978), 178.

64. Herbert Gold, "A Twenty-Year Talk With Saroyan," *New York Time Book Review*, 20 May 1979, 51.

65. Mark Harris, "Father and Son," *New York Times Book Review*, 1 August 1982, 22.

66. Richard Lingeman, review of *Obituaries*, *Nation*, 29 December 1979, 697.

67. *Forbes Magazine*, 26 May 1980, 27.

68. *Publisher's Weekly*, 26 March 1979, 71.

69. *Obituaries* (Berkeley, C A: Creative Arts Press, 1979), 283.

70. *After Thirty Years: The Daring Young Man on the Flying Trapeze* (New York: Harcourt Brace, 1964), 112–13.

71. Aram Saroyan, *Last Rites* (New York: William Morrow, 1982), 17.

72. Aram Saroyan, *William Saroyan* (New York: Harcourt, Brace, Jovanovich, 1983), 17.

73. William Saroyan, Memories of the Uppression," *Literary Review* 27 (Fall 1983): 9.

74. Margaret Bedrosian, "William Saroyan and the Family Matter" *MELUS* 9:4 (Winter II 1982): 22. In his 1991 book Edward Halsey Foster offers an alternative reading of this work.

75. *Births* (Berkeley: Creative Arts Press, 1983), ii.

76. Harry Keyishian, "Who Was William Saroyan?" *Literary Review* 27 (Fall 1983): 157.

77. Joel Oppenheimer, review of *My Name is Saroyan* and *Births*, *New York Time Book Review*, 21 August 1983, 3.

78. Oppenheimer, 3.

79. David S. Calonne, *William Saroyan: My Real Work is Being* (Chapel Hill: University of North Carolina Press, 1983).

80. Edward Halsey Foster, *William Saroyan* (Boise: Boise State University Western Writers Series 61, 1984).

81. *The New Saroyan Reader*, ed. Brian Darwent (Berkeley: Creative Arts Press, 1984).

82. Lawrence Lee and Barry Gifford, *Saroyan: A Biography* (New York: Harper & Row, 1984).

83. Aram Saroyan, *Trio* (New York: Simon and Schuster, 1985).

84. John Mills, " 'What, What-not': Absurdity in Saroyan's *The Time of Your Life*," *Midwest Quarterly* 26:2 (Winter 1985): 139–59.

85. Robert G. Everding, "The Time of Your Life: 'A Figment in the Mind of an Idiot,' " *McNeese Review*, 32 (1986–89): 11–22.

86. Gerald Haslam, "William Saroyan and the Critics," *Amelia* (April 1985): 87–92.

87. Walter Shear, "Saroyan's Study of Ethnicity," MELUS 13:1–2 (Spring–Summer 1986): 45.

88. *William Saroyan*: An Armenian Trilogy, ed. Dickran Kouymjian (Fresno: California State University Press, 1986).

89. *Library Journal*, 15 September 1986, 98.

90. Nishan Parlakian, "Saroyan's Armenians," *Ararat* 16:3 (Summer 1975): 3.

91. Leo Hamalian, *William Saroyan: The Man and Writer Remembered* (Madison, N J: Fairleigh Dickinson University Press, 1987).

92. *Madness in the Family*, ed. Leo Hamalian (New York: New Directions, 1988).

93. Margaret Bedrosian, "William Saroyan in California," *California History* 68:4 (Winter 1989–90): 202–209.

94. Harold Aram Veeser, review of *An Armenian Trilogy*, *Journal of Armenian Studies* 5:1 (Winter–Spring 1990–91): 95–108.

95. Edward Halsey Foster, *William Saroyan: A Study of the Short Fiction* (New York: Twayne Publishers, 1991).

96. Mel Gussow, "Stage View: Stratford Offers a Mix of Shakespeare and Saroyan," *New York Times*, 17 July 1983, 5.

97. *Time*, 6 February 1984, 75.

98. Jon Whitmore, *William Saroyan: A Research and Production Sourcebook* (Westport, CT: Greenwood Press, 1995).

REVIEWS

◆

Yea-Sayer [Review of *Inhale and Exhale*]

T. S. MATTHEWS*

The question before the house is this: Is William Saroyan any good; and if so, why? He has now published two books of so-called short stories, and you might think somebody would have a definite opinion about him one way or the other; but so far I haven't encountered it. Or rather, I haven't encountered it in print. The unofficial verdict of more than one reviewer has been that Saroyan is a pretty complete phony. Even his publishers content themselves with cautiously admitting that his career (so far) has been "meteoric" and that he has created "much discussion and controversy."

The fact is, Saroyan is bad news to the book-reporters. They know an out-and-out bad book when they see one; and, within the narrow limits of "publishable" stuff, they know a good one. But when something comes along that isn't really "publishable" and yet gets published, and what's more, very much published, they're apt to find themselves up a tree. A book like that, whether it's good or bad, can give them a lot of trouble; it can even show them up. It's obvious, for instance, that Saroyan is not what is called "a good writer"; people who smack their lips over good writing will never come within smacking distance of him. But it's equally obvious that what he's shouting about is not just his bumptious Armenian self but something vital. The rub comes in deciding whether he's a blasphemer or a buffoon. Or, perhaps, neither.

There was once a fellow named Walt Whitman. He billed himself as a poet, but the things he wrote were often not recognizably, not reviewably, poetry. He broke all the literary-club rules about making a scene in the reading room, and he would insist on shouting about himself at the top of his lungs. He had very bad taste, very little sense of form; he used words and ideas that were much too big for him; he ranted on like a drunken actor. He didn't seem to give a damn whether he made a fool of himself or not. He was fond of dragging in bastard words like "arriere" and "libertad" and "me imperturbe." A great deal of Whitman's writing was promissory, a great deal of it sheer brag. The professors have mummified him into a literary figure, but he was better than that. He could hardly write his name

*Reprinted from *The New Republic*, 18 March 1936: 172–73.

in their language; but he made his mark. William Saroyan is the same sort of fellow.

Saroyan's great discovery—which is an open secret, but to all intents and purposes observed by nobody—is that art is foolishness and artists are liars. "No one is reading the story of life, and no one is writing it." What they are doing is making up brilliant explanations which really fool nobody. Saroyan states his anti-literary case with violence, with exaggeration, with buffoonery. How else can such a case be stated? Like somebody who suddenly finds himself walking quietly in the company of madmen, his impulse is to dissociate himself from them violently. The case can be stated in another way—intellectually, precisely, in a still, small voice. In fact, it has been; but who listens? Saroyan's impulse is emotional: he wants to make himself heard, and he does. I suppose many if not most of those who listen hear nothing but a loud noise, but there are some who hear what the shouting is about. And to them there is something in Saroyan's cockeyed flamboyance that sounds more refreshingly natural than all the sound sense and artistry they have blinked at in half a lifetime.

Saroyan's stories are seldom simply stories: they are apt to turn into jeremiads or paeans or cachinnations or exhibitionistic caperings or poems with cuss-words. A great part of them seem to be directed at himself—with the door open. Parts of them are indistinguishable from small-boy boasting. This second book of his, with seventy-some of these "stories," abounds with poetic titles—"Laura, Immortal"; "The Gay & Melancholy Flux"; "World Wilderness of Time Lost"; "Yea & Amen"; "Taxi to Laughter & Life Unending"; "Prelude to an American Symphony." Because he almost always writes in the first person, he is accused of writing continuously about himself. To which he might reply, with Whitman: "I am large; I contain multitudes." He is always trying—though he does not always succeed—to get the multitudes up to the microphone. Sometimes he breaks off into a diatribe, as when he is writing about one of those old-fashioned movie comedies he saw as a boy, in which everybody throws pies at everybody else, and the whole thing ends up in a lunatic chase: ". . . but God Almighty it didn't seem funny to me and I sat in the darkness trying to laugh, but I kept thinking, Why are they wasting everything, why are they making all these mistakes, why is everybody so awkward and mean, what is the God damn meaning of this stuff?" Sometimes he preaches: "Brother, breathe deeply." Sometimes he talks about "the novel that must eventually be written. It will have to be about Ezra Pound and the editor of The Saturday Evening Post. It will have to be about everything." Sometimes he reminds himself of what he is trying to do: "Unless there is praying in a story it cannot be a story." Often he delivers himself of aphorisms of dubious truth or dubious importance: "Playing poker is a much better way to get to be a wise man than taking a correspondence course . . . I discovered this amazing truth, that nature is international. . . ." And sometimes he hits a note that Hans Andersen would have heard with delight, as in his story about the little whistle whose queer sound reminded the hearer of Nothing. ("In London I blew the whistle at the king's palace, and there will be no end of consequences.")

The book is well named. It is not nearly so much a book of stories as a book of breathing. To say that Saroyan is sometimes a blow-hard is to say nothing; for he draws many an honest and many a deep breath. It won't do to copy: it's not a book of breathing exercises any more than it's a model of literary calisthenics. These "stories" do not give a clear view of Saroyan's world, but they give glimpses of it, and from what I have seen I believe in its reality. Saroyan's world is not a mess but a chaos. It is not inhabited by members of lost generations nor by pilgrims night-foundered in a waste land nor by class-conscious proletarians nor by Laputan artists. Saroyan is not a Nay-sayer. In fact, he says Yea! in such a loud, glad voice that people can hardly make out whether he is cheering himself or making the great affirmation. I'll let you in on a secret: he's doing both.

New Abundance
[Review of *The Time of Your Life*]

STARK YOUNG*

Almost everyone who likes "The Time of Your Life" will speak of its abundance and be sure that he is making an original remark. Original or not, the word is inevitable for this play, which has fullness rather than power, and has flexibility rather than force, but which carries all its varied content with gusto and a kind of open delight in itself.

In something like this sense Mr. Saroyan's play is poetic, far more so than some of the blank-verse efforts that help to give what is called poetic drama a black eye. He has created a plentiful life that pours up constantly; the mind behind the play is rich with curiosity, wide music, variety, an instinct for human color, a patter of human words, and a passion, almost gay, for half-tragic human experience. As Mr. Brooks Atkinson says in The New York Times, Mr. Saroyan uses "the stage for incantation and makes an affirmation about life that he does not specifically declare." The main setting, that barroom along the waterfront in San Francisco, helps to frame and carry all this, a place whose doors all the world may stream through, and whose soul, which is alcohol, has the Dionysian function of releasing the souls, memories, moods, passions of those that come there.

The rambling technical defects of Mr. Saroyan's play make good illustrations of the inexorable—you could very well call them biological—exactions of the theatre. The theatre has its distances, physical, mental and emotional, as we have, beyond which nothing can be truly seen or felt. The needs, too, of the actors parallel those of our bodies: just as, for instance, you cannot walk out of a room without legs, so the actor cannot get out of a scene without something contrived for him to get out on. Take the case of Miss Julie Haydon, for example. She has certainly a very genuine stage quality; she is, in sum, material in which a dramatist and a director might profitably work their creative wills. We may recall her performance in "Shadow and Substance," in which she wiped Sir Cedric Hardwicke clean off the slate, what with her intense and lovely conviction, her simple and quiet approach, and her dream and knowledge of the miracle. She was for that reason a

*Reprinted from *The New Republic*, 29 November 1939: 169.

shrewd choice for the role of "The Time of Your Life's" prostitute (ending in romantic terms) and she could undoubtedly contribute a great deal in kind to the play's character, mood and elusive complexity, if only her role were written.

There is also the role that Mr. Eddie Dowling has been provided with. It must be said that Mr. Dowling's performance does indeed follow after Milton and sit in the center and enjoy bright day, though sun and moon be in the flat sea sunk. But he is, nevertheless, asked to play a part that is not really written. The sun and moon in this case are questions perfectly natural, as well as dramatic: for example, what about this man with enough money to make the others ask his opinion, though as to where that money comes from nothing in the play makes clear, this man who can sit so still and register his study of life, though we know nothing of what the springs of his life are or the sources of that deep quietness and final judgment? In that role, notwithstanding, Mr. Dowling achieves some sort of innate tenderness, stillness, sentiment and accuracy that include not only technical skill but other elements as well that defy analysis.

To pick a much simpler element technically in "The Time of Your Life": this saloon of Nick's on Pacific Street is constantly stated in the play as a favored resort; we are to believe that there is no variety of human being or number of them that does not come here. But throughout the entire play, as Mr. Saroyan has written it, we are never presented for a moment with any frequented interval, any crowded scene, in the saloon, that might without effort convince us through our eyes of this essential point.

That practical instinct that is in artists will help Mr. Saroyan to study these matters and consider, with imagination, the laborious imagery and projection special to the stage. Meanwhile his play furnishes us with an illustration of the artist as distinguished from the craftsman—in any art. Which is to say that the basic, underlying, fecundating and generalizing principle of life is there in him, in his theatre writing; and that the transition to theatrical form is but partially achieved. But it is achieved sufficiently to carry a long way already. Moreover, it should be said—and this will mean very little except to professionals—that at this stage of the game it is a certain innocence in Mr. Saroyan, as to what is hackneyed theatre and what is not—this rushing in where the angel playwrights fear to tread—that sometimes lends the play its charming and lovable quality. On the other hand Mr. Saroyan might ask us who these angels are, and make us quite sick.

The Boys in the Back Room:
William Saroyan [Review of
The Trouble With Tigers]

EDMUND WILSON*

The refrain becomes monotonous; but you have to begin by saying that Saroyan, too, derives from Hemingway. The novelists of the older generation—Hemingway himself, Dos Passos, Faulkner, Wilder—have richer and more complex origins, they belong to a bigger cultural world. But if the most you can say of John O'Hara is that he has evidently read Ring Lardner and F. Scott Fitzgerald as well as Hemingway, the most you can say of Saroyan is that he has also read Sherwood Anderson (though he speaks of having looked into a book which he bought for a nickel at a bookstore and which was in Swedish and had pictures of churches). When you remember that Lardner and Anderson were among the original ingredients in Hemingway, you see how limited the whole school is.

But what distinguishes Saroyan from his fellow disciples is the fact that he is not what is called hard-boiled. What was surprising and refreshing about him when he first attracted notice, was that, although he was telling the familiar story about the wise-guy who went into the bar, and I said and the bartender said and I said, this story with Saroyan was never cruel, but represented an agreeable mixture of San Francisco bonhomie and Armenian Christianity. The fiction of the school of Hemingway had been full of bad drunks; Saroyan was a novelty: a good drunk. The spell exerted in the theater by his play, *The Time of Your Life*, consisted in its creating the illusion of friendliness and muzzy elation and gentle sentimentality which a certain amount of beer or rye will bring on in a favorite bar. Saroyan takes you to the bar, and he produces for you there a world which is the way the world would be if it conformed to the feelings instilled by drinks. In a word, he achieves the feat of making and keeping us boozy without the use of alcohol and purely by the stimulus of art. It seems natural that the cop and the labor leader should be having a drink together; that the prostitute should prove to be a wistful child, who eventually gets married by someone that

*Reprinted from *The New Republic*, 18 November 1940: 697–98.

loves her; that the tall tales of the bar raconteur should turn out to be perfectly true, that the bar millionaire should be able to make good his munificent philanthropical offers—that they should be really Jack the Giant-Killer and Santa Claus; and that the odious vice-crusader, who is trying to make everybody unhappy, should be bumped off as harmlessly as the comic villain in an old-fashioned children's "extravaganza."

These magical feats are accomplished by the enchantment of Saroyan's temperament, which induces us to take from him a good many things that we should not accept from other people. With Saroyan the whole trick is the temperament; he rarely contrives a machine. The good fairy who was present at his christening thus endowed him with one of the most precious gifts that a literary artist can have, and Saroyan never ceases to explain to us how especially fortunate he is: "As I say, I do not know a great deal about what the words come to, but the presence says, Now don't get funny; just sit down and say something; it'll be all right. Say it wrong; it'll be all right anyway. Half the time I *do* say it wrong, but somehow or other, just as the presence says, it's right anyhow. I am always pleased about this. My God, it's wrong, but it's all right. It's really all right. How did it happen? Well that's how it is. It's the presence, doing everything for me. It's the presence, doing all the hard work while I, always inclined to take things easy, loaf around, not paying much attention to anything, much, just putting down on paper whatever comes my way."

Well, we don't mind Saroyan's saying this, because he is such an engaging fellow; and we don't mind his putting down on paper whatever happens to come his way. It is true that he has been endowed with a natural felicity of touch which prevents him from being offensive or tiresome in any of the more obvious ways; and at their best his soliloquies and stories recall the spontaneous songs of one of those instinctive composers who, with no technical knowledge of music, manage to finger out lovely melodies. Yet Saroyan is entirely in error in supposing that when he "says it wrong," everything is really all right. What is right in such a case is merely this instinctive sense of form which usually saves him—and even when he is clowning—from making a fool of himself. What *is* wrong, and what his charm cannot conceal, is the use to which he is putting his gifts. It is a shock for one who very much enjoyed *The Daring Young Man on the Flying Trapeze* to go back to reading Saroyan in his latest collection, *The Trouble with Tigers*. There is nothing in the book so good as the best things in *The Flying Trapeze*, and there is a good deal that is not above the level of the facility of a daily columnist. A columnist, in fact, is what William Saroyan seems sometimes in danger of becoming—the kind of columnist who depends entirely on a popular personality, the kind who never reads, who does not know anything in particular about anything, who merely turns on the tap every day and lets it run a column.

It is illuminating to compare this inferior stuff with the contents of a less well-known collection published in California. This volume, *Three Times Three*, consists mainly of miscellaneous pieces which the author seems to regard as not having quite come off. The result is something a great deal more interesting than the slick and rather thin stuff of *Tigers*. One of these pieces, *The Living and the Dead*, of which the author rightly says that it is not so good as it ought to be, seems to me, in spite of the fact that it miscarries to some degree, one of the best things Saroyan has written. The scene with the Armenian grandmother after the departure of the money-collecting Communist is of a startling and compelling beauty. This theme of the foreign-born asserting in modern America the virtues of an older society is one of the principal themes in Saroyan; whenever it appears—as in the short story called *70,000 Assyrians*—it takes his work out of the flat dimensions of the guy watching life in the bar; and here he has brought it into play for one of his most poignant effects. This is followed by an admirable scene, in which the young man walks out on the street and sees a child crying at a window, and reflects that for "the children of the world eternally at the window, weeping at the strangeness of this place," where the Communist must always look forward to a perfected society of the future, where his grandmother must always look backward to a world that has gone with her youth and that could never really have been as she remembers it, it is natural enough to escape into the "even more disorderly universe" of drunkenness, a state sad enough in itself. But the conception, with its three motifs, required a little doing; and Saroyan, as he confesses, did not quite bring it off. He would have had to take the whole thing more seriously and to work it out with more care; and he knows that he can get away with an almost infinite number of less pretentious pieces without having their second-rateness complained of.

Rudyard Kipling said one very good thing about writing: "When you know what you can do, do something else." Saroyan *has* tackled in his plays something larger and more complicated than his stories; but these plays seem now to be yielding to a temptation to turn into columns, too. The three that have been acted and printed have many attractive and promising features in a vein a little like J. M. Barrie's; but George Jean Nathan in the *American Mercury* has given a disquieting account of no less than five new plays by Saroyan that have already been unsuccessfully tried out. There was a rumor that Mr. Nathan had been trying to induce Saroyan to take the trouble to acquaint himself with a few of the classics of the theater, but it sounds as if the attempt had come to naught.

In the meantime, Saroyan goes on with his act, which is that of the unappreciated genius who is not afraid to stand up for his merits. This only obscures the issue. Most good artists begin by getting bad reviews; and Saroyan, in this regard, has been rather remarkably fortunate. So let him set his mind at rest. Everybody who is capable of responding to such things appreciates what is fine in his work. The fact that a number of people who do not know good theatrical writing from bad or whose tastes lie in other directions have failed to recognize Saroyan is no excuse for the artist to neglect his craft. He will be judged not by his personality act or by his ability to get produced and published—which he has proved to the point of absurdity; but by work that functions and lasts.

With his triumph there has crept into Saroyan's work an unwelcome suggestion of smugness. One has always had the feeling with his writing that, for all its amiability and charm, it has had behind it the pressure of a hard and hostile environment, which it has required courage to meet, and that this courage has taken the form of a debonair kidding humor and a continual affirmation of the fundamental kindliness of people—a courage which, in moments when it is driven to its last resources and deepest sincerity, is in the habit of invoking a faith in the loyalties of straight and simple people—Armenians, Czechs, Greeks—surviving untouched by the hatreds of an abstract and complex world. In Saroyan the successful playwright, for whom that pressure has been partially relieved, there seems to be appearing an instinct to exploit this theme of loving-kindness and of the goodness and rightness of things; and there is perhaps a just perceptible philistinism. If Saroyan, in *Love's Old Sweet Song*, has hit upon precisely the right way to make fun of *Time* magazine, he has, on the other hand, here, in what sounds like a skit on *The Grapes of Wrath*, at least grazed the familiar complacency which declares the unemployed are all bums. This is the path that leads to Eddie Guest, Professor William Lyon Phelps and Dr. Frank Crane; and let not Mr. Saroyan deceive himself: no writer has a charmed life.

Saroyan's War [Review of
The Adventures of Wesley Jackson]

HARRISON SMITH*

Twelve years ago, when William Saroyan published his "Daring Young Man on the Flying Trapeze," he became the boy wonder, the daring young genius of our newest literature. He had an exuberant love for life, for bums, tramps, and the poor and downtrodden. He looked at the world around him with dewy-eyed innocence and wonder, as if it were a miracle that the sun should shine, the stars come out at night, that men and women of the lower orders should have big hearts and noble souls, and, above all, that Mr. Saroyan should be a writer. Now approaching forty, he has lost none of his bounce, his gusto, and his Christian ardor. Edmund Wilson has said that he is an agreeable mixture of San Francisco friendliness and Armenian Christianity but has deplored the smugness and self-satisfied facility that he senses in his later work.

Of his latest novel, "The Adventures of Wesley Jackson," it can be reported that there is no trace of smugness, but plenty of narcissism, for the nineteen-year-old hero might be Mr. Saroyan himself, his own adventures in war uniform transformed by the author's usual alchemy into the conventional Saroyan pattern. It begins with young Wesley Jackson in a barracks near San Francisco, the son of a wonderful Mom and a philosophic old reprobate and drunk who is his Pop. It winds up with Jackson in England, still a private, but now a writer who can wring the hearts of the readers of his British propaganda.

Viewed by Mr. Saroyan the American army was made up of a remarkable collection of privates. They were as friendly and as naïve as puppy dogs; each one had a favorite song which he constantly whistled and sang; some were apt to burst into tears at any time, and especially young Jackson, who is the cryingest soldier on record. Most of the officers he had the bad fortune to meet were stupid or vain or both. But just as Pop is a noble drunk in the novel, so the woman who runs a house in the Middle West is a noble madam, and the lady who picks him up in New York and takes him to her

*Reprinted from *The Saturday Review of Literature*, 1 June 1946: 7–8. Copyright © GMI. Reprinted by permission.

penthouse is nobly generous and loving. The only older man in the book who rates any praise is a propaganda officer in London who convinces him that he can write.

The girl Private Jackson marries, though not with book or a candle or the consent of the army, is a half-starved runaway from a poor Gloucester family who would have become a prostitute that very night if she had not run into an American soldier. He decides immediately that she is the destined child-wife he has been looking for all his life; nevertheless, he is cautious enough to investigate the truth of her story before he takes her home with him. Indeed, most of the soldiers the reader meets are looking for a bride, of almost any kind, but especially for a girl who can give them a son. Before they are shot, they want to look into their sons' eyes. Curiously enough, not one of these philoprogenitive warriors wants to look into a baby girl's eyes.

The adventures of some of these sentimental lads in uniform are, according to strict army rules, a little incredible. For example, two of them get a free plane ride to Alaska and back, because Private Jackson tells an officer that his pal is sorrowing for his sick mother in Fairbanks, although nothing is wrong with his Mom in his home in San Francisco. Another example: a soldier trombone player is captured in Germany and is thrown into a concentration camp. He has somehow been permitted to carry his clumsy instrument with him across France. But he cannot play without a straw hat on his head; nothing comes out of his trombone except groans. The Germans search everywhere around Deutschland and finally a courier is sent to Paris and returns with a brand new straw hat "with a red band on it and a little cluster of red and green and purple feathers stuck into its band." It is Mr. Saroyan's magic that he makes you believe and love the scene that follows: "It was the most magnificent thing that anybody ever saw. . . . Wynstanley had been hungry to play," writes Mr. Saroyan. "He just wanted to play. It was the finest thing that happened in the whole war. . . . I don't know what's American as against what's something else, but I know that there is no man in the world capable of resisting the truth and beauty that came out of Wynstanley's trombone on that night of Saturday, July 22, 1944. I know the German guards couldn't resist the truth and beauty because having a hint of its enormity one of them had fetched Wynstanley his straw hat."

Now, this is a fable told in deadly seriousness and almost believed by Mr. Saroyan. In it he means to say that all men are brothers as, in his story of the mating of the pale underfed English girl, he says that all women are sisters, pure in heart, and that love conquers all.

In reading Mr. Saroyan one should gallop ahead and never stop to cogitate. What he has always been trying to say is as immortally true as the gospels or wisdom itself. If man has been permitted for centuries to soothe the savage breast with his lyre, why not grant Saroyan's soldier the same magic with his trombone, an instrument of salvation in many of Saroyan's works? Saroyan hates war, believes that the primary function of man is to love and perpetuate his species. All reasoning men agree with him. Why, then, in Saroyan's many books, in his plays, does he seem to strike a false note, to whip up so exaggerated a series of truisms that all of his latest plays, in which it is more difficult to disguise irrationality than in fiction, have been almost complete failures?

The reason for his failure to conquer, as love and dewy-eyed innocence are supposed to conquer, is that you never know where Saroyan himself stands, or where you stand with Saroyan. All of our major critics have been hacking at him for years and all of them disagree, except in finally admitting that he has genius, or whatever each one means by that. One man will say that he has been carrying on a protracted love-affair with himself for ten years; others that he is an exhibitionist or a plain fraud. No one in any serious sense believes in him any longer as a major prophet.

Saroyan might well have been one. He arrived on the American literary scene at a time when the public was tired of the destructive and cynical dicta of post-war novelists. He tried to affirm by his puckish humor, his Armenian folk-tales, his fables and his naïve emotionalism that nothing mattered in the world except love and being true to yourself. He failed because a depression followed the war and another world war followed the depression. The homelier virtues and sounder instincts of the little people, the prostitute with the heart of gold, long a convention in post-Victorian literature, the superior qualities of the uneducated man in war and in peace over the effete college-bred man have no longer a political or emotional appeal. We look today at Saroyan's men and women, at the soldiers portrayed in his latest book, and we admire their vitality, their tears, their cock-eyed behavior. We love their primitive honesty, but we lay aside this book feeling that he is a gifted teller of fairy-tales, or parables, which have little relation to a world faced with continued revolution, starvation, and the threat of another war.

Saroyan's New Mixture
[Review of *The Assyrian and Other Stories*]

Whit Burnett*

Between 1934 and 1939, when William Saroyan was a fresh young voice crying in the Western wilderness—shouting, living, breathing, too, himself upon the earth, etc.—he wrote about 500 short stories and scattered them like a free-handed sower. Many fell upon fertile ground. In his newest collection at least two of his earlier seedlings, "The Shepherd's Daughter" and "70,000 Assyrians," both in their way little masterpieces, have come up a second time with new shoots: "The Parsley Garden" and "The Assyrian."

Saroyan has stirred the mixture again, candidly, engagingly and provokingly, but something new has been added. In the Nineteen Thirties, he says in his preface, he wrote "without anxiety"; he felt "it was right to just write them and turn them loose and not take myself or the stories too seriously." To write without anxiety, he reflects now, the writer must have "implicit faith in himself, in his character and in what he is apt to write."

The something new is perhaps, for the first time, doubt. And in the best of these eleven stories there is more than the simple acceptance of life; there is a bleak and despairing contemplation of death.

Years ago the Russian writer Ivan Bunin wrote a short classic called "The Gentleman From San Francisco." The Gentleman was 58 and, wealthy but tired, he went to Europe to take a rest and expand his soul. A luxury liner took him over and a luxury liner brought him back, dead. He had waited too long and he had done the wrong things and death got him in the end.

The new thing in Saroyan's book is a disillusioned fed-upness which reaches almost masterpiece dimensions in "The Assyrian." It is a 30,000-word novella, and calls to mind other great stories in the same field, not only Bunin's "The Gentleman," and "Free" by Theodore Dreiser, but the more economical story, "The Snows of Kilimanjaro," by the Ernest Hemingway who has so evidently and belatedly influenced the new Saroyan. "The Assyrian" is as good as Dreiser's story and almost as good as Bunin's and it could have been as great as Hemingway's with better editing.

The New York Times Book Review, 22 January 1950: 4. Copyright © 1950 by The New York Times Company. Reprinted by permission.

In the preface—which contains many good things as well as advice to writers on how often to bathe—Saroyan asks if there is any "necessity" for the serious writer—that is, the poet. He thinks there is. But when a writer begins to ask that question, Saroyan feels the author is already going, not coming (alive), and when this process of dying sets in it is because the writer has been writing and thinking so hard he has grown tired and unhappy; because writers are, by their nature, lonely people, they are going to be unhappy anyway, but they should avoid trying to be exhausted.

"The Assyrian" is a study of an exhausted man, a writer-gambler, a sensualist, a visitor, a comer-and-a-goer. In Lisbon in 1949, with a new girl to help forget his third wife and child left in New York, and after a harrowing spurt at roulette, he suffers his first stroke, but, defying doctors, insists on boarding a plane, betting on the odds, and zooms East, presumably for Assyria or death.

From 1934 to 1939 there was no one alive then writing Saroyan the way Saroyan was writing Saroyan. He knew the character he was working on. Today he is two or three other fellows. Part of this is to the good, for he is still looking around, trying to get located and testing a new disillusionment.

This may not be the Saroyan you have been reading. But, minus its scratches, "The Assyrian" is quite a story, to put it mildly, and to get to such a death it took a lot of living and the effect, in the end, is here.

Look, Mom, No Hands
[Review of *The Bicycle Rider in Beverly Hills*]

It seems a long time since William Saroyan checked in his messenger's cap
and coat in Fresno, Calif., and gave up his nickname of Speed (fastest
messenger boy in town) and became a short story writer, novelist, scenarist,
traveler, husband and father. But Bill has never forgotten the flying bicycle
of his youth. Now, at 44, in a big house in Beverly Hills, with more than
100,000 miles (it says here) behind him on his Cadillac, Bill regards the
remote bicycle as the Proustian cup of tea to take him back on a soul-search
for times past.

Today Bill's son Aram is a lad of 8, and already wanting a man's-size
bicycle. His wise father points out: a boy that small can't ride a bike that
big; but Aram is determined. Nothing else will do. Finally the father buys
him the biggest bike they make, the lad climbs on, his feet hardly touching
the pedals, and off he rides, hell-bent, on the man's-size machine.

What less could one Saroyan expect of another? "If anybody could do
anything, I wanted to do it also, and do it better," Father Saroyan recalls.
"I was insecure and I must have felt unloved, for I always wanted to be
superior, self-sufficient, above emotional pain, oblivious of frustration. From
the beginning I wanted to excel."

In the streets of Fresno, thirty years ago, a youngster could learn many
things. Whizzing in the wind Bill heard "inner music," which later he
augmented by his first phonograph, the outrageous expense of which caused
his mother to run him out of the house until, listening too, and thenceforth
enchanted, she relented and permitted him to squander his earnings on a
record a week. From riding a bicycle, the author says, he learned speed,
rhythm and a literary style.

Saroyan's other books have been autobiography too, usually with the trimmings of fiction. Here the trimmings are off. If you like Saroyan, here he
is, naked to his enemies, from the age of 3. At 3, when his father, an

* *The New York Times Book Review*, 21 September 1952: 4. Copyright © 1952 by The New York Times
Company. Reprinted by permission.

Armenian Christian preacher, was just dead, the child was left for several years in an orphanage in California by his mother. There he first came to a man's realization that everything must separate sometimes in life and everything must die. But, he says, he faced the reality; he never was a chair rocker and a weeper like some of the other little kids; and not long after that he decided that if he was to "stay on his feet" (i.e., to live and not die) he must breathe deeper, stand straighter, sleep harder, run faster, sell more papers, make more money, drink more water, and pick the best and surest of the arts in order to express himself as a whole man. He was a whole man, on the way, he says, at 3. Painting, he later decided, required expensive paints, and a sculptor needed tools, but a writer needed only a pencil and paper—light to pack, ready for use.

The typewriter (bought, he told his family, to help perfect him as a business man) has long supplanted the Saroyan pencil, as the gas accelerator has supplanted the foot pedal of the second-hand bikes, but in this minor testament of an alien boyhood in America—some repetitious within the framework of the same book and some recollective of other things written before—the bicycle rider of Fresno-Beverly Hills skims by, on a paved highway now, easily, gracefully (look, Mom, no hands!), and swinging always from the concrete to the cosmic with the greatest of ease.

The Time of His Life
[Review of *Places Where I've Done Time*]

HARRY KEYISHIAN*

William Saroyan is writing his autobiography. Sort of.

Being Saroyan, he hasn't set it all down methodically, in chronological order. Rather, he's been covering the ground informally in a series of chatty, anecdotal books about his family and friends, his enemies, his career, and his changing image of himself as, to his amazement, he grows older.

The Young Saroyan—by now neatly packaged and put on his appropriate shelf in literary history—made his mark in the 1930's and early 1940's with books like *My Name Is Aram* and *The Human Comedy* and the Pulitzer Prize winning *The Time of Your Life*. He was a "romantic egotist," the mad, inspired bard of a clan of holy innocents, an exuberant primitive bearing the message that what really matters in human affairs, is beauty of character and openness to experience—and doing so in a seductive style that made writing seem the simplest and most natural of human activities.

In the late 1940's and early 1950's, in the bitter aftermath of a broken marriage, Saroyan's writing took on a darker hue. In the collection *The Assyrian and Other Stories* and in the novels *Rock Wagram* and *The Laughing Matter* he faced up to the unhappy human facts of failure, betrayal, and irretrievable loss. Mortal limitations were acknowledged: survival was not natural but required an effort of will, and a measure of luck.

In 1952, in *The Bicycle Rider in Beverly Hills*, he first tried the extended autobiographical form. His children—his son Aram, born in 1943, and his daughter Lucy, born in 1946—became his avenue to his past and gave him new eyes with which to evaluate it. "Riding a bicycle in Beverly Hills with my son made me remember the bicycle rider I was years ago in Fresno, and it made me want to keep a record of what I remember, which is this book." (A sort of *recherche du temps perdu*—the difference between riding a bicycle and dipping petite *madeleine* in tea suggesting some of the differences between William Saroyan and Marcel Proust.)

Riding a bicycle—the act producing "respect for grace, seemliness,

*Reprinted by permission from *Ararat*, Fall 1972: 23–24. Copyright © The Armenian General Benevolent Union.

effectiveness, power with ease, naturalness"—was also his education in writing, he says: "A man learns style from everything, but I learned mine from things on which I moved, and as writing is a thing which moves I think I was lucky to learn as I did." He recollects days as schoolboy, telegraph messenger, and adolescent, calling up events he used in his earlier stories.

Through the rest of the 1950's Saroyan produced fiction and drama, but got back to autobiography again with *Here Comes / There Goes / You Know Who* in 1961. ("*You*, my friend. Not me. I ain't going. I've got taxes to pay, and pieces to pick up.") There are more fresh moments from childhood, like the day the results of his intelligence tests appeared and the school found out what else they had on their hands besides trouble; later, his struggle to read his dead father's poems, written in Armenian in notebooks made of butcherpaper. He plays the famous and the obscure off against each other—like his Uncle Aram, the "most generally preposterous man" he'd ever met, and George Bernard Shaw, another clown, whose public pose became so convincing that it disguised the truly great man behind it.

In 1963 *Not Dying* appeared. (" 'And now, Mr. S.,' the Interviewer said, 'to what do you attribute your old age?' 'Not dying.' ") The Interviewer is a young man from *Paris Review*. He and Saroyan don't connect; the interview goes nowhere. Besides that, Saroyan is depressed, haunted by premonitions of his own death. He's been trying to adopt a proper stance, "to accept the messages with grace." Then his son and daughter visit him in Paris. They talk about writing and his feeling that he is falling apart. Gradually the presence of the children, and the writing of the book itself, bring him around. "I began to write the book so that the writing of it could take the place of dying, of my own literal death." Saved by involvement with family and craft, he gets moving again. "I went to work and wrote a play for money. I didn't die."

In 1963 he bought a 1941 Lincoln limousine and drove cross-country with his cousin John. The result, three years later, was *Short Drive, Sweet Chariot*, a brief travelogue with recollections occasioned by the countryside. Driving through Michigan leads to a comparison of Ernest Hemingway and Michael Arlen, as men and as writers. (Hemingway, he says mildly, "could get a little personal and mean about writers who weren't his equal"; of Arlen: "He was devoted to form in his daily life, while I had no time for it *there* at all, because of my eagerness to find it in art.")

The *Letters from 74 Rue Taitbout*, which appeared in 1968, were addressed to people he revered, like his dead father and an uncle he'd never met; people he found of interest and value, like the billionaire Calouste Gulbenkian and a boy named Sammy Isaacs he'd known in the orphanage; and people he despised, like Louis B. Mayer.

*   *   *

In the letter to his father Armenak, who died when Saroyan was three, he describes a recurring fantasy of one day meeting his father on the street. "He won't stay gone just because he's dead, he'll find a way to get back on his feet and come walking up a street and find me somewhere, because he's my father, and the way we are, we'll do a thing like that." It never happened, of course; but when Saroyan's own son was born, he seemed Armenak's replacement in the world. Years later, in the normal course of things, he and his son grew estranged: "he said my letters were a nuisance to him, so I didn't write any more"—even when visiting New York, where his son lived. And once, walking in the city, "I saw him and he saw me, and I went on up Fifth Avenue, and he went on down. I didn't smile and he didn't smile. And I didn't care and I didn't care that he didn't care." But of course he did—and a second later his son came running after him to find out what was wrong, making the fantasy come true in an unexpected way.

Days of Life and Death and Escape to the Moon, published in 1970, is a diary of days in Paris in August, 1967 and Fresno in November and December, 1968. Saroyan describes the events of those days—walks and explorations—and keeps a running log of people who died during those months: Norman Thomas and Upton Sinclair, Tallulah Bankhead and Paul Muni, songwriter Jimmy Campbell, who wrote "Show Me the Way to Go Home." But the heart of the book is Saroyan himself, noting the passage of time: "I keep thinking of myself as a very young man, and then I not only remember that I am no such thing, I *notice* that I'm not."

The latest book, *Places Where I've Done Time* (Praeger, 1972), published last March, is a set of anecdotes drawn from various stages of Saroyan's life. The focus is on places—bookshops, bordelloes, theaters, and churches—as well as on the people who make them important. More than usual in his non-fiction he lets himself go about some of them: his ex-wife, a "hungry little girl"; producer Lee Shubert, charming and helpful until box office fell off; Arthur Koestler, portrayed as betraying a friend in order to flatter Hemingway. But most are pleasant memories—of childhood picnics with his brother and sisters when they came to visit him at the orphanage; of Saturday afternoons at the Bijou (pronounced "Byjoe") Theater in Fresno, watching adventure movies and eating sunflower seeds by the pound; later, of a lady in San Francisco who whatever time he called would answer, "Come on up, the door's unlatched. If I'm asleep help yourself"; and of course long talks with his children, even as adults astounding him with "their strange lack of common sense."

If these books have a common theme it is rebirth—the quest for peace, reconciliation, and potency after periods of loss and despair. The pattern of Saroyan's search may be strictly his own—based on his identity as a writer, as a romantic, as an Armenian-American—but the trick of it, the idea of accepting his psychic ebb and flow as a condition of existence, and doing so with grace and curiosity, has great meaning. There's hope so long as Saroyan, for whom living and writing are synonymous, keeps at it, keeps passing the word—which remains, as ever with Saroyan, love. And if it's not pure and simple any more, what is? Or ever was?

We become interested in a writer because of what he writes: but eventually we become curious about what he is. For his part, the writer has frequently been very happy to display himself—even before the current trend away from fiction toward reportage and personal revelation.

In the case of William Saroyan—from the start a very "personal" writer—the shift has been natural and successful. He has produced a series of entertaining, often affecting books in which he comments directly on his past and present, his friends and children, his reactions to immediate experience, and—perhaps most of all—the consequences of his discovery of his own mortality.

Does Saroyan reveal himself more deeply or basically in these books than he had in his fiction? Probably not, because fiction is a powerful mode of getting at truth and needs no help from accidental realities. But these books are, right now, the mode Saroyan has chosen to communicate in.

ARTICLES

◆

William Saroyan in California

Margaret Bedrosian*

Like other writers who have depicted the Golden State in their work, William Saroyan seemed to describe a fantasy-land as much as an actual terrain. The California that appears in his short stories and novels fluctuates in imagery: at times it lulls us with the pastels and mist of a romantic watercolor; at other times, the imagery becomes gloomy and the landscape itself seems to brood on tensions that preoccupied Saroyan through much of his life. The sources of these tensions cannot be separated from Saroyan's family and cultural past. Much of what he experienced as an individual reflected the social and psychological challenges other Armenians faced in California during the earlier decades of this century. Saroyan's evasion of and confrontation with these challenges forms one of the central dialectics in his writing; in turn, this pattern offers a unique view of California's heartland, where landscape and aspects of local color selectively reflect the distinct currents of a writer's imagination.

Armenians first immigrated to California from the northeastern United States in the 1890s. The portion of California that attracted them most strongly was the San Joaquin Valley, a region that reminded them of their homeland in the heart of the Ottoman Empire. Here they could acquire land and farm, a simple enough desire, but one which had been suppressed for centuries in their native land, where Turkish overlords set limits on their freedom. In the next few decades, the imagery of California as a promised land of agricultural plenty spread through the Ottoman interior, while Armenian peasants dreamed of a time when they might migrate to California and start anew. Though deportation and massacre in the 1890s and most fatally in 1915 would prevent many Armenians from realizing their dream, the image had been so firmly implanted that in many cases survivors, especially children of slain parents, carried the vision of California as their final destination when they managed their escape to the United States.

No matter how they arrived in the Central Valley, once there the Armenians lost no time making up for economic deprivations experienced in the Old Country. Their primary desire was to save enough money to buy

*Reprinted with permission from *California History* 68, 4 (Winter 1989/90): 202–9.

land. All manner of comfort and leisure was sacrificed to this goal. Women worked in packing houses in the summer, men hired out for labor, and nothing extra was spent on housing. A common saying of the time was "no house can produce a farm, but a good farm can produce a house." But in the process of exerting their long-suppressed will, the Armenians managed to arouse some of the most antagonistic feelings of any ethnic minority in California. As Fresno was entering a period of full-blown prosperity, enjoying the wealth that agriculture bestowed, the pillars of the community became protective of their image as an up-and-coming All-American city, and jealous of their power to guide the area's fortunes.

Among the most aggressive of any ethnic minorities in their push to improve their fortunes, the Armenians drew most of the hostility of the "Americans" in the San Joaquin Valley. The bitterness of old-line Americans and the bemused response of the Armenians were amply documented by the sociologist Richard Tracy La Pierre in his doctoral study, "The Armenian Colony in Fresno County, California," completed in 1930. A brief sampling of some of the comments made about the Armenians by La Pierre's interviewees suggests the range of anger and distaste directed at the group:

> They always want eggs, butter, sugar, etc., at lower prices than others pay . . . except when they sell it they want a cent or two more.[1]

> If you treat them civilly they are ungracious. If you are brutal and rough with them, they respect you. Very few of them ever smile—they have a sour countenance as though every thought was mean, *not sad*, just mean. If their conduct in Turkey is as it is here, no wonder the Turks kill them. Many, many Americans long to run them out of the country (p. 341).

> You can't go into a show or any amusement place without running across a bunch of loud-mouthed Armenians that are trying to start a row. They have to be in a bunch about 6 to 1 or they are yellow. They ought to be out in a part of the town separated from us as the Russians and the Chinese who at least are keeping their places (p. 342).

In one comment that summed up the anti-Armenian feelings, one woman from Fowler (a town near Fresno) stated: "They are the only foreigners in Fowler who think they are just as good as we are. I don't know why they aren't, but we think they aren't" (p. 346).

Bearing the brunt of such hostility, the Armenians might occasionally find scapegoats of their own. La Pierre reported that Aram Saroyan, William's maternal uncle, laid the discrimination against his people at the door of the Jews, who knew that "the Armenians will become their strongest rivals in commerce" (p. 408). More commonly, though, Armenians were at a loss to explain how they had aroused such dislike. One Armenian told La Pierre, "I have mulled it all over for so long, and so often, that it has become magnified ten-fold and the prejudice existing as a reality in my mind is probably far greater than the prejudice actually found against me" (p. 413). Another, a lawyer, stated that the prejudice "has unquestionably made us self-conscious, even timid, in the presence of non-Armenians and has . . . modified the personality of all of us who have many non-Armenian contacts" (p. 413).

It was into such a social milieu that William Saroyan's immediate family moved when he was a boy of seven. By the time they came to Fresno, Saroyan and his siblings had already spent five years in an Oakland orphanage while his mother worked as a live-in maid during the week (his father had died when Saroyan was three years old). The resulting feelings of emotional deprivation, which gnawed at Saroyan for most of his life, were alternately soothed and exaggerated in the new surroundings. The Fresno that Saroyan came to know became the backdrop for a personal melodrama that resembled the trapeze act of the metaphor in his most famous short story: at one pole were those images of laden vineyards and fruit trees that shaded the Armenians from the valley sun, and at the other pole were the images of stark loneliness and loss. The former realm he rendered faultlessly in *My Name Is Aram* (1937), a collection of short stories that to this day appeals to more readers than anything else Saroyan wrote. The reason these stories are so well-liked has as much to do with what Saroyan avoided saying in them as with what he actually described. At one with nature, frozen in time and nostalgia, eating peasant fare and drinking the good water of Fresno, the book's Armenians and other ethnic characters belong to a fairy tale about how things ought to have been. Saroyan characterized Fresno in his introductory note as "the ugly little city containing the large comic world," and he leaned heavily on the comic to transform the ugly.[2]

Perhaps the most well-known story in *My Name Is Aram* is "The Pomegranate Trees." This piece is noteworthy from several points of view. At one level, it reads much like a parable about the relationship between the land of the Central Valley and the farmers who willed agriculture—and agribusiness—onto it. Early in the story, the narrator, Aram, describes the land his uncle has bought at the foot of the Sierra Nevada: "It was full of every kind of desert plant that ever sprang out of dry hot earth. It was overrun with prairie dogs, squirrels, horned toads, snakes, and a variety of smaller forms of life. The space over this land knew only the presence of hawks, eagles, and buzzards. It was a region of loneliness, emptiness, truth, and dignity. It was nature at its proudest, dryest, loneliness, and loveliest" (p. 36). This passage neatly brings together typical strains in Saroyan's work; first and foremost, it recognizes the overpowering "truth" of the desert. As the story progresses, the reader sees that this geography is much more implacable than the human will to transform it. The pomegranate trees that Uncle Melik has so poetically and romantically planted become an absurdity, totally out of place in the vastness of the dry land. Even more disheartening, their jewel-like fruit, so treasured by the Armenians, is mostly unknown to salesmen and markets. Read as a commentary on the destiny of agriculture in the valley, the story carries a strong suggestion: it is water that makes the lush illusion possible, and it is the absence of water that will eventually shrivel the fruit orchards into a barren memory that leaves one silent.

At a more personal level, the passage cited above and the story as a whole underline Saroyan's desired relationship with that land and the psychological reality it symbolizes in his own life: the "loneliness, emptiness, truth, and dignity" that are so impervious to pomegranate trees nevertheless offer a model of comportment through an emotionally dessicated life. Orphanhood is never mentioned in this story, nor anywhere else in *My Name Is Aram*, but the code of conduct required of orphans is indirectly alluded to in bits and pieces; it is a code predicated on an unsentimental appraisal of ultimate ends and a debonair creativity that responds "what the hell!" It is this resilience that unites diverse characters in other stories of the collection, such as the sad Uncle Jorgi of "A Journey to Hanford," who sits all day under the tree and plays the zither, indifferent to his father's demands to make money harvesting watermelons in Hanford; or Locomotive 38, the Ojibway Indian who patronizes Aram and takes him fishing for the sheer fun of relieving their shared boredom.

This view of life is expressed with delightful zest in "The Three Swimmers." Here Abbott Darcous, an old man educated at Yale, runs a grocery store in Malaga, an old farming suburb of Fresno, for the sake of "casual poetry." Much of Darcous' stylishness as a human being (and style was a quality Saroyan greatly admired in himself and others) emerges in the way he interacts with the three young swimmers, "foreigners" who nevertheless identify themselves as Californians. As the boys supply the grocer with information about their backgrounds, Darcous responds to each with the poetry of local color. Learning that Mourad was born near the Southern Pacific tracks, he gushes, "Well, I'll be irrigated." To Joe's comment that "we ain't educated," he replies "Well, I'll be picked off a tree and thrown into a box." And at the news that Mourad speaks Armenian, he bursts with, "Well, I'll be cut off a vine and eaten grape by grape by a girl in her teens" (p. 157). This interchange and the story in general suggests the prevailing mood of "The Pomegranate Trees"; although Malaga is not located in the desert foothills, neither has it ever been recognized as a cosmopolitan hub. Yet the charm of this story lies in the incongruity of such "different" individuals coming together by chance for a brief while and managing to create a memorable event, partaking in a communion of canned beans and water. It is this mood of "casual" serendipity that gives many of Saroyan's stories and plays their unique appeal, most notably *Time Of Your Life*, which is essentially a series of "found" moments.

But behind the generally appealing and affirmative images of *My Name Is Aram* and a host of other short stories that extol the momentary victories against emptiness are a host of other Saroyan vignettes and longer narratives that present a more sober view of the geographical and spiritual landscape. One of Saroyan's best-known stories, "Seventy Thousand Assyrians," takes us part of the way into this more twilit perspective. Significantly, this story about annihilation, American-style, takes place in a city, San Francisco, rather than in farm country, where this subject can be more easily evaded. The piece centers on an encounter between an Assyrian barber and Saroyan, a meeting that rephrases the dialectic between the void and the creative moment echoing through *My Name Is Aram*. Here, the barber represents an entire people diminishing in numbers by the forces of assimilation. Somewhat like the pomegranate orchard in the midst of the unpitying desert, the Assyrian barber, Theodore Badal, is a filament of life hanging on before an inevitable end comes to his people and to himself. As he himself recognizes, "we have no writers, we have no news—well, there is a little news: once in a while the English encourage the Arabs to massacre us, that is all. It's an old story, we know all about it." Although Saroyan ends the piece with a brave note of affirmation, saluting all those unknown individuals who carry the "dignity" and "brotherhood of things alive," the final image of Badal, "standing in a barber shop, in San Francisco, in 1933, and being, still, himself, the whole race," leaves a lingering sense of loneliness and emptiness in the reader's mind.[3]

Poised against these numerous stories and sketches that are basically positive in mood are others that more directly address Saroyan's ambivalent feelings as a young Armenian orphan growing up in Fresno. At times he is very indirect in describing the hardships his family and the Armenians in general experienced in Fresno. A chapter from one of his innumerable autobiographies, *Here Comes, There Goes, You Know Who* (1961) is representative. Entitled "The Cat," it offers a short allegory of his family's situation far away from the homeland. Describing the play of the predator cat with a mouse, Saroyan concludes: "Excelsior, the cat, the caught mouse, and us. There we were in America, never to see Bitlis again."[4] Though he continues by detailing some of the more endearing aspects of their house, such as the leaking ceilings, there is little doubt that he and his family resemble "the caught mouse" more than they resemble the cat.

A more direct description of the realities facing immigrant children in unfriendly Fresno schools in the 1910s and 1920s appears in a chapter entitled "The School." Many teachers took their role as assimilators quite seriously; during an era when the child's native culture and language were not valued in the classroom, confrontations between teachers and Armenian children could be fiery. In this sketch, Saroyan presents a classic encounter between himself in the role of feisty and clever Armenian schoolboy, and Miss Chamberlain, flirtatious yet adamant guardian of the American creed. In a running monologue that might have come from the pages of La Pierre's study, she berates Willie for not helping her keep order among the foreign children, whom she describes in the following fashion: ". . . the kids of immigrants, Armenians mainly, but others, too, a few Syrians, a few Assyrians, dark people with dark eyes you never could really understand. They kept to themselves, you never knew if you were getting through, they were still in another world, even though they were born in Fresno, and why did I encourage them to stay that way instead of opening up and being teachable, and *here*, instead of far away?" (p. 68). The little boy's retorts to this barrage reach a climax when he asserts: "But we're here, too, now, and if you can't stand the only way we can be Americans, too, we'll go right on being Armenians" (p. 69).

Behind such bravado, though, lurked a sensitivity to the pain that all children suffer when they are not accepted for who they are. A vignette in an early short story called "The Death of Children," which also takes place in Emerson School, contains some of the most touching passages Saroyan ever wrote. Introducing these sketches of children with the line, "There were all kinds of us," Saroyan captures the loneliness and victimization that children face. He describes Rosa Tapia, the little Mexican girl, who sings a song in her native language as if to substitute for all the "pointless things" she did not know; Alice Schwab, the German-Jewish girl most likely to succeed, yet least liked, who dies before she has fully lived; and most unforgettably, Carson Sampler, the sullen-faced castoff child of "no-account Southerners," whose pinched face haunts Saroyan's dreams, reflecting the depth of his own childhood deprivations.

Indeed, what the adult Saroyan took as the cost of "being Armenian" entailed much more than an occasional battle with a grammar school teacher; it was much closer to the shivers he felt watching Carson Sampler's starving face and bare feet. The rough-and-ready pose he assumed for public consumption hid considerable guilt, insecurity, and anger toward his family and his ethnic group.[5] *Rock Wagram*, an autobiographical novel from the early 1950s, suggests the tensions that Saroyan felt in mid-life. Set in Fresno, the story concerns the return home of an Armenian, Rock Wagram, who has made it big as a movie actor. Although most of the plot focuses on Rock's failed marriage and the split he feels between his Fresno "self" and the slick *chic* of Los Angeles and New York, the deepest source of the protagonist's unease lies in his past as the son of Armenian immigrants to Fresno. The story is peppered with references to Fresno's homey values and farmers' perennial worries about the water level, as well as formulaic refrains that praise grandmother and the meals of "tea, flat bread, white cheese, black olives, parsley, mint, and sliced sun-dried beef."[6] But underneath this quaint façade, Rock feels a simmering ambivalence and estrangement from his family. Although Saroyan lost his father at the age of three, he grew up in an environment where Armenians clung to unyielding family values. His father's fulfilled life in California as a minister and a would-be writer became the sore that Saroyan himself continually reopened as he flailed himself in his work. As described by his brother-in-law Aram, Armenak Saroyan's "whole ambition in the Old Country was to be able to teach the kids to learn, to obey, and to be a *man*."[7]

In the novel, Rock's unresolved feelings, his underlying doubts about *how* to be a true Armenian man, aggravate his marital problems. Asked by his aunt if he has not yet found "a nice Armenian girl to marry," Rock retorts, "Do you know one?" The woman's response again demonstrates how much separates Rock from his Fresno past: "'*One?*' the woman said. 'There are hundreds, and most of them are here in Fresno. Girls are not lacking. To marry a stranger is perhaps an adventure, but the question is, Can the daughter of people who do not understand us be a true wife to one of our sons?'" (p. 83). Symptomatic of the xenophobia that marks many immigrants, this comment also offers a measure of the psychological distance between Rock and the place of his birth. Filled with marriageable Armenian girls willing to fall into duty, Fresno is the place of inbreeding, and by implication, sterility. But doubling the ambivalence is Rock's relationship to his own roots; rejected by his father, he is no longer a "true" son. As a result, he is not prepared to meet the challenge of relating to a non-Armenian wife either. As he struggles with the decision to "take her back," to ignore her threats and desires, it becomes obvious that the forgiveness he never found in his father eludes him as well, keeping him swimming in a current that never carries him to security, or maturity. As he leaves Fresno on a trip with his grandmother, Rock comes to a bridge where long ago a young Armenian friend drowned as he tried to get to the other side of the river. Rock's thought applies as much to his own dilemma as to his dead friend's: "If he's swimming the San Joaquin River, all he's got to do is get across. All he's got to do at any time is not drop dead" (p. 169). Having entered a stream that has carried him far from his origins—both as a son of immigrants and a bartender in a city whose values are fixed—Rock Wagram has yet to find rest, especially through the family meaning he claims to want. The novel ends with Rock in barely purposeful motion, racing to catch the sunrise, devoid of hope and family, clutching a token of counterfeit humor.

The deep-seated futility that periodically engulfed Saroyan's work reaches a nadir in his succeeding novel, *The Laughing Matter* (1953), his most pessimistic story. Here the brooding vineyards of the San Joaquin Valley form an apt backdrop to the torment and bitterness of the main character, who significantly envisions his ethnic group, the Assyrians, as a dying race. Though, characteristically, Saroyan would no sooner find himself in such a pit than he would take a flying jump to the other extreme, these polarities suggest just how complex his view of California, the Armenians, and his family was. Fundamentally at odds with himself, his depictions of the Armenians, other ethnic groups, the "mainstream," and the San Joaquin Valley are given many distinct shadings in his work. What remains consistent in his writing, beginning in the earlier works and trickling into the very last ones, are the sentiments of a local boy shaped by the tensions common to other Armenians of his generation in California. Like them, Saroyan tried to hold onto a pugnacious, absurdist, and perhaps absurd, creed that made the best of exile in the Golden West. As Father Kasparian, a character in his play, states, "Armenians in dispersion all over the world, but especially here in California, in Fresno, will continue to be Armenians, they will not become so foolishly American that being also Armenian will ever be an embarrassment to them, and something to forget as quickly as possible, by marrying foreigners and bringing up children who neither know nor care that they are Armenian."[8] However, as Saroyan was all too aware through his own childhood and his experience of marrying outside the tribe, life in California only highlighted millenia of history, wherein Armenians did not always have the choice of carrying the banner of their identity intact. Instead, they, like he, took refuge in self-images, spirited, yet contradictory, that enabled them to take leaps of faith into a landscape where illusions can thrive—until the basic void closes in, and leaves them speechless.

Notes

1.   Richard Tracy La Pierre, "The Armenian Colony in Fresno County, California: A Study in Social Psychology" (Ph.D. diss., Stanford University, 1930), 337. Subsequent page references to this work appear in the text.

2.   William Saroyan, *My Name Is Aram* (New York: Harcourt, Brace and Company, 1937), vii. Subsequent page references to this work appear in the text.

3.   William Saroyan, "Seventy Thousand Assyrians," in *The Saroyan Special* (New York: Harcourt, Brace and Company, 1944).

4.   William Saroyan, *Here Comes, There Goes, You Know Who* (New York: Simon and Schuster, 1961), 125. Subsequent page references to this work appear in the text.

5.   See Margaret Bedrosian, "William Saroyan and the Family Matter," *MELUS Journal*, No. 4 (1982): 13–24. Saroyan's attitudes toward his family, his ethnic group, and his home were ultimately inextricable from one another. Examining one inevitably involves the others.

6.   William Saroyan, *Rock Wagram* (Garden City, New York: Doubleday & Company, Inc., 1951), 65. Subsequent page references to this work appear in this text.

7.   Quoted in Lawrence Lee and Barry Gifford, *Saroyan* (New York: Harper & Row, 1984), 171.

8.   William Saroyan, "Armenians," in *An Armenian Trilogy*, ed. Dickran Kouymjian (Fresno, California: California State University Press, 1986), 59.

William Saroyan and the
Theatre of Transformation

JAMES H. JUSTUS*

Zip! Walter Lippman wasn't brilliant today;
Zip! Will Saroyan ever write a great play?
—*Pal Joey*

Lorenz Hart's question in 1940 contained its own implied answer: *no*. In the 60s, though the answer may still be the same, the Saroyanesque play as a unique amalgam of sentiment and fantasy deserves the attention of a new generation of readers. From the beginning, critics praised Saroyan for his freshness, irreverence, and promise, and from almost the same time condemned him for vagueness, egoism, and lack of discipline. In the 30s alone both praise and condemnation could be sufficiently and indiscriminately confirmed by a long list of short fiction—seven major volumes—and two produced plays in 1939, *My Heart's in the Highlands* and *The Time of Your Life*. Before the decade was over, despite the favorable reception of the two plays and the wider popular success of the stories, perhaps only Saroyan himself maintained a consistently favorable opinion of his contributions to American literature.

Like Steinbeck, Caldwell, Farrell, and the dramatists of social protest, Saroyan had a distinctive voice which spoke of and for the 30s. But where others were unremitting in their castigation of specific evils of American capitalism, Saroyan was merely occasional in his accusations. However deeply he felt about fascism and the abuses of political power, the literary treatment was usually generalized and moral. Placed against the programmatic social protest of Maxwell Anderson's *Winterset* (the moneyed classes pervert justice) and *High Tor* (the business world is ruthless in the name of economic progress), Paul Green's *Johnny Johnson* (the military and its mad supporters crush men of good will), John Howard Lawson's *Success Story* and Clifford Odets' *Golden Boy* (capitalism corrupts individual integrity), a play like *The Time of Your Life* seems mild indeed. Saroyan suggests, hints at, alludes to specific

*From *The Thirties: Fiction, Poetry, Drama*, ed. Warren G. French (Deland, FL: Everett Edwards, Inc., 1967). Reprinted by permission.

social wrongs, and then nearly always in comprehensive moral contexts (such as the deadening effects of materialism) which tend to dilute the anger with nostalgia and irony. A characteristic speech is the closing line of *My Heart's in the Highlands*; after their eviction, when Johnny and his penniless father take to the road, Johnny says: "I'm not mentioning any names, Pa, but something's wrong somewhere."

It was clear to The Committed that Saroyan was not effectively angry— he could not write *The Grapes of Wrath*, for instance. Neither was he interested in exploring the potential revolutionary spirit of the rural or urban dispossessed in the manner of *Studs Lonigan* or "Kneel to the Rising Sun." Most clearly, he was not interested in ideology—the determining motive behind *Awake and Sing!* or *One Third of a Nation*. Moreover, Saroyan was too bumptiously independent, he was too addicted to the vitality, rather than the privations, of children and immigrants, and he indulged himself too freely in a rhetoric that could only inspire fantasy and dreams. The Saroyan method, made clearer in the 1940s and after, is finally not frontal, but oblique; and the major mood it establishes is not anger, but poignancy.

Lack of money—and therefore food and shelter—is more the occasion for sorrow at The Way Things Are and indefinable longing than it is for a plea to correct those things. In *Love's Old Sweet Song* (1940) even the pathos of the uprooted is changed into vaudeville as Cabot Yearling, fresh from Oklahoma with a pregnant wife and fourteen children, claims squatter's rights to an already occupied house. If Saroyan is remembering the plight of the Joads here, he gives Steinbeck little comfort for his role as their chronicler. Accompanying these Dust Bowl paisanos are a *Life* photographer and a newsman who keeps saying things like "The pitiable plight of these unfortunate people is not the concern of one man alone, but of the whole nation." Furthermore, the view is conservative when it is not merely comic; Cabot denies that he is unfortunate, proclaims his proud integrity, and boasts of being able to "shift for ourselves, the same as ever." Only in his best play, *The Time of Your Life*, does Saroyan resemble those dramatists who were choosing viably realistic situations which invited larger, symbolic readings. For all their differences, Harry Van of Robert Sherwood's *Idiot's Delight* and Gimpty of Sidney Kingsley's *Dead End* both anticipate Joe of *The Time of Your Life:* the little man of essential decency who understands the human predicament and who despite that gloomy knowledge idealistically clings to the hope of man's improvement. Entrapment, the common informing metaphor in the lives of those people herded together in a remote Italian lodge and the tenements along the East River in New York, fails to be the dominant metaphor for the habitués of Nick's San Francisco saloon simply because the hopes for escaping the trap are more stubbornly voiced.

Since the early 40s the familiar Saroyan stories have continued to flow, a few novels have appeared and been variously received; and plays both produced and unproduced, with seemingly tireless admonitory prefaces, have been published—all reminders that Saroyan is not only still around but that he is still the same old Saroyan. And, except for the tone of his non-dramatic work, which has grown increasingly solemn and self-conscious, and a few stories written in bile, Saroyan's is indeed the same voice heard in the 30s: there is grief aplenty, but man is a miracle, and merely living confirms life's miraculousness. That which seemed so distinctive to the spirit of the 30s no longer strikes us with the same relevant hopefulness, although such an observation may say more about our times than it does about Saroyan's themes, which were and still are largely prescriptions for ills which the author sees as endemic to no particular time.

In both his narratives and his dramas, Saroyan's sphere of significant action is a theatre of transformation in which he presents a celebratory enactment of man's affective victory over the timid conventionalities, compromises, and evasions of his life. He sings of man's release into a new vision of the "miracle" of the rebirth: "Let him walk and talk and think and sleep and dream and awaken and walk again and talk again and move and be alive." His vision ("the glorious truth of mere being") is never passive; it activates other men into new areas of awareness. Saroyan's vision receives full—if rambling—definition in the hortatory confessions of the memoirs, *The Bicycle Rider in Beverly Hills, Here Comes / There Goes / You Know Who*, and *Not Dying:*

Life may or may not be a tragic thing—the question is "still open." Man is captured only once, at birth, "only that capture is also a setting free." Merely living, "an enormity not to be slighted," involves wholeness— good vision, good hearing, swiftness of mind and spirit, laughter, "the fact of *being*." Although man is an "accident" on the earth, an element of the "deliberate" is sufficient to compel him to correct the "wrongs of the accidental" in him and to "cherish, accept, recognize, employ, extend, enlarge, improve, and thrive upon the accidental *rights* which were also born into him, the principal one of which is to continue. . . ." Because the "each" of anything is unique, man must honor other men, whatever possibility may be discovered in the "less great, the non-great, the anti-great, the anonymous, the unimportant, the insignificant, the useless, the unfortunate, the ill, the mad, or the wicked." His duty is to live fully, forever pushing aside irrelevant boundaries and dedicated to finding himself, others, the world, time, and space as a "dramatic, satisfying, and good" experience.

This vision of man—a premise in *The Time of Your Life* but a force which competes riotously, luxuriantly, with the action itself in most of the other plays—is conventional enough, though its sources are perhaps more complex than in most writers who share it with Saroyan. Behind this vision are the stoicism of an enduring minority in a new land, the Biblical sense of humility and joy in contemplating God's creation, the sincere arrogance of the special man who has been mystically touched by grace, the received literary-philosophical conventions of nineteenth-century Romanticism.

Out of these varied backgrounds—and from Saroyan's own experience—comes the persistent and often sentimental reverence for the innocent, the helpless, the down-and-out. In summoning up his wild array of con men, unknown artists, exuberant youths, impractical Greeks and Mexicans, sad Jews, dreaming streetwalkers, unemployed actors, and indigent drunks, Saroyan has always celebrated a single type of which these are representative: the beautiful people. Silent or incorrigibly loquacious, they are those who understand the mystery of being, treasuring the rare moments of illumination. And they are not *merely* representative, for while Saroyan is insistent on the miracle of life itself and its essential wholeness, the intensity of his scorn is in proportion to the world's demonstrated indifference to individuals. His people tend to be extravagant, eccentric, improbable—even those little people of decency and honesty whose simple minds and kindly hearts should make great claims on the world's attention.

If Saroyan's concept of the beautiful people tends toward the simplistic and the sentimental, his picture of the world they must live in is complex, involving the forces which at once assault them maliciously and test them providentially. If they survive the sheer facts of incompleteness, disease, violence, indifference, and the pervasive fear of death, their beauty is earned and is thus worth Saroyan's effort to celebrate it. In *My Heart's in the Highlands* the reminders of human misery—the gnawing need for cheese, bread, fruit— impinge upon and constantly threaten the superior claims of art—the medium for transforming loneliness into community. In *The Time of Your Life* the transients attempt to impose the order of charity in the artificial world of Nick's saloon, but constantly intruding is the disordered chaos of the great world where there is, in the Arab's reiterated observation, "No foundation. All the way down the line." The disinterested generosity of Joe extends to all those bruised by the world, but the hurt is more persistent than the healing. There is a touch of the futile and the desperate in the facile way Blick is dispatched; the bullying forces of evil, made more horrible by public sanction, are even here, in Saroyan's most realistic play, routed by concerted wish-fulfillment. Barnaby Gaul of *Love's Old Sweet Song* reminds Ann of the "great troubles" of man—panics, famines, floods, hurricanes, and "fury and stupor in the heart." He reminds the *Time* salesman that he brings "news of world-wide madness and horror to the living every Friday," but the only antidote Gaul can offer is the con man's nostrums—bottled hope that will somehow cure disgrace, disease, and wretchedness.

Saroyan's examples of forces and alliances which threaten man are less often social than moral—not banks and loan companies, but "wretchedness," not Hitler, but "the madness of war," not Wall Street, but "despair in the heart." When the mice in *The Beautiful People* (1941) cry for a lost brother,

Owen, a writer of one-word novels, advises his sister Agnes not to interfere: "Things end. They change. They spoil. They're hurt. Or destroyed. Accidents happen . . . Sooner or later everybody's got to know that death is with us from the first breath we take." But despite this mature realization, Owen is an artist of affirmation who reaches the peak of his awareness when he can write a *two*-word novel, *My Brother*. Jonah the father proclaims: "We are alive with all things alive, from the mite to the whale." The transforming power of love extends to the inarticulate boy with whom Agnes falls in love. When she complains to her father, "He's bewildered and shy and full of terrible sorrow, and his shoes don't fit," Jonah replies: "But his feet within them do." Misery and joy are in delicate balance always, but Saroyan insists upon the poet's right to change whatever in the world is changeable, to preside over man's potential rebirth. *The Beautiful People* is the most obvious of Saroyan's parables of man's necessity for love, the transforming agent; the victory of its action is worthy of awe: "Aye," says an old drunk, "the wonder and the beauty of it."

In this theatre of transformation, Saroyan's most familiar technique is that of first juxtaposing, then merging, two orders of reality: the eccentric, the unusual, the singular, and the familiar, the usual, the commonplace. In the astonished mingling of the two orders comes the blurring of distinctions, and mankind stands revealed in unity as the eccentric grows familiar and the familiar becomes an object of awe. It is not only a twentieth-century version of what the poets of *Lyrical Ballads* were striving for; it is also the triumph of a faith in both unity and variety—the residual tradition of Emerson and Whitman. A waterfront saloon may be the natural arena for the banal—prostitutes, longshoremen, and ordinary but persistent young men who risk their nickels in telephones and pinball machines—but it is also the stage of opportunities, not only for the swaggering Kit Carson with his endless flow of tall tales, but also for Joe himself, who believes the stories and whose commitment is to the daily "rehearsal" necessary for "man to get to be himself."

Saroyan's theatre of transformation is any place where the world's misfits and outcasts gather together in huddled need and where, often, the world's proud spiritual cripples—bankers, vice-presidents, voice teachers, construction workers—also wander in to reveal their even greater need for rebirth. It may be an ordinary house in Bakersfield or Fresno, a bar or an apartment in San Francisco, a New York restaurant, or a vacant theatre itself. And presiding over the ceremony of rebirth is Saroyan's priest, touched by madness or grace, God's own elect who points the true way. He is Jasper MacGregor (*My Heart's in the Highlands*), Joe (*The Time of Your Life*), Barnaby Gaul (*Love's Old Sweet Song*), Jonah Webster (*The Beautiful People*), Michael Sweeney (*Sweeney in the Trees*), Jim Dandy (*Jim Dandy: Fat Man in a Famine*), the King (*The Cave Dwellers*). In Saroyan's dramatic enactments of these romantic premises, it is perhaps inevitable that the results are so often maudlin. The

Good Heart has ever been a difficult notion to make interesting, and Standing in Awe of Life is easier to affirm than it is to render.

Saroyan has always been fond of saying—and the early critics were eager to agree—that his work is of its time and place, its particular moment of reality. That his work should reflect the desperate days of physical and spiritual unease is only natural. There is disillusion and there are suggestions throughout his work of the 30s of the larger world outside the California setting: the threats of dictatorship, oppression, and hatred organized for war. In its aggressive optimism and its very popularity, *The Time of Your Life* arrests the mood of America in crisis, particularizing genetic evils and celebrating the momentary but fragile victory of charity and good will.

But unlike Dos Passos, Farrell, and most of those writers who lost moorings, found new ones, and lost even those in the 30s, Saroyan was relatively untouched by social disorder and political disenchantment. Moorings he had and kept. His disillusion, hurt, and fear were not the exceptionally personal ordeals of most of his fellow writers. The difficulty of earning one's precarious way and making orderly lives in the midst of dominant American social and political patterns were for Saroyan givens of life. The Armenian community, in conjunction with other minority groups, made itself felt in the whole processes of Saroyan's attitudes toward life and, so naturally with Saroyan, his attitudes toward art. Endurance, no mean virtue, became a matter to be understood; withstanding the cruelty of the world became a matter for ingenuity and laughter. The claims of "the others" always impinge on those of "the beautiful people," and the confrontation is often tender and sentimental but sometimes corrosive and brutal. If laughter is the characteristic response to such situations, it is often laughter that verges on crying.

The close identification with his origins which has constantly shaped Saroyan's vision of man—endurance in the face of the great trial of living and the "miracle" of simply being part of humankind—has also shaped the form of his work. What man is and does is reflected in everything of Saroyan's: the short fiction, the novels, the plays, the memoirs, the songs. More often than not, the organization is not related to cumulative development of character and plot but the smaller units of form: the set piece of rhetoric or incantation, tableaux vivants enlivened by music, the tall tale, the fable, the anecdote, the interlude, the vaudeville "set." It should not be surprising for those now accustomed to the plays of Genet and Ionesco that Saroyan characteristically uses the play as a kind of repository in which all these formal units meet, mingle, and compete. But for an occasional grim exception—such as his first dramatic attempt in 1935, *Subway Circus*, and the brutally pessimistic *Hello Out There* of 1942—Saroyan's plays are spectacles: the grand assembly, the concatenation of voices and types, the particulars, eroded and made featureless, reduced to their generalities. Man in his clumsy and wobbly experience on earth is made to order in a handful of types. There is a profusion of faces and masks, shifting identities, caricatures, stereotypes: all representative of Essential Man. The fleshing out is done according to the patterns of myth and dream, not those of realistic character portrayal, a strategy which permits extreme individuality to function as emphasis for the common strain beneath it. The shifting, jostling juxtaposition of the real and the unreal not only justifies Saroyan's cheerful borrowings from the theatrical traditions of expressionism and surrealism, but also points up the technique, if not the substance, of what has turned out to be the dominant theatrical mode since World War II—the theatre of the absurd. Saroyan's plays—the sunny absurd—are dedicated to the underlying principle that though man's living may be tragic, his dying certainly is not. Saroyan investigates how many may best live, and the formula in *Jim Dandy* is characteristic—plunging beyond the mere acceptance of man's lot (*be-beget-begone*) is the resolution that comes of enlightened rebirth: "I will confound time and change with love and patience."

Saroyan may never write "a great play." His scorn of the commercial theatre and his indifference to the formal conventions of the genre render his exercises in the drama interesting, stimulating, provocative—and also platitudinous, unintegrated, impressionistic. But they are of a piece; they celebrate repeatedly the miracle of what one character in *Jim Dandy* describes as "that perfect defective thing whose breed is man." Saroyan's strengths are also his weaknesses—whimsy, spontaneity and improvisation, the exploitation of all the tag-ends and scraps of man's vitality as a human and social animal. They belong to a tradition of highly structured formlessness that recurs now and again and finds common cause in such diverse phenomena as the *commedia dell' arte* and the plays of Ionesco and Beckett.

Purists who suffer through a Saroyan play may find comfort in Gide, persuaded as he was—at least in 1920—of the impossibility of making a theatre piece into a work of art; but if the play can be thought of as a vehicle of man's celebration of himself, Saroyan must be suffered. In Saroyan's incantatory world, what is hurt and imperfect in man is transformed by love into a celebratory ritual which defines his potentialities for a "good" survival. Everyman's rebirth, like Fishkin's in *Jim Dandy*, proceeds from the lament over the cosmic trick of having to inhabit "this Fishkin flesh" to the song of transformation: "This world's home and we are lucky tenants of the house." The sentiments are stubbornly cheerful as prescriptions for survival in a mad world. They reflected the needs of the 30s, but Saroyan persisted in his belief that those needs were more general than specific and did not somehow disappear at the end of that decade. Out of the vagaries of whimsy and moralism, Saroyan has always demonstrated an agile sense of experimentation in structure and form in his art, but he has never seen fit to alter his theme: "To have been born is surely our end. To die is beside the point. And to live is our pleasure and law."

Whitman and Saroyan:
Singing the Song of America

DICKRAN KOUYMJIAN*

"When was the beginning of American writing?" William Saroyan asked in an essay of 1956. His answer: "Opinions must vary. Facts themselves must vary, at least in how they are interpreted.

"In my opinion American writing began when the unschooled took to the business. This leaves out Emerson, but not Whitman.

"Leaves of Grass could not have been written in England, Wales, Scotland, or Ireland.

"Whitman himself probably couldn't have written what he wrote anywhere else in the world. In America, European man had an arena at last in which hope could be limitless, and anybody with sufficient intelligence, energy, and ability was free to achieve almost anything."[1] Saroyan's "anybody" was himself. America was his limitless arena, and he was European man. He had achieved. He regarded himself a direct literary descendent of Whitman. Whitman's struggle for recognition was like his own; Whitman's battle with the establishment was followed by him boldly; Whitman's universalism was his, too.

There are several ways to approach the relation between Saroyan and Whitman: by enumerating the parallels in their lives; by analyzing Saroyan's references to the poet who died sixteen years before his own birth; by examining Whitman's influence on Saroyan's writing; by comparing their world view.

Like Walt Whitman, William Saroyan was born into an honorable, if poor, middle-class family. His father became a Protestant minister as a result of American missionary work in his home town, the city of Bitlis in the western part of historical Armenia. Saroyan was the youngest of four children and the only one born in the United States, where the family sought refuge after having correctly anticipated the continuation of Ottoman Turkish oppression that was to lead to the Armenian genocide just ten years after the Saroyans' arrival in America. At thirteen, disenchanted by the public school

* This essay was written specifically for this volume and is published here for the first time by permission of the author.

system, Saroyan, like Whitman, was able to escape it before his imagination was permanently crippled. Both men undertook practical protoliterary employment: Saroyan with the Postal Telegraph Company, Whitman as a printer's journeyman.

Because the two refused the conventional academic path into the world of American letters, they shared a lifelong disdain for those institutions that guided literary fashions and dictated behavioral norms. Saroyan was passionate and boisterous. He rejected conformity. He was immodest. He had little use for the niceties of polite society. He would not flatter to advance his career. He would not follow the accepted way of doing things if it was unprincipled or not to his liking. He was stubborn about his personal integrity. Saroyan probably imagined that Whitman had similar personality traits.

One consequence, no doubt, of the meager formal education of both Saroyan and Whitman was their rejection of the accepted canons of literary composition, precisely those learned in classrooms. Free of formalism, they were able to liberate the forms in which they wrote. Whitman's innovation in the use of free verse—long rhythmical lines with a natural organic structure—his fresh subject matter with its glorification of the body and exaltation of sexual love, find their parallel in Saroyan's rejection of structure and plot in his stories and in the formlessness of his plays. Both writers used prefaces to explain their work to reader and critic.

Whitman published his first book, *Leaves of Grass*, at age 37, and it was a failure. Saroyan published his first book, *The Daring Young Man on the Flying Trapeze* (1934), at age 26, and it was a great success. Literary critics were quick to see Whitman as a new and audacious voice in American literature; Emerson, by then a member of the establishment, endorsed him. Saroyan also garnered critical acclaim, but too often academics were confused by his works, especially the plays, and accused him of neglecting form, being too facile, indulging in surrealistic fantasy, and working too quickly and carelessly. The New Critics, with their insistence that great literary work can be evaluated according to conventions of form and technique, were especially hard on him.

In the essay "What Makes American Writing American," quoted above, Saroyan goes on to say: "There's no telling what doubts may have been in Whitman's heart about the kind of poetry he was writing and how it would be received. It isn't unlikely that he sometimes believed he was making a fool of himself, because even in our time even our best writers, whenever they hit upon a new order of writing which they feel they must pursue, have doubts about what they are doing, and what the critics and the public will think about it."[2] In this passage the California writer is again talking as much about himself and his new order of writing as he is about Whitman.

"Whitman published Leaves of Grass at his own expense," says Saroyan. "It was an instantaneous flop, although Emerson hailed it in a letter to

Whitman. Emerson might accurately have said the stuff wasn't poetry, but he didn't. And the fact is it didn't matter whether it was poetry or not. No Englishman, not even an unschooled one, could have written as Whitman had, because none would have been willing to do so; none would have been willing to be so likely to be taken for a lunatic."[3]

By attributing the merits of Whitman's creativity in part to his lack of schooling, Saroyan is again referring to himself. Only someone with a streak of insanity would have undertaken such a task; Saroyan often boasted about the madness in his own clan, and by implication in himself. Thus again he fits the profile of Whitman as writer.

In his concluding remarks on Whitman, there is further reinforcement of the parallels between himself and the poet:

> Whitman did not belong to the world of art. Whatever it was that he wrote, it just wasn't understood to be the proper subject of poetry. As for his manner of writing, it was practically anarchistic. Whitman belonged to the world. He and his work were the same thing, as in the founder of a religion. If he was anything at all he was a personality or, if you prefer, a personage, in the European sense—a personage without any inherited, social, or economic right to such a designation. He was Whitman, pure and simple. He was Anybody become Somebody by saying so, which is the essence and meaning of America. He may in time be named the first true American—the upstart with great if impudent confidence who does something different that turns out to be more than merely eccentric or ill-mannered.[4]

The subjects of Saroyan's own stories and plays were not the accepted ones either, and he too was an upstart who made his success by willfulness. "This ego push is by no means obsolete among us," says Saroyan. "It persists all over the place, in areas of potential magnificence no less than in areas of inevitable absurdity—from subtle discoveries in science to acts of attention-attracting for what is known as publicity." Again, seeing himself in Whitman, Saroyan concludes: "Whitman was a loner, as most Americans are at heart. He belonged to no school, and founded none."

The dedication to the 1958 anthology, *The William Saroyan Reader* begins, "To the writers who impelled me to write, Jack London, Guy de Maupassant, Charles Dickens, Anton Tchekhov, Mark Twain, August Strindberg, Maxim Gorky, Ambrose Bierce, Leo Tolstoy, Molière, George Bernard Shaw, Walt Whitman, Henri Fréderic Amiel, Henrik Ibsen, Sherwood Anderson, and Solomon, the son of David, who wrote *The Book of Ecclesiastes*."[5] This is perhaps the most complete catalogue of literary influences to which Saroyan ever admitted. Three years earlier, in "Earthly and Heavenly Voices" (written for *High Fidelity Magazine*), he commented, "If records of the voices of the writers of the past were available, whom would I want to listen to? Well, I would especially like to hear voices of Guy de

Maupassant, Leo Tolstoy, Jack London, Mark Twain, Anton Chekhov, Charles Dickens, Goethe, Strindberg, Ibsen, Hamsun, Ambrose Bierce, Joaquin Miller, Maxim Gorky, Balzac, Walt Whitman, Poe, and O. Henry."[6] Even earlier, in the 1948 story "A Walk in New York," published only in 1968, he says "What young ghosts of great men the walker greets as he goes: Washington, Franklin, Lincoln, Poe, Stephen Foster, O. Henry, Walt Whitman, Jack Johnson, Caruso, Knut Hamsun, George Bellows, Sousa,. . . ."[7] In that same year, 1968, Whitman turns up again in Saroyan's letter to Carl Sandburg published in the *Saturday Evening Post*. "When I had been a telegraph messenger in Fresno, aged thirteen, working the nightshift after school . . . I used to write poems on the company typewriters, because I had read everything on the poetry shelf at the public library—Walt Whitman, Vachel Lindsay, Edgar Lee Masters, and Carl Sandburg, among others, and I believed I ought to write stuff like that, too, but in the end it turned out that my first book was a collection of short stories, and after that I wrote fewer and fewer poems and hardly ever offered them to an editor."[8] In *Obituaries*, a vast reflection on death published in 1979, Saroyan speaks of his disappointment that Franklin Roosevelt read mystery stories: "In those days (the late 1930s) . . . I had the notion that a President of the United States, with such an affection of fondness for the people, or at any rate the majority of the people, would find it in order to go continuously to the waters provided by Walt Whitman, Mark Twain, and, for instance, O. Henry."[9]

Beside these almost casual references were more serious ones, like the essay on American writing already cited, which reveal Saroyan's appreciation of Whitman and his debt to him. In *After Thirty Years: The Daring Young Man on the Flying Trapeze* (1964), a reprint of his first great success accompanied by thirty-eight short reminiscences on writing, Saroyan attributes the poetic quality of his early prose to Whitman: "The thing I knew in 1934 was that it was necessary to write a story every day. . . . There were no other restrictions. The story could be a letter. . . . Each nevertheless was also a story. Some of the . . . stories were jazz, pure and simple, but jazz in writing. Some were prose poems, something like Walt Whitman's broken prose, or poetic prose, but more in feeling than in the use of language."[10] The theme of poetry writing is picked up again on the last page of Saroyan's last book, the posthumous memoir *Births*:

> Rembrandt was an Armenian, the Armenians say . . . there is evidence that he was, there is also evidence that he wasn't. He was born, that's all. And so were you. Forget it. Skip it. Let it go. I forget. I even forget what I dreamed last night, and what a loss that must be to you, Oh friend in the future, as Walter Whitman would say, or Mr. Walter Whitman had he also been an executive at a bank or at an insurance company, like T. S. Eliot and

Wallace Stevens. Everybody who writes a poem isn't a bum, you know? Some of the boys settle themselves into chairs of responsibility and even authority. God bless them, and you, is all I can say. God really really really bless them.[11]

From Saroyan's use of Whitmanesque conceits in his first stories to his respect for Whitman the poet at the end of his life, there was a consistent and constant evocation of the author of *Leaves of Grass*. This book he held in such high esteem that it came first in his list of nondramaric works for theatrical production. In 1941 *Theatre Arts* invited Saroyan to suggest a repertory for a national theatre. He offered a list of twelve items. It was published the following year in the preface of his book *Razzle-Dazzle:*

They are . . . potential American theatrical material, . . . these should constitute the beginning of a real American stage art, with a basis in the past, a present direction, and a constant potential for the future. I am choosing my plays from those artful and real sources of the temper and texture of inner and outer American life that seem to be urgently in need of isolation and absorption by the American race. . . .
1. Leaves of Grass, by Walt Whitman; adapted by Christopher Morley and William Rose Benét; all people in the play will be anonymous; no story; no plot; pure theatre. Instead of sets, colors and projected images, probably by Boris Aronson. No intermissions. A couple of hours straight through. Music by Paul Bowles.[12]

By choosing *Leaves of Grass* first, Saroyan was choosing his own work. *The Time of Your Life* had just won him the New York Drama Critics Award and the Pulitzer Prize. The play had no story and little plot. The characters seemed to make their stage entrances as haphazardly as customers might have entered Nick's Bar. Paul Bowles had written the music for *My Heart's in the Highlands*, Saroyan's first play. Thus, the identification of Whitman the poet and the poetic Saroyan was firmly established at the beginning of the California writer's career and was to endure to its end.

What parts of Saroyan's style and subject matter can be in part attributed to his reading of Whitman?[13] Saroyan's use of catalogues is like Whitman's, though often they are merely lists of names and objects or just synonyms. Saroyan championed the common man in all of his writing; he insisted that no man or woman is more important or more worthy than any other. He often provocatively professed his belief in the singularity of all humankind. In *Haratch*, one of the posthumously published plays, Saroyan (as a character in his own play) is asked if he did not say more than once that everybody is Armenian. He replies "Oh, yes, I did, but I was informed that a Jewish writer had said that same thing . . . before I had done so . . . and how right he was: Everybody is a Jew. In other words, everybody is everybody else."[14] The idea is even more dramatically advanced in the same play. In response to the question "Who is an Armenian?" a character answers, "An Armenian is a Turk who says I am an Armenian."[15]

The urge to identify the self with the universe, the "universalizing" of experience, is a quality Saroyan shares with Whitman. That we are all the same person underneath the superficial masks of daily social interaction is for him a visible truth. Behind this vision of life is the conviction that we are all tied together by the bonds of common humanity—within each human breast beats the same cosmic energy.

Whitman's focus on the self fitted Saroyan well. He wrote of the self and from the self. The dozen or so autobiographical books by Saroyan repeatedly review the major events of his life with special existential focus on how he became himself. In Saroyan's last play, *Warsaw Visitor*,[16] written in 1980 only months before his death, the three main characters are all himself: Moustache, an American writer named Saroyan traveling to Warsaw, the Devil serving as the writer's alter ego and foil, and Saroyan, the author of the play, who from time to time comes onstage to talk to the audience.

The celebratory impulse in Saroyan's writing can be traced directly back to Whitman's song of the self in *Leaves of Grass*. Saroyan seeks the experience of being; he wants to go straight to the core of things, energetically, immediately, passionately. He is, in Philip Rahv's conception, a "redskin" like Whitman and William Carlos Williams. He is emotional, naturalistic, nativist, energetic, and in some sense uncultured.[17]

Saroyan's work is thus a great deal more complex and diverse than many critics have acknowledged. His writing is a blend of the affirmative, mystical, and rambunctious qualities of the American romantic sensibility, but tinged with the sorrow of the Armenian experience. As David Calonne has remarked, "He praises and broods, moves outward toward the world in extrovert fashion and holds closely inward to himself the loneliness of the poet."[18]

Whitman supplied Saroyan with a model of transcendence and bravura. In the essay story "Myself upon the Earth" from the *Daring Young Man on the Flying Trapeze*, Saroyan writes: "Every life is a contradiction, a new truth, a new miracle, and even frauds are interesting. I am not a philosopher and I do not believe in philosphies; the word itself I look upon with suspicion. I believe in the right of man to contradict himself."[19] The thought and the language is from Whitman's *Leaves of Grass*: "Do I contradict myself? / Very well then I contradict myself, / (I am large, I contain multitudes)." For Saroyan as for Whitman, the contradictions of experience must be embraced; life's paradoxes cannot be overcome by forcing them into "systems" or philosophies. The inner self must be allowed to grow free of the false twistings and "proofs" of logical constructions.[20]

Saroyan emphasized imagination and the idea of play in his dramatic work. It confounded the critics and sometimes even the audiences. Nevertheless, this concept is very much a part of the American literary tradition. It is an echo of Whitman's "I loaf and invite my soul," and his exaltation of the limitless potentialities of a life lived with improvisational easy and spontaneity.[21]

Saroyan's first success, the story "The Daring Young Man on the Flying Trapeze," has (as he himself acknowledged) a Whitmanesque feeling. Its short first part, subtitled "Sleep," is a grand catalogue of the life-images of a writer.

> Horizontally wakeful amid universal widths, practising laughter and mirth, satire, the end of all, of Rome and yes of Babylon, clenched teeth, remembrance, much warmth volcanic, the streets of Paris, the plains of Jericho, much gliding as of reptile in abstraction, a gallery of watercolors, the sea and the fish with eyes, symphony, a table in the corner of the Eiffel Tower, jazz at the opera house, alarm clock and the tap-dancing of doom, conversation with a tree, the river Nile, Cadillac coupe to Kansas, the roar of Dostoyevsky, and the dark sun.
>
> The earth, the face of one who lived, the form without the weight, weeping upon snow, white music, the magnified flower twice the size of the universe, black clouds, the caged panther staring, deathless space, Mr. Eliot with rolled sleeves baking bread, Flaubert and Guy de Maupassant, a wordless rhyme of early meaning, Finlandia, mathematics highly polished and slick as a green onion to the teeth, Jerusalem, the path to paradox.
>
> The deep song of man, the sly whisper of someone unseen but vaguely known, hurricane in the cornfield, a game of chess, hush the queen, the king, Karl Franz, black Titanic, Mr. Chaplin weeping, Stalin, Hitler, a multitude of Jews, tomorrow is Monday, no dancing in the streets.
>
> O swift moment of life: it is ended, the earth is again now.[22]

Throughout the story, the physical body of the starving young writer, with all his senses put in relief by hunger, is contrasted to the artistic flight of his literary imagination, his soul. Surely Saroyan was working in Whitman's realm. In the end the writer dies. The final lines describing this death are transcendent, almost as mystical as Whitman in section Five of "Song of My-Self."[23] "Then swiftly, neatly, with the grace of the young man on the trapeze, he was gone from his body. For an eternal moment he was all things at once: the bird, the fish, the rodent, the reptile, and man. An ocean of print undulated endlessly and darkly before him. The city burned. The herded crowd rioted. The earth circled away, and knowing that he did so, he turned his lost face to the empty sky and became dreamless, unalive, perfect."[24] The recent tendency to consider Saroyan an ethnic writer ignores his obsession with American letters. Today, ethnic writers are often dismissed by academics and critics. Why should the general reader bother with works labeled "ethnic"? The very term "ethnic" literature is taking on a pejorative meaning. Such an optic ignores Saroyan's influence on a generation of American writers and filmmakers—Kerouac, Salinger, Brautigan,

Peckinpah. The strong Whitmanesque affirmation of the self is evident in Saroyan's prefaces, pronouncements and autobiographical memoirs. We are dealing here with an American trait shared by Whitman, Thoreau, Wolfe, Miller and Saroyan.

Nothing underlines this attachment to American letters more than Saroyan's respect for Whitman, his homage to the individual who forged a new path in American poetry, one that he followed and extended into the areas of the story and the stage. Like Whitman, Saroyan sang America, an America diverse in its pursuits and universal in its reach. If Walt Whitman looked West, one young Californian—William Saroyan—caught his glance, understood its meaning, and incorporated the message into his own creation.

Notes

1. *I Used to Believe I Had Forever, Now I'm Not So Sure* (New York: Cowles, 1968), 134; reprinted from the *Reporter* (September 1956).

2. *I Used to Believe*, 135.

3. *I Used to Believe*, 135.

4. *I Used to Believe*, 135.

5. *The William Saroyan Reader* (New York: Braziller, 1968).

6. "Earthly and Heavenly Voices," *I Used to Believe I Had Forever*, 49–50. Originally in *High Fidelity* (January 1955).

7. *I Used to Believe I had Forever*, 199. The list continues: Ty Cobb, J. P. Morgan, [Arshile] Gorky, William Jennings Bryan, Eugene O'Neill, Christy Mathewson, John Barrymore, Billy Sunday, Theodore Dreiser, George Gershwin, Babe Ruth.

8. In the 24 August 1968 issue, as part of six letters later incorporated into *Letters from 74 rue Taitbout or Don't Go But if You Must Say Hello to Everybody* (New York: World Publishing, 1969), 125–32.

9. *Obituaries* (Berkeley: Creative Arts, 1979), 122.

10. *After Thirty Years: the Daring Young Man on the Flying Trapeze* (New York: Harcourt, Brace and World, 1964), 124–25.

11. *Births* (Berkeley: Creative Arts, 1983), 121.

12. *Razzle-Dazzle* (New York: Harcourt, Brace, 1942), xxii.

13. Howard Floan, Saroyan's first biographer, in *William Saroyan* (New York: Twayne, 1964), was also the first to add Whitman's name to those of Sherwood Anderson, de Maupassant, George Bernard Shaw, and Mark Twain as a major influence on the writer. David Calonne, in his *William Saroyan: My Real Work is Being*, with a foreword by Dickran Kouymjian (Chapel Hill: University of North Carolina Press, 1983), pursued the matter.

14. *William Saroyan. An Armenian Trilogy*, edited by Dickran Kouymjian (Fresno: The Press at California State University, Fresno, 1986), 169.

15. *William Saroyan: An Armenian Trilogy*, 153. The passage goes on to say: "It is a decision open to all people, and only Armenians have ever wanted to be Armenians, everybody else has not made a decision but has gone right on being whatever it was he believed he was, anyhow."

16. *William Saroyan, Warsaw Visitor and Tales from the Vienna Streets*, edited by Dickran Kouymjian (Fresno: The Press at California State University, Fresno, 1991).

17. The information is found in Stephan Axelrod, *Robert Lowell: Life and Art* (Princeton: Princeton University Press, 1978), 10–11, as quoted by Calonne, *William Saroyan*, 8–9.

The full citation is: "American literature composes itself into a debate between 'palefaces' and 'redskins.' The 'palefaces' (Henry James, T. S. Eliot, and Allen Tate would belong to this party) produce a patrician art which is intellectual, symbolic, cosmopolitan, disciplined, cultured. The 'redskins' (Walt Whitman and William Carlos Williams would tend to belong here) produce a plebeian art which is emotional, naturalistic, nativist, energetic, in some sense *un*cultured. . . . All such formulations attest to a basic bifurcation in American literature between writers who experience primarily with the head and those who experience primarily with the blood."

18. Calonne, *William Saroyan*, 8–9.
19. *After Thirty Years*, 162.
20. Calonne, *William Saroyan*, 21–22.
21. Calonne, *William Saroyan*, 73.
22. *After Thirty Years*, 136.
23. The precise quotation: "Swiftly arose and spread around me the peace and knowledge that pass all arguments of the earth."
24. *After Thirty Years*, 142.

Saroyan, Stein, and Language in Motion

Edward Halsey Foster*

There are passages in William Saroyan's work where he speaks with such passion or intensity that he seems to nearly lose control of his material:

> A story is not this man did this thing and this was the consequence. A story is this man did this thing and this was the consequence and this man might have done another thing and there might have been another consequence, or a story may be this man who did this thing is not and only this man who is awake and aware of this man who did this thing is a truth, and the unbeing of this man who is not is the being of this man who is awake, and the truth of man, the being of man.[1]

Passages like this are extreme instances of Saroyan's principal assumption about literature: namely, that it can be, and indeed should be, the direct, unmediated expression of the writer's self. Saroyan wrote as quickly as he could (in fact, he learned to type in order to write even faster) so that his writing would be an immediate record of his feelings at the moment of composition. In their biography of Saroyan, Lawrence Lee and Barry Gifford described plays like *The Time of Your Life* (1939) (which was written in six days) as "rumpled, unmade,"[2] and in formal sense that is true, but it was not formal structure that Saroyan wanted. His writing was to be as deeply subjective as he could make it.

In works ranging from the stories in *The Daring Young Man on the Flying Trapeze* (1934), *Inhale and Exhale* (1936) and *Three Times Three* (1936), to the late memoirs such as *Letters from 74 rue Taitbout* (1969) and *Obituaries* (1979), Saroyan repeatedly sought moments of great rhetorical and emotional intensity. "Resurrection of a Life," for example, the first story in *Inhale and Exhale*, opens, "Everything begins with inhale and exhale, and never ends, moment after moment, yourself inhaling, and exhaling, seeing, hearing, smelling, touching, tasting, moving, sleeping, waking, day after day and year after year, until it is now, this moment, the moment of your being, the last moment, which is saddest and most glorious."[3] *Births* (1983), pub-

---

*This essay was written specifically for this volume and is published here for the first time by permission of the author.

lished nearly half a century later, opens with similar rhetorical display: "A birth is a birth, and any human birth is the same as any other. It is anonymous, in short, and it might be said to be the birth of somebody supreme in the land of lore and legend, the son of God, that is to say, or the daughter of Heaven, and the mother might be said to be the mother of God. These are matters of words and sayings."[4]

By comparison, a more conventional book, *The Human Comedy* (1943), opens, "The little boy named Ulysses Macauley one day stood over the new gopher hole in the backyard on Santa Clara Avenue in Ithaca, California. The gopher of this hole pushed up fresh moist dirt and peeked out at the boy, who was certainly a stranger but perhaps not an enemy."[5] Saroyan's less conventional writing is rarely seen in works like *The Human Comedy*, which were written to sell, and in which he was careful to maintain a conventional, restrained prose style. Here he was the kind of writer characterized by his son, Aram Saroyan, as a writer with "his own perennial bag of tricks," the celebrity with a major role in American popular culture.[6]

The Saroyan of *Three Times Three* and *Births*, on the other hand, was too aware of popular taste to think that what he was doing would find a large following. It is these books, particularly their moments of rhetorical exhilaration, that have earned him a significant place in the history of American expressionism, which has its origins in Walt Whitman, whom Saroyan considered the first truly American writer. Here, for example, is a passage from one of Saroyan's better stories, "Antranik of Armenia": "And it was nowhere and everywhere. It was different and exactly the same, word for word, pebble for pebble, leaf for leaf, eye for eye and tooth for tooth. It was neither Armenia nor Russia. It was people alive in that place, and not people only, but all things alive there, animate and inanimate."[7] "Inanimate" things are "alive"? As absurd or nonsensical as this passage seems, its real value lies in its ecstatic tone and cadences—very much the sort of thing one finds throughout Whitman's work. Here, for example, is the conclusion to Whitman's "Great are the myths":

Great is life . . . and real and mystical . . . wherever and whoever,
Great is death. . . . Sure as life holds all parts together, death holds all parts
    together;
Sure as the stars return again after they merge in the light, death is great as life.[8]

Whatever these lines may mean literally (one wonders if Whitman himself knew), their force certainly has less to do with what they say than with tones and cadences of conviction and energy.

As I have discussed in my book on Saroyan's short fiction,[9] there is a close link between the aesthetics of Gertrude Stein and Saroyan. In part her theories reached Saroyan through Sherwood Anderson, who modeled his own work on Stein's, but Saroyan also read her work closely enough to write a very good parody of it in his essay "Poem, Story, Novel" in *Inhale and Exhale* (1936). He met Stein twice during her lecture tour of America in 1934, and it is likely that he heard her deliver one or more of the pieces collected and published the following year in *Lectures in America*. There are close parallels between Saroyan's work and the theories she outlined in those lectures.

Stein in effect took Whitman's poetics and refurbished it with theoretical underpinnings, bringing his expressionistic manner into the twentieth century and thereby setting the foundations for a tradition that extends through Anderson to William Faulkner, Thomas Wolfe, and Jack Kerouac as well as Saroyan. Stein believed that "[t]he business of Art" was "to live in the actual present, that is the complete actual present, and to completely express that complete actual present."[10] The objective was not mimesis or objectivity. A literary work, that is, should not simply be about something but should embody and manifest the occasion of its writing in the movement or process of its words. According to Stein, the words should possess "a movement lively enough to be a thing in itself moving."[11] Movement, not meaning, was then the essential focus: "I am inclined to believe," she concluded, "that there is really no difference between clarity and confusion, just think of any life that is alive, is there really any difference between clarity and confusion."[12] As the poet Lyn Hejinian has remarked, "Stein wanted to understand things not in isolated rigidity, which falsified and monumentalized conditions which were fluid, but as present participants in on-going living—fountainous living."[13]

One must not claim more for Stein's work more than was actually intended. Fredric Jameson identified Stein as a postmodernist *"avant la lettre,"*[14] but she was not that, although her experiments, grounded ultimately in romantic expressionism, have been very useful to postmodernist writers. Stein believed that language was always in flux because the personality of the writer was always in flux.

Expressionism depends on the notion of a "unified" or independent self, which a truly postmodernist writer would question. Stein's work, like Saroyan's, is firmly subjective. "Poetry and Grammar," for example, one of the essays in *Lectures in America*, is about the ways in which poets learn to give things their "true names"—words, that is, that somehow embody the essence of the thing to which they refer. Stein singled out Whitman as one who "really wanted to express the thing and not call it by its name," and she cited the title *Leaves of Grass* as an instance of his having done so. She wanted her prose poems in *Tender Buttons* to do much the same thing: "I had to feel anything and everything that *for me* was existing so intensely that I could put it down in writing as a thing in itself without at all necessarily using its name."[15] In doing this, she found that she "could be very gay." William Gass has shown that what she meant by "gay" has exactly what one means now; many of the "things in themselves" are presented in words which encode her homosexual feelings and perceptions.[16] The "thing in itself" is then something uniquely perceived by an individual, and writing is a matter of personality, individual perception, and expressivity: the writing and the self, as in Whitman, are one.

Stein wanted writing to be a record of unmediated perception; in Saroyan's more ambitious work, that was his objective as well. In "Quarter, Half, Three-Quarter, and Whole Notes," published in *Three Times Three*, he avoided conventions of subject matter and narrative and tried to write as freely as Stein had in *Tender Buttons*. Even in his conventional works there are occasional moments when words are forced into powerfully emotional cadences where there is little or no "content." The "thing in itself" is at this point essentially an expression of the author and his perceptions, modulated in time:

> I'm here to tell you and I'm telling you in simple language it's dirty and rotten, but it's the only thing, and you're going to live forever because even after cities are swallowed by the earth and civilizations forgotten the father of life is going to rise from sleep and walk quietly through the desolation and build a house and pause there and into this house the mother of life is going to grow with seed and another tribe of man is going to stand upon the surface of the earth and one of these is to be yourself and there is nothing you can do about it. You can die but that is less and less an end and more and more a beginning. . . .[17]

In "Psalms," Saroyan wrote that his concern in his work was simply "the change taking place, now"; art, he said, "is a seeming to say."[18] The work of art, that is, offers not ideas but movement: "substance [i.e., language] in motion"[19]—and that, of course, is exactly what Stein argued. As she said, "there is really no difference between clarity and confusion"; what matters, in short, is not the literal intention in the language.

Saroyan turned to Stein's aesthetics in such autobiographical works as *Short Drive, Sweet Chariot* (1966), *Days of Life and Death and Escape to the Moon* (1970), *Places Where I've Done Time* (1972), *Chance Meetings* (1978), *Obituaries* (1979), and *Births* (1983). Sometimes his reminiscences are conventionally structured, but there are other occasions (particularly in *Obituaries* and *Births*) where the ostensible subject (a place where he had lived, for example, or a man he had known) is little more than an excuse to write, and the writing in turn is, in Stein's phrase, "a seeming to say": the true subject is "the change taking place, now."

In *Births*, written at the end of his life, Saroyan said that what he needed was a "gimmick" or "procedural system" so that "the writing [would be] inevitable, unavoidable, and even appealing every morning first thing in the day."[20] "[T]he thing that matters is the writing that has come out of the employment of the procedure," he argued: "the purpose of this kind of writing is to beguile you [i.e., the writer] *into finding yourself.*"[21]

Notes

1. *Inhale and Exhale* (New York: Random House, 1936), 287.
2. Lawrence Lee and Barry Gifford, *Saroyan: A Biography* (New York: Harper & Row, 1984), 14.
3. *Inhale and Exhale*, 3.
4. *Births* (Berkeley, CA: Creative Arts, 1983), 2.
5. *The Human Comedy* (New York: Harcourt Brace, 1943), 11.
6. Aram Saroyan, *William Saroyan* (New York: Harcourt Brace Jovanovich, 1983), 35.
7. *Inhale and Exhale*, 265.
8. Walt Whitman, *Complete Poetry and Collected Prose* (New York: Library of America, 1982), 145.
9. Edward Halsey Foster, *William Saroyan: A Study of the Short Fiction* (New York: Twayne Publishers, 1991).
10. Getrude Stein, *Lectures in America* (New York: Random House, 1935), 104–5.
11. *Lectures in America*, 171.
12. *Lectures in America*, 174.
13. Lyn Hejinian, "Teo Stein Talks," *Temblor* 6 (1986): 132.
14. Fredric Jameson, *Postmodernism or, The Cultural Logic of Late Capitalism* (Durham, NC: Duke University Press, 1992), 4.
15. *Lectures in America*, 242; my emphasis.
16. William Gass, *Habitations of the Word* (New York: Simon and Schuster, 1985), 85.
17. *Inhale and Exhale*, 198.
18. *Inhape and Exhale*, 377.
19. *Inhale and Exhale*, 378.
20. *Births*, 110.
21. *Births*, 113; my emphasis.

Saroyan's Study of Ethnicity

WALTER SHEAR*

At one time William Saroyan was America's most famous ethnic writer—more famous than ethnic, perhaps. In the late 1930s and early 1940s Saroyan exploded onto the literary scene as a true wunderkind, the writer who was singlehandedly revolutionizing the form of both the short story and the drama. He was the man who refused the Pulitzer Prize and argued with Louis B. Mayer over the issue of artistic integrity. As a literary personality, he had an instinctive desire to be a part of the American cultural scene, to feel that he counted on such a stage. Yet at the same time he felt apart from it, hating the entrepreneurs of culture and his writing rivals with such a passion he was often dismissive of the popular mainstream culture of his day. In these moods he was apparently satisfied with his own artistic ego and his quieter working out in his fiction of his own cultural dilemma.

Saroyan's ethnic writing, which is in essence his emotional record of what it means to be a member of the Armenian subculture, is scattered throughout the corpus of his work, appearing in almost every form his protean talent produced—short story, novel, novella, memoir, essay. While his later fictional works (especially his novels) tended to regard ethnic existence as a problem—sometimes as a state racked by irreconcilably conflicting values—his earlier work, while not always optimistic, tended to emphasize a seemingly immortal quality in his ethnic heritage and the capacity of recent immigrants for adjustments. In one of his earliest stories, the mother tells her family in Armenian, "It is no use to cry. We have always had our disappointments and hardships and we have always come out of them and always shall."[1]

The Saroyan book which investigates most intensively the relationship between the young ethnic and the mainstream culture is a collection of short stories written fairly early in his career, *My Name Is Aram*. Its analysis of the ethnic's position is deceptively elaborate and thus this aspect of the book has often been overlooked. The only two literary critics who have studied the book in detail stress its wavering between romantic allegiances and realistic constraints. Howard Floan points to "the conflicting claims of dream

*Reprinted from *MELUS* 13, nos. 1 and 2 (Spring–Summer 1986), 45–55, by permission of *MELUS: The Society for the Study of Multi-Ethnic Literature in the United States.*

and reality" in the stories, while David Stephen Calonne believes the romantic elements dominate since the central character's "activities celebrate the triumph of freedom over restraint, of the intense over the quotidian."[2] While not dismissing these considerations, I will concentrate on the book's analysis of the relationship between the ethnic community and the mainstream culture and its examination of the social interaction within each group. In his investigation Saroyan employs a second generation ethnic, the Armenian-American boy, Aram, as narrator and a schematic division of the arenas of social action into: 1. an official world of status and socially-defined relationships; and 2. a community evoked and defined by personal relationships. These two overriding frames are, in most stories, paralleled and given public enhancement by the social divisions between the American mainstream world and the Armenian ethnic world. To avoid rejecting the values of any group, Saroyan opens the plot form of these stories so that at the end of each there is a suggestion of continuance rather than conclusion. Saroyan dramatizes his ethnic society as a total system functioning according to particular principles, but he views it as depending on inconsistencies for its operation.

Saroyan's official world is partly defined by those Calonne refers to as "the mediocre instruments of society's institutions," but in a broader sense it is that arena where one comes to terms with one's social role.[3] The personal world is characterized by a free and innocently irresponsible activity of the human spirit, an expression which seems connected with the ethnic's desire to articulate another kind of community. In general the characters in the stories exhibit a persistent concern for one another's personhood, a caring that may be related to the social conditions of the 1930s, but which seems more particularly tied to the social uncertainties in the position of the American ethnic. Whatever the reason, the characters often respond to each other by developing and elaborating attitudes of seriousness and mock-seriousness which successfully avoid risking anyone's personhood. The stories show people taking care of one another in a psychological sense, a nurturing that is reflected figuratively in the concern for health and physical condition which is a pervasive motif for the stories.

As the official world and the personal community interact, what they demonstrate is the necessity for lying (or keeping silent)—that is, for temporarily suppressing the claims of one world so the other might occupy center stage. In this manner each world can proclaim its status without contradicting the other world. The first story of the collection, "The Summer of the Beautiful White Horse," directly confronts the problem of consistency and honesty. On seeing his cousin Mourad with a new white horse, Aram is dumbfounded because theirs is a proud and honest family and "I *knew* my cousin Mourad couldn't have *bought* the horse, and if he couldn't have bought it he must have *stolen* it, and I refused to believe he had stolen it."[4] As the quotation implies, logic is not much help. At first it seems to cancel itself out. Then it seems to conclude that Mourad and Aram must be in some jeopardy, for obviously the horse is stolen. But again worldly logic is suspended as the boys' enthusiasm for the horse is such that they avoid facing the legal (official) view. In the same spirit of suspension, John Byro, when he sees the situation, only hints at his own position as owner—to show his good will for the name of the family and to avoid a direct, official confrontation. This intermittent concern with consistency works. Finally it is personal concern—not any official logic of right and wrong—which unites Byro again with his horse.[5] Later, in "Locomotive 38, the Ojibway," the Indian title character also suppresses a fact, his ability to drive, in order for Aram to have the fun of actually experiencing some of his aspirations. Both the Indian and Byro, an Assyrian, seem to have an instinctive feeling for the world of these Armenian boys.

The world of personal relationships is invariably activated by a nonethnic official society, but it is also generated by structures in the ethnic group, where social relationships are, because of the eroding authority within the group's social structures, always contingent, always in need of some improvisation. For the ethnic, therefore, the personal seems to be inevitably effacing the official. While this can seem a natural condition to the children, it evokes pathos in the adults. Since it is only contingently official, the Armenian ethnic society seems in the American social order defined by the more personal interactions of an extended family, a group which in its affections and its tendency to accept people for what they want to be seems to imply a version of the family of humankind. It has in common with the personal world a feeling of being psychologically inside, at a remove from conventional American society.

The major family is the Garoughlanian because the main character— the first person narrator in all the stories—is Aram Garoughlanian. It is a family who, we are told, "come by all their wisdom naturally, from within" (80), a condition that accents the tie between family identity and personal idiosyncrasy. As a boy (in most of the stories he is between 10 and 14), Aram is still spontaneously a member of both Armenian and American societies and thus can function as a kind of understanding go-between. From his Armenian background, he has inherited a feeling for the personal world, for characters like his cousin Mourad who "enjoyed being alive more than anybody else who had ever fallen into the world by mistake" (10). But he also understands how the official world operates and its non-Armenian rationality. For example, he and Joey accept their strappings at school because they've broken the rules and they want to "be fair and square with the Board of Education" (102). Most often Aram is not a protagonist, but rather a witness to the drama of the fears, dreams, and inclinations of others.

Typically, the stories concern what doesn't happen—how Aram's uncle fails to raise pomegranates, how another uncle doesn't get a job, how his cousin doesn't get in trouble for stealing a horse, how two people don't fall in love, etc. What doesn't happen is not failure, however—the personal world, say, defeated by a more ruthless and indifferent official world. And it is in this respect that the forms of the stories can be considered open; that is, the narratives deliberately evade the kind of final closures implied by a triumph of personal desire or a rejection of an official sort. Further, the characters retain their role as agents even though their aims may not be achieved, for their agency consists chiefly in the improvising of relationships to the official world and thus guaranteeing the continuity of existence on a personal level.

Instead of hostilely confronting each other and concluding with someone's sense of failure, both the mainstream world and the Armenian world open with a feeling of multiplicity and freedom. Aram is not imprisoned by old country perspectives, but neither does he reject his heritage. Because of this, he comes to understand the necessity of some distance between the official world and the personal world, to see that an authentically-lived existence in one world creates more freedom in the other. When Aram humorously comes to the realization that he is losing the 50 yard dash and that his fellow racers are not simply there to contribute to his triumph, he is finally released from the bondage imposed by his egotistically subjective response to the I-must-triumph-over-my-competitors paradigm of the official world. At the end of "The Summer of the Beautiful White Horse," when the boys realize that John Byro is not going to press charges against them, all three come to share in the recognition that personal dreams can in the right human context become fundamental claims.

Within the context of the ethnic world, the figure of the family patriarch is used to dramatize an official force transformed into a purely personal effect. Uncle Khosrove, the most prominent of these types, is the loudest in a series of uncles and grandfathers who pour out their stylized version of a wisdom calculated to regulate family activities. Theirs, however, are no longer iron, absolute commands. In fact, the strength of the orator's insistence seems only to signify a corresponding fading of official status. Although these characters are overly accepted and acknowledged as authority figures, no member of the family follows their advice completely.

Because of their diminished status, these characters bring out most strongly the juggling of logic, the social manipulation of what is recognized and what is not, that results from the interaction between external convention and internal evaluation. For example, Uncle Khosrove's publicly stated attitude toward games, that one should not take winning or losing too seriously, seems a recognition that personal attitudes should never be bound tightly to one's objective fate as a game player. But he pretends to a stoicism he does not possess: he is in fact the worst loser in the world. The fact that he "himself lost *his* life when he lost a game" demonstrates the lack of personal command which results from the precarious nature of his present social status (140). There is a kind of logic in the fact that this inconsistency between idea and behavior leads directly to Khosrove's most intensely personal relationship, that with the Arab, who comes to represent the loss of everything external. The narrator imagines that the Arab, by losing a game of *tavli* to his uncle (thus officially opening the possibility for a personal relationship), comes to a recognition of status: the Arab "understood *who* my uncle Khosrove was—without being told" (142).

The uncle and the Arab come to enjoy a silent communion. As Aram's mother explains, "They understand one another and don't need to open their mouths" (145). When Aram seeks an objective fact, the Arab's name, Khosrove screams as if he is being murdered, reacting as if the relationship to be preserved must remain totally private. What the two friends share is the old social world—literally, the old country—now gone but still alive personally, reduced to an unspoken understanding. When the Arab dies, Aram concludes, "He died an orphan in an alien world, six thousand miles from home" (147). As Calonne notes, the gap between their old world, personal, silent communion and Aram's leafing through American advertisements becomes a symbolic image for "the developing gulf between the two generations," and thus, for a kind of pathetic failure of the personal in this version of the ethnic family (69).

The context of the old world and the new world is used more overtly in "Old Country Advice to the American Traveler," where Uncle Garro gives advice to the younger Uncle Melik about the dangers of travel on a train.

" 'Several moments after the train begins to move . . . two men wearing uniforms will come down the aisle and ask you for a ticket. Ignore them. They will be imposters.'

'How will I know?'

'You will know. You are no longer a child' " (135).

A man, Garro says, will offer a cigarette. Don't take it, he advises. "The cigarette will be doped" (135). He further envisions a young woman intentionally bumping into Melik. This woman will be a whore.

On the actual journey, Melik not only finds that none of this happens, he himself offers another young man a cigarette, goes out of his way to sit with a young lady, starts a poker game, and has a wonderful trip. Yet at the end of the story he tells Uncle Garro that he has followed his instructions. The story ends with Garro saying, "I am pleased that *someone* has profited by my experience" (137). There is an obvious irony in the events, and yet the reversing of much of the advice does not cancel it esthetically. It remains the embodiment of the old world of Garro, still *his* experience. In an important sense the difference in characters, and in their relationship to the new world, means that each has his own truth.

The personal comes to have several shades of meaning in this collection. Most of the patriarchs are smaller scale variants of Uncle Khosrove, "an enormous man with a powerful head of black hair and the largest mustache in the San Joaquin Valley, a man so furious in temper, so irritable, so impatient that he stopped anyone from talking by roaring, *It is no harm; pay no attention to it*" (12). With its massive, total dismissal of the external world, his seems the voice of pure psychic energy, the voice of completely internal power. However, the family reaction to Khosrove tends to imply that such articulation is really a kind of reaching after lost official power. The ranting intensity in his official role tends to seem that of an imprisoned voice, to become a personal comment on present status. In these stories, which are largely paced by dialogue, many of the characterizations are basically voices. All articulate a felt relationship to the ethos of their world, but while some convey a strong sense of active agency, others suggest an isolated self and like the silence of the "poor and burning Arab" convey the pathos of those deprived of or denied social status. They remind us that to come to the New World is to lose most of one's former social status.

Several of the stories are direct examinations of the community as the arena for weighing personal desire. Using Aram's low-keyed concern, the early stories of the volume analyze critically, but sympathetically, qualities of the dream of the self. In "The Summer of the Beautiful White Horse" the typical (and typically impossible) boy's dream of riding a horse is permitted to happen through an almost miraculous suspension of feelings about property rights. John Byro, the owner of the horse, is an outsider to some extent ("an Assyrian who, out of loneliness, had learned to speak Armenian") (16), but he comes to a kind of understanding as he looks at the returned horse. "I do not know what to think. . . . The horse is stronger than ever. Better tempered too" (19). Somehow the horse being stolen had been a good experience for all involved.

The following story, "The Journey to Hanford," features a playful interaction between two comic extremes: 1. Aram's grandfather, who orates—in such a way, again, as to imply a diminished official force—the practical view of life; and 2. Uncle Jorgi, who is tolerated by the family but considered a fool because his only ambition is to play a zither. The prominent refrain in the story is the grandfather's complaint about unrealistic writers: "When you read in a book that a man who sits all day under a tree and plays a zither and sings is a great man, believe me, that writer is a liar"; "When you read in a book . . . that a woman is truly a creature of wonder, that writer has turned his face away from his wife and is dreaming. Let him go" (21). It is soon apparent that even though he may be articulating the truths of realism, his comments are essentially psychological declarations of his status.

There is little response to the statements and the story's plot also features an evasion of conflict. Uncle Jorgi is sent to Hanford to get a job, the journey here, like those in other stories, being the movement to the world beyond the ethnics. With little suspense, it transpires that Jorgi is saved from having to work, though it is Aram who has to explain to this naïve zither-player that the farmer has lied to him about all the watermelons being harvested: "He didn't want to hurt your feelings. He just said that because he knew your heart wouldn't be in your work" (28).

The story ends with the harmony of the family restored, the two philosophies reconciled because appearances indicate that at least Jorgi has tried to get work. Aram observes, "When I came back to the parlor the old man was stretched out on the couch, asleep and smiling, and his son Jorgi was singing hallelujah to the universe at the top of his beautiful, melancholy voice" (30).

In "The Pomegranate Trees" a foolish dream of Uncle Melik, to grow pomegranates in vast quantities and sell them to an eager public, comes, as one expects, to failure. And yet, through the casual dialogue between Aram and his uncle in which each comes to learn gradually, sympathetically about the other and about the world around them, the experience comes to have a value of its own. The marvelous quality of the story is its concealment of the exact time the uncle knows the dream is doomed and the underplaying of the moment, finally, when the two realized that in a crucial sense this failure doesn't matter.

Not simply a pretty lie, the personal dream evokes the psychological debt connected with social dignity or status. (One begins to owe a consistency of identity to others and to a degree their expectations become demands for some assimilation of their values.) "My Cousin Dikran, the Orator" concentrates on the uncertain mixture of the precious and the precarious in the ethic's movement into mainstream society. Here public speaking is the sign of the emergence from a more private tribal identity. Aram observes a farmer leap to his feet to make his pledge: "Gone are the days of poverty for this tribe from the lovely city of Dikranagert—the five Pampalonian brothers—twenty-five cents." After having made this overt commitment to a common cause, the farmer goes home, "his head high, and his heart higher. Poor? In the old days, yes. But no more" (77). Though the amount is paltry by mainstream standards, the new-found pride in identity is the essential value. Although the actions here are restricted to the ethnic community, the people, by officially indicating what they feel they have become, are risking themselves in the movement from their old-country identity. A more public dream, life in a new society, can now be lived and shared.

As the story develops, the emphasis shifts to Dikran, a second generation figure, and the same kind of social movement is traced, this time one step closer to assimilation into the American mainstream. Here, however, the story is much more critical of the movement. Aram's family is pleased when the boy Dikran (aged 11) becomes adept at giving speeches. Nonetheless, the patriarch of the family is still dissatisfied, because all the boy's knowledge is from books, impersonal. Dikran's speech at the school program is "the best thing of its kind—the best of the worst kind of thing"—for the boy concludes that the World War, in which several million were killed, was a good thing for the world (83). In spite of his pride in the boy's achievement in an American ritual, the old man feels he must speak to the boy out of what he knows: "Continue your investigation of the world from books, and I am sure, if you are diligent and your eyes hold out, that by the time you are sixty-seven you will know the awful foolishness of that remark [about the war]—so innocently uttered by yourself tonight" (84). Certified social achievement is a good thing, but in this case the status of the elder in the ethnic community permits personal sensitivity to have the final word by articulating a truer wisdom.

The stories "A Nice Old-Fashioned Romance with Love Lyrics and Everything" and "The Circus" concentrate on characters working out the social fictions which their roles in the official world force upon them. Both utilize favorite materials of Saroyan's, the classroom and the confrontation between students and teachers. Here and elsewhere in Saroyan the American classroom is another arena where one's personal behavior can win a form of status, providing one can manipulate official structures. In "The Circus" the narrative is always uncomfortably on the verge of a serious confrontation as the boys openly challenge the rules by fleeing from school (instead of sneaking out). They imagine that their punishment this time may involve the removal to a more indifferent (more absolutely official) environment, the reform school. But at the end the institutional patriarch (the principal, old man Dawson) turns more personally understanding, whipping them with more blows, as required for such an offense, but with a gentler stroke. He also pays tribute to their bizarre concern for him: "I'm awfully grateful to you boys . . . for modulating your howls so nicely this time. I don't want people to think I'm killing you" (108).

In "A Nice Old-Fashioned Romance" Aram is accused, unjustly, of writing on the blackboard a poem, saying that his teacher, Miss Daffney, is in love with Mr. Derringer, the principal in this story. The fact that Aram is actually innocent means nothing because to both teacher and principal his past behavior in the classroom makes him guilty. His punishment, however, is not the issue; rather the question in the story is whether the two authority figures will be able to acknowledge that the poem in fact objectifies their secret feelings. The story ends with Miss Daffney's removing herself from the scene, apparently because of her inability to make what is an obvious truth into a sufficiently public feeling that it might form the basis for a positive bond.

One of the complications in the story occurs when Miss Daffney surprises Derringer beating a chair instead of Aram. As she suspects, a small deal between the principal and the boy has been negotiated. Derringer wants Aram to be more "gracious" about Miss Daffney's appearance in "his" poems. Aram, who has not written the poems, sees a chance to strike a personal bargain on the level of the official lie. "If you punish me," he tells Derringer," then I won't be gracious" (71). Derringer agrees not to punish him, but so that no one gets suspicious, he gets Aram to howl while he straps the chair.

Miss Daffney, bursting in on this private scene, regards Derringer's action as a falsification of his school role (and perhaps as a personal betrayal of her as well). In this instance, however, as she might have figured out, turning the social ritual into a more personal relationship is not a bad idea, for it also opens the possibility for the surfacing of some feelings of affection in the sorting out of what is going on.

As is the case in several other stories, the movement around and about the official social situation creates the playfulness of a game situation. The advantage of turning a social situation into a kind of game is that all parties can see that the official rules and outcomes are not the absolutely confirming measurements they can seem. Characters involved are more apt to appreciate the ingenuity, the active intention, and the persistence of the other person. They are inevitably moved to an attempt at understanding. The great danger is the tendency of the ego to draw the official world into its private domain, as is the case with Uncle Khosrove's attitude toward the games. At one time Aram, encouraged by Lionel Strongfort's advertisements, imagines himself becoming the most powerful man in his neighborhood. Not until he has alarmed his relatives, irritated his neighbors, provoked advice from his Uncle Gyko and stories from his grandmother, and lost the key race to the other boys does he begin to understand that the dream in this case cannot be more. Sometimes the greater strength of external reality is simply in the fact that, while it cannot be exceeded, it can be naturally and democratically shared.

In this story Uncle Gyko is an adult mirror of Aram's ego dreams. Believing that the secret of greatness is "the releasing within one's self of those mysterious vital forces which are in all men" (54), Gyko deludes himself that he is getting wisdom from God. In fact, as Aram informs us, he gets all his ideas from "the theosophy-philosophy-astrology-and-miscellaneous shelf at the Public Library" (57). His concluding advice for Aram is the great secret of the private world—but also, as Aram eventually sees, its supreme delusion: "We are a great family. We can do anything" (62). In this story, and throughout the book, Saroyan's fascination with the desire to achieve is tempered by his witty awareness of the terms the world dictates to its social inhabitants.

Heinrich Straumann has remarked that a prominent and ultimately unfortunate strain in Saroyan's work is a tendency to try to escape from reality (200). It is perhaps the most formidable kind of negative criticism of Saroyan since it implies that his weakest work is his most characteristic. The argument of this paper is that Saroyan is essentially a modernist in that he regards his fictional reality as multifaceted and that his awareness of the claims of the ethnic community pushed him in this direction. His aim in *My Name Is Aram* is to show how his main character, possessed both of a heritage of values and an active imagination, senses himself moving psychologically between an old order and a new possibility. Much of the maneuvering is done through conversation, a crucial activity which keeps the characters alive to their environment as a community and invaluable to one another as individuals. And it is further enriched by humor, that detached awareness of the individual that both sets of ethos, ethnic and mainstream, are, as cultures, inherently peculiar.

Even though Saroyan has said that the characters are based on his own memories, their dialogue seems less remembered talk than improvisation, the sketching out in the writing process of an increasing communal awareness and an increasing communal crisis. The book seems based primarily on Saroyan's recollections of people's infinite capacities for manipulating their conventions. In it he creates, through a rhythmically comic interchange of internal values and social perspectives, a version of how culture might work. He ultimately suggests, through the narratives' postponing and suspending of judgments on people, that some measurement systems are valuable only when they function intermittently.

Notes

1. William Saroyan, *My Name is Saroyan: A Collection* ed. James H. Tashjian (New York: Harcourt, 1983) 53.

2. Howard R. Floan, *William Saroyan* (New York: Twayne, 1966) 83; Heinrich Straumann, *American Literature in the Twentieth Century*, 3rd ed. (New York: Harper Torchbooks, 1965) 200–02; David Sadkin, "William Saroyan," *Critical Survey of Short Fiction*, ed. Frank N. Magill (Englewood Cliffs: Salem P, 1981) 2190.

3. William Saroyan, *William Saroyan: My Real Work Is Being* (Chapel Hill: U of North Carolina P, 1983) 65.

4. William Saroyan, *My Name is Aram*, Rev. ed. (New York: Dell, 1966) 11.

5. This tendency to handle controversy in an idiosyncratic fashion may have been a part of Saroyan's own temperament. Years later in *Chance Meetings* he tells a reader that "to this day I am very easily willing to keep silent and to walk around what looks like totally meaningless, useless, ridiculous trouble. Don't hate—ignore. Don't kill—live and let live." *Chance Meetings* (New York: Norton, 1978) 86.

William Saroyan: Romantic Existentialist

THELMA J. SHINN*

William Saroyan is a contradiction of terms. He is unabashedly romantic, yet his romanticism is portrayed within the frequently sordid realism of the run-down bar and the lives of derelicts and prostitutes, escaped convicts and gamblers. He is buoyantly optimistic (an attitude violently attacked and rejected by the egotistical view that modern society is the first society to recognize the hopelessness of life and the destructiveness of man), yet he writes of murder and disillusionment. He uses the simplest, most realistic dialogue and characters in plays with little discernible reality of plot and—sometimes—setting.

In a word, Saroyan's philosophy is not a resolution of but a recognition and acceptance of the contradictions of life. He tells us that life is both funny and sad, both violent and tender, and that generally the contradictions are present in the same scene, the same person, at the same time. Consequently, critics could not define Saroyan's plays—to give one interpretation would conceal the other interpretations simultaneously maintained by the symbolism. This led many critics to reject Saroyan's works because they felt that the plays, in appealing to the irrational and to the emotional in the audience rather than to the intellectual and rational, could be dismissed as mere Romanticism. The more perceptive critics, however, suspected that there was more to Saroyan than sentimentality. Like George Jean Nathan, they began by asking "Is Saroyan crazy?" and ended by asserting that "in this William Saroyan, crazy or not crazy, the national theatre, I believe, has discovered its most genuinely gifted new writer."[1]

Today's theater seems to be the new generation of Saroyans that Saroyan predicted in his introduction to "Hello Out There," where he acknowledged a similar debt to George Bernard Shaw. The nonplot symbolic dramas of Pinter, of Beckett, of Ionesco with their usually unrelieved pessimism are remarkably similar to the "romantic fantasies" of Saroyan. Saroyan displays the same disregard for spelling out meanings to the audience, the same freedom with scenery and plot, the same concentration on the individual. Much of modern drama is considered existential because the individual is trying to find for himself some meaning in this absurd universe—and the

*Reprinted from *Modern Drama* 15 (September 1972): 185–94, by permission of the editors.

meaning, if any, appears to be within himself. In this sense, at least, the existential theme is precisely what most concerns Saroyan.

Saroyan's departure from modern theater, as well as from the theater of the 30's and 40's, is his remarkable—his critics say unrealistic—ability to find a note of affirmation, to testify finally to the rejected ideal of human dignity. It is this unforgivable sin which caused critics to dismiss his plays before they had even attempted to cull the depths of his drama for the insights he might have had which enabled him to draw such seemingly unsupportable conclusions. A look at those insights in a few of his plays perhaps might show that Saroyan had a deeper and more significant message for drama and for the world today than even his most positive critics saw.

Saroyan's first play, *My Heart's in the Highlands*, already demonstrated both the unique contributions of his talent and the characteristics which were going to offend many of the critics. These did not always differ: as Joseph Wood Krutch noted in his review of the play, "Mr. Saroyan's farragoes of sentiment and slapstick, ingenuity and impudence, are not only *sui generis* but highly entertaining to all those whom they do not exasperate."[2] It is strange that an audience which had been exposed to Thornton Wilder's *Our Town* in 1938 could be so shocked and upset by Saroyan's freedom with the set and "sentimentality" a year later. But what seemed to offend most was that the play could not be reduced to one logical interpretation. The several attempts made were, as Brooks Atkinson notes, all valid interpretations, but not just because—as Atkinson is inclined to add—Saroyan was lucky enough to have a capable director interpreting the play for the audience through his presentation.[3] The multiplicity of meanings reflects the symbolic import of the play, a symbolism—as that in the poetry of Hart Crane— exclusively American. Saroyan explores the themes of economic inequality, the plight of the artist, individual integrity, the search for beauty and the growth of awareness in a seemingly haphazard way in the simple international American stock of a small neighborhood. The Scotch bugler, the Armenian-speaking grandmother, the Polish grocer are all beautifully American. The setting is representative rather than realistic; the simple dialogue is intuitive rather than logical.

The economic inequality is implicit in the poverty of the family, which forces them to beg credit from the local grocer to provide for themselves and for their hungry guest and which forces them out of their home at the end of the play. But the manner of dispossession, when compared with that in Elmer Rice's "Street Scene," reveals that Saroyan's interest lies not so much in the inequality indiscriminately arising from the indifference of the external world as it does in the individual's ability to turn even this into a vehicle for the expression of human dignity. The mother and children in *Street Scene* were ignobly emptied into the streets into the waiting and re-stricting clasp of "charity," while Johnny's father gallantly leaves his furni-ture too as much to help the poor family moving in as to pay the back rent.

One gets the impression that he might have given them the furniture whether or not any back rent was due, and that his decision to leave at all was prompted not so much by the economic reality of eviction as by his decision to start anew somewhere else after the rejection of his poetry by *The Atlantic Monthly*. In other words, the dispossession in Saroyan's play emphasizes the brotherhood of man and the dignity of the individual, the human relationships rather than the social "realities."

The plight of the artist theme is also treated in a universal manner by Saroyan. Though Johnny's father represents the artist, he is not alone. Saroyan recognizes the artist—the sensitive awareness to living—in each of the characters, as Johnny merges with his father, as Mr. Kosak and Esther are moved by the poetry and recognize the value of the artist even before they know what he has produced, as Mr. MacGregor creates beauty with his bugle, and as the townspeople instinctively recognize and worship it. Saroyan identifies the artist as the man sensitive to the beauty which can be found in the world. His plight is in the rejection by the world of his attempts to express this beauty, and that rejection is equally wrong—or at least equally possible—whether the man is a first-rate or a tenth-rate poet. The townspeople instinctively recognize the beauty of MacGregor's music, while the "world" of the institutionalized charity of the "Old People's Home" takes the bugle away from him.

This search for beauty within the individual which Saroyan recognizes comes close to being the element of the divine in humanity. MacGregor, who achieves recognizable expression of beauty in his music, has his "heart in the highlands," and goes there at the end of the play. The townspeople implicitly recognize the divine origin of this gift when they bring the food as sacrifices to it. The father has created his successful poem in the person of Johnny and in himself—thus they are in this sense identical and thus MacGregor wants to come to their home to die because that is the closest he can come to the divine perception in this world.

It is Johnny's father who gains the most complete awareness of the value of the individual and of the search for beauty in this play. Though he has failed to be recognized by the world, he has gained his one reader in Mr. Kosak and he has not deserted his calling. He knows that he is right as he answers Johnny's inquiry of where they were going with: "Never mind Johnny. You just follow me." Johnny himself, as he ends the play with "I'm not mentioning any names, Pa, but something's wrong somewhere," has only grasped half the truth—the easiest half according to Saroyan. His recognition of the injustice of "a world that prevents good people from dwelling together peacefully in the goodness of the universe" is the stopping point of most modern views of the world. Saroyan goes on to assert that man's search for beauty can carry him beyond the ugliness of the world to the divine within himself and within his fellow men. If this attitude must be romantic and sentimental, then Saroyan is both—and so is Emerson,

Thoreau, Hart Crane, any artist who believes that man can transcend the injustice of the external world by looking within himself and that man can find a beauty within himself that is within each man. Saroyan tries to reach this inner beauty, and if he does not appeal to it with logical arguments, it may be because beauty is beyond logic. If he couches his appeal in what seems sentimental and romantic, it is because inner beauty is the source of whatever sentiment and romance man can know. Even this first play shows that Saroyan is not simply saying that life is beautiful and all men love each other. He says rather that in each man with any sensitivity there is a desire for beauty and that this desire should be followed and nurtured if there is to be any positive reality of beauty in this absurd world.

Saroyan's greatest success, *The Time of Your Life*, carries the same message as *My Heart's in the Highlands*, or messages rather, since the simple statement above can scarcely represent the levels of meaning presented in Saroyan's symbolic dramas. Again the characters and the situation reflect the economic conditions of the period and the inequalities of modern society. The cast includes a prostitute, a drunk, a society couple out slumming, a longshoreman, a policeman to mention just a few. The central set is a run-down bar where the central character sits drinking champagne and watching people. Every person (with the exception of Blick, the depersonalized symbol of the authority of the external world reminiscent of Kafka's bureaucrats) is seeking for beauty. However, it is not at all easy to dismiss this as romanticism either, even the most "apparently" romantic situation of the prostitute with the heart of gold who gets a new life through the sincere love of a man. The ingredients are romantic—because they deal with that desire for beauty within the individual which is the source of all romance—but Saroyan's treatment of the material reveals more perception than is usually attributed to him. The prostitute remembers the beauty of her childhood—when her childhood wasn't beautiful:

> I dream of home. Christ, I always dream of home. I've no *Home*. I've no place. But I always dream of all of us together again. We had a farm in Ohio. There was nothing good about it. It was always sad. There was always trouble. But I always dream about it as if I could go back and Papa would be there and Mamma and Louie and my little brother Stephen and my sister Mary. I'm Polish. Duval! My name isn't Duval, it's Koranovsky. Katerina Koranovsky. We lost everything. The house, the farm, the trees, the horses, the cows, the chickens. Papa died. He was old. He was thirteen years older than Mamma. We moved to Chicago. We tried to work. We tried to stay together. Louie got in trouble. The fellows he was with killed him for something. I don't know what. Stephen ran away from home. Seventeen years old. I don't know where he is. Then Mamma died. What's the dream? I dream of home.

The beauty of her home remained despite the economic inequality imposed by the external world; the relationship of individuals was its main expression.

Here Saroyan's admiration for family ties is apparent, but most apparent is that the word "home" epitomized for Kitty her search for beauty. Her perception of the indefinable beauty of her family and her childhood—despite the trouble and the sadness—was her artistic achievement, her communication of beauty where it is not immediately discernible. As Joe encourages her to pursue this desire for beauty within herself despite the efforts of the world—despite Blick—to rob her of any personal integrity (an effort which is answered and supported within herself by her loneliness—by the recognition of alienation), he does not attempt to predict the outcome. The one obvious thing is that whatever the outcome may be the attempt is infinitely better than the alternative, than the prostitution of the individual by the depersonalized destructiveness of the external world.

Saroyan's ending to this play, however, if not condemned as sentimentality, will have to be recognized as pure wish-fulfillment. We can perhaps accept Johnny's father's perseverance in his thus far unsuccessful attempts to be a poet, or Mr. MacGregor's ascent to the highlands through death, or even Kitty's attempts to preserve the element of the divine in herself with the help of a weak-witted truck driver who loves her for it; but to believe that the imaginative liar Kit Carson could successfully destroy Blick and all he stands for is nearly impossible. Thus *The Time of Your Life*, despite its charm and its dreaminess which led Harold Clurman to recognize it as a "little classic of the American theatre" sixteen years after he had refused to produce it,[4] is somewhat more guilty of the criticisms directed at Saroyan's works than are most of his plays.

Certainly no critic could claim that *Hello Out There* or *Across the Board on Tomorrow Morning* are examples of exuberant optimism. The senseless but inevitable murder of the romantic gambler in *Hello Out There* is later to be echoed in one of the three plays Saroyan wrote during his residence at Purdue University in 1961—by far the best of the three plays despite its disastrous opening speech—*Death Along the Wabash*. *Across the Board on Tomorrow Morning*, which offers a birth rather than a death, is, however, equally pessimistic.

In these three pessimistic plays Saroyan openly admits that his romantic individualists in their search for beauty do not always succeed—and this is perhaps why he said later that he repudiated *Hello Out There*—but the value of their attempts contrasted with the rest of the world still places them far above the other characters. The most romantic of these three is *Hello Out There*, where the young man says to the girl that with her he could be good—but in the light of Saroyan's other plays this can be raised above its typically sentimental interpretation. The young man's recognition of beauty in the girl makes her a symbol of his unique expression of beauty, of his poem or song, and therefore of the true goal of his restless search for beauty. He attempts to give her to the world by sending her to San Francisco, but his attempts are as unsuccessful as were those of Johnny's father to get his poems published. The insensitive and dishonest world (represented by the woman who falsely accused him of rape) which destroys him also rejects his perception of beauty, as the woman slaps the girl and pushes her to the floor, saying "Listen to the little slut, will you."

But we should avoid placing only one interpretation on Saroyan's symbols; the girl must also be seen in relation to Mr. Kosak of *My Heart's in the Highlands*. She is the one person who has listened to the young man, who has in a sense read his poetry and therefore given value to it. Thus at the end she blends with him through their shared perception of beauty and her last line is the same as his first line—"Hell—out there!"—which is both an attempt to communicate with the world and an acceptance of the alienation of the individual.

Across the Board on Tomorrow Morning is even more symbolic than *Hello Out There*, leaving realistic presentation far behind as the audience becomes part of the play and time is suspended so that a new-born baby appears as a young man and buys a Scotch before he returns to his mother and the seven pound infant which is himself at the end of the play. The most obvious theme is the conflict and identification of illusion and reality. Saroyan maintains in this play a precarious balance between the external and internal world, and the success of the play is that he doesn't reject either as illusory: in the delightfully drunken perception of Fritz the cab driver, "illusion or reality, no illusion or no reality, one more drink before I go."

However, in attesting to the illusoriness of the external world at all, Saroyan is taking his stand for the internal world as before. Whether Kitty's dream of home is an illusion, whether each man's search for beauty is illusory, it is an illusion which many—Saroyan included—honor by such titles as divinity, as art, as inspiration. Simultaneously, for Saroyan at least, whether the external world is irrelevant and is going to disappear tomorrow morning or not, it is within the context of that world—with all its "delicate balance of despair and delight"—that inner reality must be expressed: "It's worse, getting worse every minute. But it's so in a way that's irresistible to me, like her freckles. And, for one reason or another, irresistible to you, too."

Harry's appreciation of beauty—the beauty even of her freckles—enables him to produce his son Cavanagh—who, like Johnny is to his father, is both his poem and his search for beauty transmitted to the next generation. This is revealed when Cavanagh addresses Harry as "Myself. My father. My son. Yourself. Each of us."

The final lines of the play, in which Fritz places a bet on Tomorrow Morning, show that Saroyan had passed beyond the wish-fulfillment he allowed himself in *The Time of Your Life*. In *Across the Board on Tomorrow Morning*, which shares many features with the earlier play, Fritz realizes that he will lose the bet, as Piper did at the beginning of the play, but he is going to bet anyway, because he likes the name. Since Tomorrow Morning has been used in the play as the point at which the "eye was blind to the irrelevant and open to everything else," Fritz's bet symbolizes Saroyan's willingness to gamble on the desire for beauty in mankind despite his realization that the odds are against him and that he has lost before.

Death Along the Wabash is the most pessimistic of Saroyan's plays. *Hello Out There* recognized the world's rejection of the artist's perception of beauty, but held out the hope that the search for beauty would still be carried on by the individual. In *Across the Board on Tomorrow Morning*, despite the lighter tone, the conclusion that the enlightened view will not come until tomorrow morning and that all odds are against its winning at all is even more pessimistic. This is only relieved by Fritz's willingness to continue betting on the losing horse anyway.

In *Death Along the Wabash*, no one is left to search for beauty anymore, and the world refuses to gamble on the individual. Instead, it destroys him, ostensibly because it is helping him to reach his goal—which is only attainable in heaven, or at least out of this world. The Hobo as the representative of the world is right when he says that he has destroyed the idealistic, Negro, escaped convict Joe in self-defense: a complete perception of the beauty possible within oneself does destroy the external irrelevancies for that individual, and in this sense Joe was threatening the Hobo's existence.

And the Hobo is much worse than Blick, because he is not depersonalized. At one point he is even identified with Joe's father. He is terrifying because he is a person capable of perception who has chosen the other alternative, who has rejected the inner self for a clean suit of clothes and sixty dollars. This play, so reminiscent of Pinter, surpasses both the obvious theme of murder for materialistic satisfaction and the topical theme of racial discrimination—of the Hobo representing society's specific persecution of the Negro. It is the somewhat superficial concentration on the racial theme which weakens all three of the plays Saroyan wrote at Purdue. Saroyan transcends this in *Death Along the Wabash* because he is not so much trying to write as a black man as to portray the individual persecuted by the world, the individual searching for beauty who has been his main concern in the other plays. Consequently, portraying a hero that is black rather than a black hero enables Saroyan to point out parallels between discrimination against minority groups and discrimination against the individual. Except for the blatant exposition in Joe's first speech, the play is powerfully written. The speeches are generally longer and weightier than those usually found in Saroyan's plays, and the conclusion of unrelieved pessimism is hardly recognizable as the work of this affirmative playwright. Joe's romantic search, which he hopes will lead him to Jaurez and love and freedom, is lost because he decides—what he must decide—to trust the Hobo. Although he is a finer person than the Hobo, Joe is destroyed, and his love has been put into an insane asylum. The Hobo's argument is that he *has* helped Joe—that by murdering him, he enabled Joe to reach Jaurez while still superior to the people who give up. This powerful portrait of that portion of mankind which recognizes the external world as the only reality ("They'd catch you before you got to Terre Haute") and thus destroys the inner reality in others and in themselves is especially significant because the Hobo's arguments appeal strongly to logic, to the rational perception of the world. Those critics who argued that Saroyan was not logical should read this play—they might note an undercurrent of resentment here of the artist who was criticized for appealing to the heart. This play gives modern society what it claims to want—a realistic pessimism and the destruction of the idealistic and romantic in mankind.

In fact, the pessimism of this play strikes deeply because Saroyan's multi-level symbolism enables him to reflect parallels between many forms of persecution and discrimination and at the same time to show the close relationship between the persecutor and his victim. Saroyan not only realizes that, as in this play, the sensitive individual, the artist, the economically oppressed, the black man or Armenian in search of something beyond what society has allotted him, will more likely than not be destroyed by the world before he can reach his goal; but even more painful is Saroyan's recognition that this destruction is likely to be at the hands of the individual's own father—from another man who could have chosen to search for beauty or fight for freedom but who sold out to the world instead for materialistic reasons.

This is not a new discovery Saroyan made just before writing *Death on the Wabash*. The world had always opposed his individuals; it is only that he has preferred to place his bet on beauty, on humanity, on tomorrow morning despite the odds. He reaffirms the value of the individual in his most recent play, *The Cave Dwellers*, and if one reviewer derides it for imitating Beckett by calling it "an affirmative '*Waiting for Godot*' " it should be remembered that Saroyan was writing plotless symbolic drama many years before *Waiting for Godot* appeared in 1953. It is true that several of Saroyan's general situations reflect other plays—Wilder's *Skin of Our Teeth* is strongly recalled in *High Time Along the Wabash* and Hart and Kaufman's *You Can't Take It With You* provides the source for much of the merriment in *The Beautiful People*. Despite these recognizable influences, Saroyan's plays, as Joseph Wood Krutch affirms in his review of *The Beautiful People*, are still very original and carry different messages from their models.[5] This is equally true of *The Cave Dwellers*, where the characters resemble nothing so much as characters in other Saroyan plays. The artists this time are actors—a clown, an actress, and a prize fighter, joined by a girl who shakily sings "How do you do, my partner?" The new generation is born on stage, reminiscent of *Across the Board on Tomorrow Morning*. The central event is the eviction of the main characters from an old theater, and this, along with the robbery of the milk, recalls *My Heart's in the Highlands*.

The Cave Dwellers, however, lacks the power of Saroyan's earlier works except in isolated moments. The ingredients are there, the intention is there, but somehow the use of romanticism has become an immersion in romanticism. Saroyan is pushing too hard: as Walter Kerr observed, "The sentence beginning 'Love is . . . ' occurs more times in eleven scenes than I could count, try though I did."[6] Critics have frequently argued that Saroyan tends to state his message rather than present it dramatically, and statements do detract from the effect of this play, anyway. In fact, Saroyan protests too much this time, perhaps because he had become increasingly more aware of the loneliness of his affirmative position and the difficulties of maintaining it in the face of current conditions. Joseph Wood Krutch had once proclaimed his admiration for the sincerity of Saroyan's affirmation and had added that, from a person less convinced of the rightness of his stand, the attitude might prove disastrous.[7] If the three plays Saroyan wrote at Purdue, particularly *Death Along the Wabash*, can be considered as indications of Saroyan's doubt in his affirmation, we might validly wonder who he is trying to convince in the *Cave Dwellers*, the audience or himself?

However, allowing for the intrusion of sentimentality and didacticism in *The Cave Dwellers*, on the whole Saroyan has succeeded remarkably well in using romantic material symbolically. To one who automatically identifies any affirmation with romanticism, he is a romantic. But to recognize the world for what it is, to admit the apparent hopelessness of an affirmation of the individual, yet still to be willing to gamble on human dignity because of the value of the attempt itself sounds more like courage than romanticism. Out of place though he seems, in a consideration of the pessimism of much of modern drama, Saroyan might find a kindred spirit in the "black is beautiful" movement, with the young men willing to risk prison or exile by refusing to follow their society's command to kill people for peace, with the "flower people" and others who dare affirm love and the ultimate value of human relationships over the material rewards of social conformity. He might even find an acceptable niche in the literary history of the world.

Notes

1. *The Magic Mirror* (New York, 1960), pp. 216, 227.
2. Brooks Atkinson, *Broadway Scrapbook* (New York, 1947), pp. 118–9.
3. Atkinson, p. 119.
4. Harold Clurman, *Lies Like Truth* (New York, 1958), pp. 57–9.
5. "God is Love, or Why Worry?," *Nation*, CLII (May 3, 1941), p. 538.
6. "Saroyan in a Hard Sell," *New York Herald Tribune* (Sunday, October 27, 1957), reprinted in *The Cave Dwellers* (New York, 1958), p. 91.
7. "Play and No Play," *Nation*, CLV (October 10, 1942), 357.

Joe as Christ-Type in Saroyan's *The Time of Your Life*

Kenneth W. Rhoads*

William Saroyan's 1939 play *The Time of Your Life* would certainly have to be included in any compilation of the outstanding works of modern American drama. Winner of both the Critics' Circle Award and the Pulitzer Prize,[1] the play is compounded of passion and poetry, ingredients vital to a work of dramatic significance. Critical opinion, both initially and over the years, has, while frequently observing certain weaknesses of structure, generally judged the play a work of imagination and insight. Its primary qualities are almost unanimously perceived to inhere in its characterization, dialogue, and a sense of situation, of the moment. The varied, intense characters with which Saroyan has peopled Nick's bar in San Francisco, reacting to the conditions of life, express their profoundest fears, frustrations, aspirations, and triumphs in speech which is always colorful, usually direct, often poetic. The essential anguish and joy of their lives is revealed with an immediacy which evokes a profound sense of the human condition.

It is therefore surprising that in this play—generally acclaimed the finest work of a dramatist whose forte has always been strong characterization—the central character Joe should have presented a critical enigma never satisfactorily resolved. For, although Joe is the prime mover of what little well-defined plot exists in the play and is clearly the unifier and focus of dramatic action up to the point of crisis, critics have been unable to develop a consistent thematic rationale which reconciles certain seeming ambiguities of Joe's character and behavior. His vague origins, for instance, a certain inscrutability in his nature, his physical deficiency, and his inability, at the moment of crisis, to take the only action possible and resolve the conflict by eradicating the evil Blick and all that he symbolizes, have resisted all efforts to fit the protagonist neatly into either the society of Nick's bar or the larger ethos of the play.

Brooks Atkinson, in his opening-night review of the original production, saw Eddie Dowling (who created the part of Joe) "in a bar-fly role" and described Joe as "a well-heeled, steady drinker who fancies that he is a

*Reprinted from *Essays in Literature* 3 (1976), 227–43, by permission of the editors.

student of life. He is quixotic and mystic with some oddments of philosophy rattling around in his generally befuddled head."[2] A few days later, in a fuller consideration of the play, Mr. Atkinson discussed Joe as "the discursive, well-heeled stranger . . . an enigmatic man of some means who has a profound sense of dissatisfaction with the ways of the material world. He regards himself as a student of life; the others defer to his judgment, probably because he has money." Proposing that a central weakness of the play derived from certain deficiencies in the major protagonist, he further observed that *"The Time of Your Life* would be a sturdier play if Mr. Saroyan were less romantically indifferent to the practical details of the central character. Since it wields so much influence on the drama as a whole, Mr. Saroyan ought to tell us where it got all that money, which is one of the most essential facts of life."[3] The latter statement is especially puzzling, since Joe does make clear the source of the money he dispenses with such largesse—a point which is highly pertinent to his philosophy of life.

Wolcott Gibbs in his review referred to Joe as "an alcoholic philosopher" and noted, "The actor of the evening is Eddie Dowling, but not even he can give complete reality to a character who sometimes seems to be God but a good deal of the time just a man who has been drinking too much champagne on an empty stomach."[4] Other reviewers expressed similar judgments, equally limited and equally circumscribed by an apparent fixation on Joe's drinking.[5] Nevertheless, despite their generally quizzical view of the play's protagonist, most critics found both the role and Eddie Dowling's realization of it delightful, as they did the play itself.

The lapse of years, with further productions of the play, including the 1948 movie version in which James Cagney played Joe and the 1955 revival by the New York City Center Acting Company, seems to have brought little additional insight into the character of Joe for most critics even though the play itself continued to grow in critical favor and scholarly esteem. Thus, Ward Morehouse, in *Matinee Tomorrow: Fifty Years of Our Theater*,[6] sees Joe as merely "the mysterious man with money in his pocket," and John Mason Brown, in *Broadway in Review*,[7] while praising the enormous vigor and the beauty, compassion, humor, and insight of Saroyan's script, encompasses his interpretation of Joe in the statement, "[Saroyan's] fable is no more than how a man, a strange, kindly, and inquiring fellow, a delectable, heartsick, Irish Mr. Fix-It, whose search, between gulps of unexplained champagne, is for happiness and an answer to the far-reaching enigmas of life, manages to marry a two-dollar prostitute off to his amiable henchman and thus save her from the pryings of an odious busybody on the Vice Squad."

Plainly, the standard critical judgment of the central character Joe in *The Time of Your Life* evinces general perplexity, and no coherent view as to Joe's nature and his real function in the drama. Further, that judgment is frequently distorted: for nothing in Saroyan's script—either the dialogue or the stage directions—indicates Joe to be an alcoholic or ever lacking full control of himself, nor did Eddie Dowling play him as such. One is tempted to speculate that perhaps the critical brotherhood succumbed to the ubiquitous stereotype of the barroom Irishman. In any event, it is difficult to reconcile such superficial interpretation with the character which Saroyan actually created, for a consistent and satisfying explanation of who Joe is and what he represents within the play's larger thematic context lies readily available in the text. A careful reading shows that Joe may be seen as a valid Christ-figure—not a literal Christ, for *The Time of Your Life* is no Second Coming, nor even an allegorical Christ, but a type of Christ, essentially realistic and certainly very human—whose nature and behavior are completely consonant and who takes on stature as heroic protagonist within such a mode. Whether Saroyan consciously created Joe as Christ-figure is immaterial; this is the character which emerges and which the script projects—by allusion, by indirect revelation, by implicit scriptural parallel in Joe's motivations and the shape of his life, and by specific episodes whose relevance to the meaning of the play is carried by their symbolic content.

In fairness it must be noted that critical opinion has not been completely impervious to such suggestion, although little more than a glimmer of the full implications has ever been revealed. The reviews quoted above contain passing references to Joe as "mystic" and as "a character who sometimes seems to be God," and to his "deep quietness and final judgment." George R. Kernodle, in "Plays for War and Peace Time," described Joe as "a rich guardian angel [who] sits all day and all night in a dockside honky-tonk to seek out goodness. He gives money, but also what is more important—faith, the courage to believe in dreams."[8] The *Time* reviewer, discussing the movie version of the play, referred to Joe as "a sort of bush-league saint (James Cagney) who tries to make people happy."[9] In connection with the 1955 City Center revival, in which Franchot Tone played Joe, *Time*'s critic noted that "[Saroyan's] wealthy drunk plays both God and Maecenas to prostitutes and bums."[10] Concerning the same production, Wolcott Gibbs, lamenting that Franchot Tone played the part merely as "an inspired drunk" and seemed specifically drunk, as opposed to Eddie Dowling's "indefinable moon-struck quality" in the original production, observed, "The difference might be described as that between an extremely intelligent actor playing a boozy mystic and a wonderfully bemused and spiritually cockeyed Irishman playing himself."[11]

John Gassner has apparently seen the Christ-figure implications of Joe more fully than any other scholar of the theatre. Writing in *Dramatic Soundings: Evaluations and Retractions Culled from 30 Years of Dramatic Criticism*,[12] he defines Joe as the cohesive element of the play, the "sensitive film and focus" on which every event and presence impinges. "He is many things in one," says Gassner, this man who has acquired money and sickened of it, who is alone and inscrutably so. . . . Out of his loneliness and sensitivity he has developed a pity for all mankind and a feeling of brotherhood; and having money and time at his disposal, he has made himself a paraclete or comforter of his fellow creatures, giving understanding where it is needed and material help where it is imperative. . . . He has a mystic prototype in the Paraclete of Evreinov's *The Chief Thing*, and a realistic one in the interfering Luka of Gorky's *Night's Lodging*. There is, in short, a subtle integration in the play.

Here, however, Gassner rejects further exploration of the fruitful course his inquiry has taken. "One cannot," he decrees, "attribute supernatural or social leadership to this figure. But as a very human person, he is the catalytic agent of a large portion of the play."[13] Seemingly, Gassner's refusal to see Joe as a literally supernatural or divine presence, as God incarnate—a valid critical judgment, certainly—also deterred him from developing the ideas suggested by his sound critical intuition. Thus, unfortunately, while his analysis discloses an incipient awareness of the wider implications of Joe's nature and function, it fails to explore fully the significance of this central character within his complete dramatic context.

The initial fact of any Christ-type—be it Osiris, Prometheus, or Christ himself—is that his origins are vague, mysterious, or at the least unusual or ambiguous. This is true of Joe. He seems to have come from nowhere, and his coming into the world of Nick's bar has been sudden and with no immediately apparent purpose. Joe's parentage, too, is obscure; he tells Mary L. only that "I'm Irish on both sides,"[14] and, like Christ, he has only a first name—Joseph.

At this point in Joe's life he seems—like Christ—to have no apparent means of support, although he tells Nick, significantly, that he has "the full co-operation of the Good Lord" (p. 116) in his vocation. The nature of that vocation while never explicit is gradually revealed in unmistakable terms, as the conflicts of the play develop, to be a ministry to his fellow-man, and particularly to the poor, the outcast, and the oppressed. His only personal conflict is with the corrupt authority which exploits and threatens the lost ones to whom he has committed himself.

Although, as with Christ, the facts of Joe's past essentially comprise a lacuna in his life up to the point of his ministry, he does reveal that—like Christ the young carpenter—he had once worked but ultimately gave it up. And the nature of that experience bears directly on his having rejected that life for his present endeavors. The commercial world brought him only disillusionment and a deep sense of guilt derived from his very success. For although he had learned how to make money, he found material success to be achieved only at the expense of others. When Tom asks Joe where he gets the money he dispenses so charitably, Joe, *"looking at Tom sorrowfully, a little irritated, not so much with Tom as with the world and himself, his own superiority,"* tells him:

> Now don't be a fool, Tom. Listen carefully. If anybody's got money—to hoard or to throw away—you can be sure he stole it from other people. Not from rich people who can spare it, but from poor people who can't. From their lives and from their dreams. I'm no exception. I *earned* the money I throw away. I stole it like everybody else does. I hurt people to get it. Loafing around this way, I *still* earn money. The money itself earns more. I *still* hurt people. I don't know who they are, or where they are. If I did I'd feel worse than I do. . . . Money is the guiltiest thing in the world. It stinks. Now, don't ever bother me about it again. (p. 149)

Thus Joe is a type of scapegoat for the sins of his fellow man. He distinctly bears a burden of guilt for those who exploit and hurt others, and suffers in full empathy with the injured and the have-nots. Consequently he has, as he tells Tom, gained "a Christian conscience in a world that's got no conscience at all" (p. 149). His anguish over the proceeds of material wealth, and its ambiguity of financial gain and investment (the fruits of his work, although earned, turned sour because they were concurrently stolen), inevitably recalls Christ's parable of the talents (Matthew 25: 14–30): the "good and faithful" servants who invested the talents entrusted them by their master doubled his money in each case, but the "wicked and slothful" servant, not knowing that his master reaped where he sowed not and gathered where he strawed not, hid his talent in the earth and thus failed to return his master's money "with usury." Inescapably, as Jesus advised his disciples, "unto every one that hath shall be given, and he shall have abundance: but from him that hath not shall be taken away even that which he hath."

Now enlightened as to the moral nature of the struggle for money and material success, Joe can no longer participate in that world. But his withdrawal leaves him frustrated, for, as he says, "I've got money. I'll always have money, as long as this world stays the way it is. I don't work. I don't make anything. I drink. (*He sips.*) I worked when I was a kid. I worked *hard*. I mean hard, Tom. People are supposed to enjoy living. I got tired. . . . Well, you can't enjoy living unless you work. Unless you do something." So, like Christ, Joe seems to be suspended between two worlds—those of the flesh and of the spirit. Unlike Christ, Joe is not conscious of a well-defined purpose to his life; he says to Tom, "I don't do anything. I don't *want* to do anything more. There isn't anything I can do that won't make me feel embarrassed. Because I can't do simple, good things. I haven't the patience. And I'm too smart" (pp. 149–50). But Joe's very lamentation reveals in him the humility which Christ taught and himself displayed; ironically, Joe does perform those simple, good things out of his concern and compassion for others, in the process effecting rebirth and salvation in very concrete, real terms for the people his life touches. Perhaps the pertinent point here is that he, a twentieth-century Messiah of sorts, has, like Christ, no Messiah complex.

A multitude of passing allusions and episodes augmenting the major motifs of the play pervades *The Time of Your Life*, contributing to an accretion of Joe's Christ-image. Throughout the play, with the exception of one brief scene in Kitty's hotel room, Joe spends his entire time seated at his table in Nick's euphemistically named Pacific Street Saloon, Restaurant, and Entertainment Palace at the foot of Embarcadero on San Francisco's waterfront. Thus, as Christ found his mission not in the houses of the rich patriarchs or the elite council of the Sanhedrin, but rather on the shores and in the fields among poor fisher-folk and sweating farmers, ministering to the leprous, the ill, the dying, so too Joe finds his greatest compatibility with the common people of his world—the bewildered, the frustrated, the agonized, the lost, the outcasts who find in Nick's bar a refuge from the chaos and brutality of life outside. Nick, perceiving in Joe an innate superiority, is perplexed by Joe's proclivity for this environment and those who inhabit it, just as the Pharisees could not understand why Jesus ate with the publicans and sinners (Matthew 9:11). "O. K., professor," he muses as he brings the champagne Joe has ordered for Kitty, whom Nick can only see as a "two-dollar whore" (p. 34) even while accepting her at face value, freely and with no animosity, as he does all the habitués of his establishment: "Why you come to this joint instead of one of the high-class dumps uptown is more than I can understand. Why don't you have champagne at the St. Francis? Why don't you drink with a lady?" (p. 35). But the Lady and the Gentleman from uptown society who come to Nick's bar slumming for a vicarious thrill find absolute nothing in common with Joe. Their only response to his instructions for Tom to take the gun he has purchased and give it to some good person who needs it, and to bring back this week's *Life*, *Liberty*, and *Time*, all the flavors of chewing gum, all the different colors of jelly beans, six of the longest panatelas he can find, and to give the news-kid a dollar, give some old man a dollar, and give the Salvation Army people in the street a couple of dollars and request them to sing "Let the lower lights be burning, send a gleam across the wave, / Some poor, dying, struggling seaman, you may rescue, you may save," is: that Joe must be "absolutely insane" (pp. 150–54). The savior-figure is ever mocked and rejected by those who fail to understand his altruism, his compassion, his ingenuous idealism.

That Joe drinks only champagne—a seeming incongruity in a waterfront honky-tonk where everyone else takes beer or hard liquor—is not a gratuitous circumstance. Champagne is, of course, wine, as Joe refers to it at least once (p. 35), a drink traditionally associated with Christ both literally and symbolically. In offering Kitty champagne Joe is extending to her his understanding, and, symbolically, the wine of communion and redemption—a redemption, or salvation, which he is shortly to effect for her very literally. It is significant that when Nick brings the wine to the table he tells Kitty, "This guy doesn't belong here. The only reason I've got champagne is because *he* keeps ordering it all the time. Don't think you're the only one he drinks champagne with. He drinks with *all* of them" (p. 36). This wine of salvation which Joe offers to all the outcasts may be seen in its eucharistic context as the blood of Christ. This is made almost overt in the scene in which Joe and Kit Carson examine the monstrous revolver which Joe has purchased. The scene is crucial to the crisis and resolution of the play since it reveals Kit's adeptness with guns (although he must bluff his way through with Joe's big and unfamiliar pistol) and, by the removal of the bullets after Kit's demonstration of the gun's operation, prepares for Joe's inability to kill Blick at the moment of truth. This in turn prepares for the eradication of Blick by Kit, the old man from America's mythological frontier past who embodying all the heroic values needed to resolve the situation—courage, readiness for action, good in an absolute sense capable of striking down evil—kills the sadistic symbol of fascist oppression with three shots from his old pearl-handled revolver. The two men have previously established a close communion in preceding discussions (pp. 106–13). Joe, whose all-encompassing sympathy immediately embraces Kit on his arrival at Nick's, is the one—the only one—who assures the old man that he believes the preposterous tales of his earlier exploits; the affecting old frontiersman's response to Joe is warm and intuitive. Now, before the climactic event which will part them forever, their final meeting becomes a symbolic last supper, at which the champagne with which they toast each other becomes the wine of communion. Joe pours the wine, they touch glasses, and partake of the symbolic drink—just as the Salvation Army chorus outside begins to sing "The Blood of the Lamb." Then, in ritual response *"at the proper moment,"* the two celebrants join the singing, *"sipping champagne, raising hell with the tune, swinging it, and so on"* (p. 155) in a crazy but sincere barroom Mass which seals an unspoken compact between them.

Other passing allusions and brief incidents suggest and augment Joe's image as type of Christ. Joe, like Christ, who said "Judge not, that ye be not judged" (Matthew 7:1; see also Luke 6:37), will not judge and condemn his fellow men. When the longshoreman McCarthy, who attacks the "tribe" of writers as trouble-makers and potential despots and who tells him, "I hate the tribe. They're mischief-makers. Right?"—Joe answers, "Everything's right. Right and wrong" (p. 89). Joe, capable of an objective view which encompasses all sides of a situation, and understanding all motivations, cannot resort to simplistic condemnation. He might well have answered, after Christ, "Ye judge after the flesh; I judge no man" (John 8:15); that is the essence of his seemingly ambiguous response. On another occasion Joe tells Mary L. that he has been trying "for three years" to find out if it is possible to live a civilized life that will not hurt any other life; and further states, in response to her inquiry as to whether he has responsibilities, that he has "*one*, and *thousands*. As a matter of fact I feel responsible to everybody. At least to everybody I meet." One recalls that the recorded ministry of Christ encompassed a period of just three years—from his 30th to his 33rd year of life—years dedicated in their entirety to fulfilling the responsibility he felt in serving his fellow man. Replying to Mary's subsequent question, "You're famous?" Joe says: "Utterly unknown, but very famous" (p. 77). Joe's paradoxical remark, given point within the context of a play which laments man's failure to exhibit the (Christian) ideals which he so blatantly professes, evokes the virtual commonplace that if Christ were to return today he would go unrecognized and rejected. Another time Joe speaks significantly of "this realm" and his duty. Expressing his feeling of responsibility to Tom, whose life he has earlier saved, and who has become his devoted follower and *Johannes Factotum* who wants, in fact, to become just like Joe—a disciple of sorts—Joe remarks, "In this realm there's only one subject, and you're it. It's my duty to see that my subject is happy" (p. 114). Tom is perhaps the "*one*" of the responsibilities to which Joe had earlier referred.

The evidence for Joe's awareness of the other realm, the spiritual one, is more than just implicit in his humanitarian impulse and compassion for others, or even in his pointed differentiation between this realm and some other unspecified one. That Joe differs from other people in some very fundamental way is recognized by Tom, who observes, in response to Joe's determination to extricate Kitty from her sordid life, "You're a different kind of a guy" (p. 117). That Joe's difference perhaps resides in his connection with a realm other than the worldly one is suggested by his preceding rather veiled remark to Tom, who has commented on Joe's aversion to ambulatory movement (his difficulty in walking approaches physical disability) and de- lighted amazement at Joe's intention to seek out Kitty at her hotel. "At my best, Tom," he says, "I don't travel by foot" (p. 117). Joe refers explicitly and pointedly to the spirit during his first meeting with Kitty Duval, to whose inner purity and innocence he penetrates immediately and intuitively through the tough, encrusted karma of her angry, defensive, spiritually- crippled exterior. Responding "*gently but severely*" to her initial suspicion of his intent in offering her the champagne, he says, "It's not in my nature to be unkind to another human being. I have only contempt for wit. Otherwise I might say something obvious, therefore cruel, and perhaps untrue." And then, in reply to her admonition to be careful what he thinks about her, Joe tells her, with a sincerity which she finds strangely affecting, "I have only the noblest thoughts for both your person, and your spirit" (p. 33). When the champagne is brought and Joe offers her the symbolic wine of salvation, his toast, "*sincerely*," is "To the spirit, Kitty Duval" (p. 36). Her outward response is a grateful "Thank you"; inwardly, an understanding of Joe's nature and real intent begins to illuminate the soul he has touched.

Joe seems to possess an uncanny perception, transcending time, into the future and the past, which suggests a supernatural omniscience. On a somewhat mundane level, he can predict precisely and unerringly (and without recourse to *The Racing Form* which so absorbs Nick) what horse will win any race at Laurel—even when the worst horse, ridden by the poorest jockey, and carrying the longest odds, proves the winner! His matter-of-fact acceptance of his clairvoyance, so in contrast to Nick's incredulity, is revealed to stem from an incontrovertible source when, in answer to Nick's bewilderment Joe roars, "Faith. Faith" (p. 59). His prescience of the future is again suggested by his reassuring consolation when Nick is driven nearly to exasperation by his inability to understand Joe's solicitude for the prostitutes: "Nick, I think you're going to be all right in a couple of centuries." To which Nick responds, "I'm sorry, I don't understand your English" (p. 36). A psychic memory of the past is revealed when Joe is drawn into the argument between McCarthy, the intelligent, idealistic union longshoreman and his friend Krupp, the slow but honest cop who is not comfortable in his job and who does not perceive the reason for the orders he is given, but knows only that he must follow these orders. Now his orders are to keep peace on the waterfront—why, he does not know, but only that it must be kept. Krupp can only reply, "For citizens," and when McCarthy points out that he, McCarthy, is a citizen asserts that he is keeping the peace for him. To which McCarthy responds, "By hitting me over the head with a club?" and then turns to Joe, asking, "Right?" Earlier in the scene McCarthy has elicited Joe's sympathy by receiving his sorrowful assent to a similar oblique request for agreement; now, *"melancholy with remembrance,"* Joe can only respond with a tenuous "I don't know" (pp. 85–86). The implication of the mood specified by the stage directions is that the discussion of the current strife on the docks has stimulated, somewhere deep in Joe's primordial memory, the recollection of a time and place where another champion of human rights was scourged and driven by the duly-invested agents of established authority who, armed with spear and whip rather than gun and club, carried out diligently *their* orders to keep the peace. Perhaps two thousand years may, after all, constitute only a brief jump from a crown of thorns to a possibly lethal blow on the head. In this light a previous reference to the growing labor strife gains added meaning. In the first scene of the play Tom tells Joe that he has been out in the street listening to all the talk about the trouble on the waterfront, adding excitedly, "Joe, one guy out there says there's got to be a revolution before anything will ever be all right." The response from the mentor, who again seems to draw on the memory of another revolution from some time long past, is a simple "I know all about it" (p. 26).

The episode involving the mysterious Mary L.—tenuous and apparently without point within the overt plot of the play—gains considerable significance when Joe's nature and function as type of Christ is recognized. Joe and Mary L. are mutually reinforcing in this context. From Mary's initial entrance she and Joe establish an immediate and intimate rapport; they seem, in fact, intuitively drawn to each other. When Joe attempts to guess her name from the initials on her handbag, and tells her his initials are J. T., she promptly guesses his first name—"Joseph?" He replies, "That's my first name, but everybody calls me Joe. The last name is the tough one" (pp. 69–71). Significantly, the "tough" last name is never revealed; the initial itself only strengthens the allusion, since a T has often been used to symbolize a cross. Nor is Mary's last name disclosed. Joe inquires, "Is it just plain Mary?" When she acknowledges that it is, Joe's response, "Mary's one of my favorite names" (p. 71), seems almost to make explicit the building allusion to the various Marys with whom Christ was so closely associated— Mary, the mother who gave him birth, Mary the mother of James and Salome, and Mary Magdalen—the Marys who were so much a part of his ministry and his last years, who lamented his death at the foot of the cross, who together first learned of the miracle on the first Easter morning. Joe proceeds to tell Mary L. about another Mary whom he had once met in Mexico City and whom he had loved, but who married someone else. He reminisces about his speculations on the kinds of "kids" they would have: "My favorite was the third one. The first two were fine. Handsome and fine and intelligent, but that third one was different. Dumb and goofy-looking. I liked *him* a lot. When she told me she was going to be married, I didn't feel so bad about the first two, it was that dumb one" (pp. 71–72). Here the implicit parallel with Christ is marked: Joe's major concern and compassion was for the odd child, the different one, while it was Christ who said, speaking of the man who shall leave his ninety-nine sheep to go into the mountains to seek the one sheep which has gone astray, "And if so be that he find it, verily I say unto you, he rejoiceth more of that *sheep*, than of the ninety and nine which went not astray" (Matthew 18:13). Within this context it also seems pertinent that Joe speaks of the imaginary children as "kids," a slang term perhaps, but most apt as reminder of Jesus' metaphorical sheep.

The revelation of Joe's affection for children is by no means restricted to this episode, but has been previously suggested by his fascination with children's toys, in which he takes a childlike delight. At one point he sends Tom out to buy a selection of toys, and spends a good share of his time during Act I blowing the whistles, winding up the mechanical toys, and playing the music box which Tom brings back. Perhaps it is no accident that Mary L. enters as Joe is explaining the essence of toys to Nick, who has become intrigued with the marvelous gadgets. Including Mary L. in his audience, Joe expounds, "Nick, this is a toy. A contraption devised by the cunning of man to drive boredom, or grief, or anger out of children. A noble gadget. A gadget, I might say, infinitely nobler than any other I can think of at the moment. (*Everybody gathers around Joe's table to look at the toy. The toy stops working. Joe winds the music box. Lifts a whistle: blows it, making*

a very strange, funny and sorrowful sound.) Delightful. Tragic, but delightful"
(p. 67). Joe's obsession with the playthings of children thus reveals a poignant
depth which goes far beyond the surface naiveté of ingenuous delight. He
experiences the toys as metaphor for a tragically lost innocence in a world
(basically wonderful but now gone corrupt from the unconscionable power
of evil men) which cries out for redemption.

Here again a parallel with Christ is suggested. Jesus' love for children
is frequently cited, and he also saw the innocence of childhood as a metaphor
for the purity of soul necessary for spiritual salvation. "Suffer little children
to come unto me," he said, answering his disciples' rebuke for wasting his
time administering to infants, "and forbid them not: for such is the kingdom
of God" (Luke 18:16). Again, when his disciples came to him asking to
know who is the greatest in the kingdom of heaven, he called a little child
to him, set him in their midst, and said, "Verily I say unto you, Except ye
be converted, and become as little children, ye shall not enter into the
kingdom of heaven. Whosoever therefore shall humble himself as this little
child, the same is greatest in the kingdom of heaven. And whoso shall
receive one such little child in my name receiveth me. But whoso shall
offend one of these little ones which believe in me, it were better for him
that a millstone were hanged about his neck and *that* he were drowned in
the depth of the sea" (Matthew 18:3–6).

Joe's very real love for children is shown by his kindness to the young
newspaper boy, from whom he invariably buys all of the boy's papers and
tips very generously. When the newsboy, who wants to be a "great lyric
tenor," auditions for Nick, Joe is greatly affected by his singing of "When
Irish Eyes Are Smiling." When Nick, who has also been moved by the song,
exclaims, "Joe, people are so wonderful. Look at that kid," Joe responds
with great feeling: "Of course they're wonderful. Every one of them is
wonderful" (pp. 80–83).

The scene between Joe and Mary L., brief though concentrated (pp.
69–80), develops strong overtones of Christ's relationship with Mary Magdalen. Mary L., like her Biblical counterpart, has lived in the world and known
carnal satisfaction—in fact she now has two children; and it becomes quickly
evident that she is strongly attracted to Joe, as he is to her. But, just as
Christ's commitment to his mission caused him to sublimate his physical
feeling for Mary and deny any sexual fulfillment of his love, it is clear that
Joe and Mary are destined only for one brief moment of spiritual recognition
with no possibility of physical consummation. This is emphasized when
Joe, who has asked Mary if she would like to dance, and has expressed
disappointment when she assents because he did not think she would like
to, tells her that he is sorry but he does not dance. Joe's inability to engage
in this kind of sensual activity has been previously established: Kitty, responding to Joe's compassion on their first meeting, asks him to dance with
her, but Joe tells her that he never learned to dance and expresses regret

that, while fond of her, he cannot accede to her request that he hold her in his arms (pp. 51–52). Thus, Joe's self-denial of the sexually related pleasures is pointedly manifested, and the contrast of Mary L.'s sensual orientation reinforces the implicit Biblical parallel. Now, during a moment of quiet communion, Mary recognizes Joe's unspoken love for her, but Mary has a husband who awaits her. Joe is anguished over her departure, yet she cannot stay and, slowly and regretfully, takes her leave, disappearing forever into the macrocosm. The depth of Joe's love is apparent as he stands, in grief and silence, staring for a long time after his vanished Mary.

One need not insist on a too-direct parallel, and certainly not an exclusive one, between Mary L. and Mary Magdalen, although the allusion is a strong one. Mary L.—mother, confidante, and lover—suggests all of the Marys—the mother, the friend and follower, the object of sublimated love—who were so close to Christ, generalizing within herself aspects of all three. And certainly it is not incongruous that Mary should appear suddenly and mysteriously in a honky-tonk saloon on the San Francisco waterfront; Mary the Virgin, Mother of Christ, is after all the patron saint of mariners. Too, with respect to Joe, the suggested allusions are multiple. A meeting of Joseph and Mary inevitably evokes Biblical associations with respect to Christ. Another Joseph, who was thrown into a pit, kidnapped, and sold into slavery in Egypt, but who rose to become a savior and leader of his people, was also a type of Christ. And one can hardly resist a certain mischievous symbolism that suggests Joe the Christ-figure as his own father, Joseph.

The larger, more general, parallels between Joe and Christ in terms of their inherent natures, their attitudes and actions, and their missions, should present no problem of dramatic plausibility. But what may validly be concluded about the many suggestions of Joe's supernatural powers, and how may they be reconciled with his stature as a very human *dramatis persona* in this intensely human comedy? One may certainly infer that Saroyan was not trying to put a literal Christ on the stage, nor did he need to. After all, there *are* saints among us; all of them have lived centuries or millennia in the past. One of the characteristics of a saint, in addition to a higher spirituality which most of us understand only abstractly, is his or her humanity. Joe's essential quality, too, is his intense humanity—his awareness of other people and his sensitivity to their inner agonies as well as their outer struggles. This was also true of Christ, but to have endowed Joe overtly with incarnate divinity would have shifted the grounds of the play and introduced an element incongruous with its dramatic and thematic premises. Thus, the hints of Joe's supernatural qualities, the suggestions that his realm of existence somehow transcends this material, mortal one, need not—should not—be taken literally. These hints and suggestions do, nevertheless, recur with frequency and insistency. Consequently, they function effectively to enrich Joe's character through meaningful ambiguity: an ambiguity which, by the very air of mystery it imparts, serves to establish Joe's awareness of a higher, spiritual level of existence and to augment his inherently Christ-like nature. Ambiguity in dramatic character, in the wrong hands, can obscure and confuse, and it is not always well-managed; but when adroitly handled it serves not to diminish but to enhance character. Hamlet, while if not Shakespeare's greatest tragic hero, is probably his most intriguing one, and it is Hamlet's very ambiguity which gives him such depth and susceptibility to varied levels of interpretation. Were Hamlet subject to precise definition his character would be correspondingly limited. Within the realistic context of *The Time of Your Life* Joe is a vital human character with his share of the passions and the foibles that mark the human animal; at the same time he is endowed with a consummate humanitarian concern for all his fellow beings. Through meaningful ambiguity Saroyan manages to suggest the transcendent spiritual quality—the greatness of heart and soul—which sets Joe apart from other men, while he keeps him firmly rooted in the real world.

While structurally Joe's dramatic function is diffuse and varied (he seems at one and the same time to be objective observer of life, interested, even passionate, participant in the swirling action, dissociated chorus, perceptive commentator on life's pains and joys, father-figure, and ingenuous child) his connection with the plot action most specifically concerns Tom and Kitty and his ultimately successful maneuverings to bring about their physical and spiritual union and effect their escape from a hopeless past and present to a new life in San Diego. His relation to the two young people strongly reinforces his image as Christ-figure throughout the play. Joe is literally a savior for Tom and Kitty in both a spiritual and a factual sense. He has in the past—three years ago, it is pointedly stated (p. 24)—saved Tom's life when Tom was sick, hungry, and dying. Interestingly, chicken soup, that traditional health cure-all of the Jewish mother, was the agent of Tom's recovery. Then Joe took Tom to the doctor, gave him money for food and clothes, and paid his room rent. Now he is in good health and eats three times a day—sometimes four, sometimes five. Unlike Yeats's Lazarus, Tom, the subject of Joe's miracle, is grateful to have been resurrected. A *"great big man of about thirty or so who appears to be much younger because of the childish expression of his face: handsome, dumb, innocent, troubled, and a little bewildered by everything"* (p. 23), an adult in years but seemingly still a boy, clumsy and self-conscious, Tom is not quite ready for independent existence. So he devotedly serves the man who saved his life, and although he sometimes questions the rationality of Joe's demands on him and wishes he understood the reasons for the "crazy" things he is often asked to do (pp. 27, 103), he continues to learn from Joe. Certainly Tom has been changed by his master; Joe readily perceives Tom's ingenuous but sincere love for Kitty and, giving his approval, admonishes Tom, "But take care of yourself. Don't get sick that way again" (p. 53). The sickness, then, from which Tom had suffered and for whose cure Joe had been responsible was venereal disease, an affliction not merely of the flesh, but one contracted (within a context of traditional morality) in consequence of the sin of sensual lust, and a transgression against the divine law. The change in Tom's character by Joe's tutelage thus constitutes a kind of spiritual regeneration: once, Tom had used other Kitty Duvals as objects merely to satisfy his physical desires, in the process violating both their bodies and spirits; now he sees only the essential goodness, still uncorrupt, of this fallen but shining angel, before whom he trembles and stammers like a schoolboy and whose virtue he will now, in his *"almost religious adoration of her"* (p. 30), protect with his life.

Perhaps in the relationship of Joe and Tom one may be permitted to see at least an oblique reference to another disciple, also traditionally a big man—Peter, the big fisherman—a dedicated follower of *his* master who called him away from one mode of life to devote himself to a higher one. He also "questioned," i. e., denied, that master (three times, in fact) and who, through his master's tutelage, gained a wisdom and understanding which enabled him, when the inexorable course of events separated them forever, to attain to a life of fulfillment and independent achievement.

Joe's relation to Kitty through the course of the play recalls not only Christ's understanding and forgiveness generally, but also suggests the specific episode of the woman taken in adultery, whom he refused to condemn. The scribes and Pharisees, perceiving only two opposed alternates of judgment and hoping to trap Christ into either a repudiation of his own teaching of mercy or a violation of Hebraic law which demanded that she be stoned to death for her sin, brought the woman to him for judgment; Jesus, neatly evading the snare, advised that he who was without sin among them be first to cast a stone. Thus confounded by their own consciences the accusers were rendered impotent, and Jesus, having saved the woman's life, then told her "go, and sin no more" (John 8:11). Similarly, Joe undertakes nothing less than Kitty's complete salvation, which begins with his befriending her and offering her the symbolic champagne immediately on their first meeting. From the beginning Joe sees, not Kitty Duval, once queen of the burlesque circuit from coast to coast (as she so desperately and pathetically insists) and now prostitute drumming up two-dollar tricks on the San Francisco waterfront ("the most beautiful lay in the world" for drunken sailors on shore leave), but rather Katerina Koranovsky, home-loving farm girl from rural Ohio, fresh-cheeked, innocent, with ribbons in her hair, still as pretty as the seven-year-old charmer who smiles from the picture she keeps at the foot of her bed. It is significant that when Joe and Tom go to Kitty's hotel room so that Tom may tell Kitty of his love and ask her to go away with him to a new life, Joe brings Kitty a toy carousel, which he winds up and plays for her, and which makes a *"strange, sorrowful, tinkling music"* (p. 120). The carousel, a traditional symbol of childhood innocence, here evokes concretely and with great pathos the essential virtue which Joe sees in the anguished girl. Joe understands, as even the tolerant though gruff Nick cannot, that while the world has driven the music out of her soul, *"putting in its place brokenness and all manner of spiritually crippled forms,"* under the harsh reality of what she has become remains a goodness, a beauty, *"that element of the immortal . . . which no circumstance of evil or ugly reality can destroy"* (p. 29). Kitty is a dreamer, which Joe intuitively recognizes: *"clearly, slowly, with great compassion,"* he asks her, "What's the dream?" (p. 32). The dream is of home and the innocence of a lost childhood, and Joe knows that the dream is the true reality of Kitty Duval / Katerina Koranovsky—a reality exempt from total destruction and susceptible to retrieval and revitalization. The agent of that regeneration is a twofold love: on an immediate level the powerful overt love of the adoring Tom, and in a wider, all-embracing manifestation the spiritual love of the Christ-like Joe.

Joe, then, is prime mover in the union of the two young people. Savior of both of them in a very literal sense, he also effects a kind of rebirth for them individually and in their new life together. Tom, educated and strengthened through Joe's tutelage, may now end his discipleship and go forth to a life of independence and self-achievement; Kitty, cleansed and released from the prison of her former life, may now realize the long-suppressed dream in the return of innocence. Together, now in this time of their lives, they will be fulfilled by the strength and purity of their mutual love. In short, they will have attained, through the power of Joe's love and compassion, both the inner peace and the outer joy in living which all the habitués of Nick's Pacific Street Saloon, Restaurant, and Entertainment Palace so desperately seek but so rarely find. [15]

One major critical problem which has existed regarding Joe is his failure to kill Blick at the climactic moment, when all the complications of the final act have built to that expectation. The justification for Blick's literal eradication has been fully developed; even aside from the larger implications of Blick as representative of Hitler and the growing Nazi terror (a thematic element barely implicit and recognizable only within the play's original time context) the portrayal of Blick as evil in a complete and absolute sense has been sharply drawn. Now his sadism has built to an intolerable point: he has harassed the girls, man-handled the newsboy, beat up old Kit for coming to Kitty's defense, bestially forced Kitty to disrobe and perform for his lascivious gratification, and is now viciously beating Wesley, the young Negro pianist who dared intervene in Kitty's behalf. It would seem that the time of Joe's life to kill has come—the time, in the words of Saroyan's headnote to the original script, to "kill and have no regret" (p. 15). That same headnote admonishes: "Despise evil and ungodliness, but not men of ungodliness or evil. These, understand. . . ." Yet Blick may be killed—not as a man, since his humanity has ceased to exist, but precisely because he has come to stand for disembodied existential evil. Now, Joe takes the revolver out of his pocket and looks at it. *"He cocks the revolver, stands real straight, holds it in front of him firmly and walks to the door. He stands a moment watching Blick, aims very carefully, and pulls trigger. There is no shot"* (p. 189). At this point Nick enters, grasps the situation, and wrests Joe's gun from him. In answer to Nick's amazed "What the hell do you think you're doing?" Joe replies (*"casually, but angry"*), "That dumb Tom. Buys a six-shooter that won't even shoot once" (p. 189). Joe has, apparently, completely forgotten that he had earlier removed the bullets from the gun and put them back in the box.

If this scene is considered within the frame of reference so far developed with respect to Joe, no moral contradiction exists. For, as type of Christ, whose power is for good and whose acting force is love, it is not appropriate or even possible for him to kill. Joe's nature, after all, is not that of the Old Testament God of wrath and retribution, but rather that of the merciful and forgiving Christ; his killing of Blick would provide the real incongruity. Nevertheless, while Christ's greatest violence never approached homicide, he was very much a man of real flesh and blood (whatever else he might have been) who when his sensibilities were sufficiently aggrieved could become enraged and respond by physical assault. Joe, like Christ, is a passionate man. The magnitude of Blick's crimes certainly far surpasses that of the moneychangers who defiled the Temple; thus, it is not inconsistent with Joe's character that his immediate response to the outrageous human indignity inflicted by Blick is to expunge the evil by the means closest at hand. Nor does his action diminish his essential benevolence: Joe, after all, is a *type* of Christ, and a very human one—he is not the prototype. Perhaps under a condition of such extreme provocation the Christ-impulse and the human impulse within Joe come into conflict, and the outcome may even momentarily hang in the balance. But the Christ-impulse dominates, having earlier turned to action by Joe's removal of the bullets from the revolver. This action may be seen on one level as symbolic of his inability to actually perform the lethal act. More literally, it has perhaps been psychologically motivated as a defense against commission of something so diametrically opposed to his essential nature. And, even in his moment of angry passion, Joe may well recall subconsciously that the gun is empty and know that his destructive action is incapable of fulfillment.

It is true that Joe expresses no regret over Blick's demise, nor does he condemn Kit for his violation of the Fourth Commandment. This does not necessarily present an inconsistency. Since Blick has come to represent unrepentant evil, the Christ-impulse in Joe would not lament its eradication, and Kit's action might even be viewed—wryly, perhaps—as a minor harrowing of hell. At the same time, Joe does not expressly approve of the killing, nor does he participate in the general exultation which it precipitates. Again, he does not judge.

The final aspect of any Christ-figure is that his ending, whether it be

in death or mere disappearance, is, like his origins, obscure. Joe's departure
from Nick's bar similarly carries an aura of vagueness and mystery. Following
the report of Blick's death—"Somebody just shot him, and none of the cops
are trying to find out who"—Joe, ignoring the offer of champagne from the
delighted Nick (the wine of communion and salvation is, after all, inappropri-
ate for the consecration of death), rises slowly from his chair, takes his hat
from the rack, and puts his coat on. Nick, perplexed over Joe's strange
demeanor, his refusal of his wonted drink, and his early departure, evokes
only laconic, tentative replies from his usually loquacious friend.

NICK: What's the matter, Joe?

 JOE: Nothing. Nothing.

NICK: How about the champagne?

 JOE: Thanks. (*Going.*)

NICK: It's not eleven yet. Where you going, Joe?

 JOE: I don't know. Nowhere.

NICK: Will I see you tomorrow?

 JOE: I don't know. I don't think so. (pp. 192–93)

Then, following Kit's re-entrance and his revelation, unequivocal although
couched as another of his incredible tall tales (that he had once on Pacific
Street in San Francisco killed a man named "Blick or Glick or something
like that" with his old pearl-handled revolver because he could not stand
the way he talked to ladies, after which he had had to throw the beautiful
revolver in the bay) Joe hands Kit his own revolver and then walks slowly
to the stairs leading to the street, turns, waves to the group, and silently
exits. Thus, as suddenly and mysteriously as he had arrived from places
unknown and never disclosed, he leaves without explanation for an unrevealed
destination. He has touched the lives of these people briefly, with a touch
which has brought them understanding and healing, and those lives will
never be the same. But his ministry here, at Nick's saloon on the San
Francisco embarcadero, is at least for now finished; other Toms and Kittys
in other places need him, and a new mission calls. He cannot delay.

   The Time of Your Life is a play of intense romanticism and unashamed
sentimentality; one must, in fact, accept Saroyan here on his own grounds
if the play's full potential for an affecting emotional involvement is to be
realized. Saroyan is not for the cynic or the iconoclastic realist. The interpretation of Joe advanced in this discussion is not only consonant with such a
dramatic mode, but it may be seen to gain therein considerable dramatic
depth. Any Christ-figure—as is Christ himself—is highly romantic in concept. Everything that he is and symbolizes, and all that he does, is strongly
stimulating to the imagination and the emotions, capable of communicating

simultaneously intellectual, moral, and spiritual meaning. Certainly other interpretations of Joe may be validly advanced (although so far they seem not to have been).[16] Nevertheless, Joe as Christ-figure is solidly grounded in the evidence from the script which has been cited here and whose very bulk and pervasiveness seem to belie coincidence. Above all, seeing Joe as type of Christ not only removes critical ambiguities heretofore existing in the absence of an alternate viable rationale, but more importantly reveals a focal character of greatly augmented stature and meaning and increases immeasurably the ideative and emotional dimensions of the play.

Notes

1. Saroyan refused the Pulitzer Prize in protest against the singling out of one of his works in particular, and awards to artists in general; artists are workers, he asserted, whose rewards should be no different from those of other working people.
2. *The New York Times*, 26 Oct. 1939, p. 26.
3. *The New York Times*, 5 Nov. 1939, Section 9, p. 1.
4. *The New Yorker*, 4 Nov. 1939, p. 27.
5. The *Time* reviewer tersely described Joe as "a wealthy drunk . . . with a generous purse" (6 Nov. 1939, p. 32), while the *Life* critic cursorily characterized him as "a philosophical barfly" (4 Dec. 1939, p. 46). In the view of Joseph Wood Krutch, "All the characters are, to be sure, simply the author in disguise. . . . What we get, then, is Mr. Saroyan as the philosophical spectator (played with delightful unction by Eddie Dowling) . . ." (*The Nation*, 4 Nov. 1939, p. 505). In Stark Young's appraisal of the central character, "we know nothing of what the springs of his life are or the sources of that deep quietness and final judgment . . ." (*The New Republic*, 29 Nov. 1939, p. 169). According to Grenville Vernon, Joe is "an alcoholic philosopher and philanthropist [who] sits at a table drinking champagne" (*The Commonweal*, 10 Nov. 1939, p. 78), while Charles Angoff saw him as "a wealthy patron, a chronic dipsomaniac . . ." ("Drama," *The North American Review*, 248 [Winter 1939–40], 403).
6. New York: Whittlesey House, 1949, p. 265.
7. Freeport, N. Y.: Books for Libraries Press, 1969, p. 191.
8. *The Yale Review*, 30 (1941), 422.
9. 14 June 1948, p. 98.
10. 31 Jan. 1955, p. 71.
11. *The New Yorker*, 29 Jan. 1955, p. 44.
12. Introduction and Posthumous Editing by Glenn Loney (New York: Crown, 1968).
13. All quotations from Gassner are on p. 409.
14. William Saroyan, *The Time of Your Life* (New York: Harcourt, 1939), p. 71. All further citations will be placed directly within the text and are to this edition, which contains a Preface and a headnote by the author.
15. Even the most recent critical consideration of *The Time of Your Life* remains strangely oblivious to some of the essential facts about Joe. Thelma J. Shinn, for example, in "William Saroyan: Romantic Existentialist," *Modern Drama*, 15 (Sept. 1972) [reprinted in this volume], discussing Kitty's search for beauty, states, "As Joe encourages her to pursue this desire for beauty within herself despite the efforts of the world—despite Blick—to rob her of any personal integrity (an effort which is answered and supported within herself by her loneliness—by the recognition of alienation), he does not attempt to predict the outcome" (p. 189). Any "prediction" of the outcome by the seemingly omniscient Joe is entirely beside

the point. Far beyond merely encouraging Kitty from an existential orientation to the world, he purposefully undertakes the resurrection of that dormant beauty, whose essence he fully understands, which precedes and underlies the surface reality of Kitty's existence.

16.   Over the past two to three decades scholarly work on William Saroyan has, sadly, greatly diminished; currently a real dearth exists. For example, neither the 1973 nor 1974 MLA International Bibliography (the latest issue published at this writing) lists a single article on Saroyan.

The Time of Your Life:
"A Figment in a Nightmare of an Idiot"

ROBERT G. EVERDING*

In *Razzle Dazzle* Saroyan describes his vision of the world, a vision that forms the thematic foundation of his major work *The Time of Your Life*: "The world which everyone other than myself seems to have identified and accepted as The World is in reality a figment in a nightmare of an idiot. No one could possibly create anything more surrealistic and unbelievable than the world which everyone believes is real and is trying very hard to inhabit."[1] This condemnation of contemporary reality is developed in two essays appended to the printed edition of *The Time of Your Life*. In "On Reality" Saroyan declares that behavior went astray some two thousand years ago when mankind continued to cling to an ethic that no longer responded to human needs. This ethic is based on concepts of nobility that have their roots in the attitudes and actions of the heroes of classical literature. The masses consider this ethic "heroic" because it gives their suffering a significance and occasionally provides the illusion of personal victory; such behavior is called "pathetic" by Saroyan because "it makes of living a game in which the values are nothing" with the result that the "Life of our time is so wretched it's not worth talking about."[2] Comparing life to a card game, the playwright calls this outmoded approach to life a "bluff" and warns that this bravado is inevitably called and exposed by the realities of modern life.

In "Two Theatres" Saroyan criticizes the individual for living life as though he or she were actors in a bad melodrama in which "There is always the outward play of truth. There is always the pretense of virtue, dignity and nobility." He laments the fact that people confuse reality with the fictions of Hollywood by assuming the films' romantic and heroic attitudes and by expecting human endeavors to have the same perfect endings. In contrast to this theatre of illusions, Saroyan sees that "There is only one theatre, the world" and that "every man has one character to play, himself." For Saroyan, then, the world's most pressing need is the exposure and elimination of the black comedy of our present reality because "it makes it so tough to get order into the other play, the real one."[3]

* Reprinted from *The McNeese Review* 32 (1986–1989), 11–22, by permission of the editors.

A change in perception is, for Saroyan, the requisite beginning for any improvement in the human condition. He explains in "How to See" that, since the source of all reality is vision, the world's shabbiness is the result of our careless perception and our blind acceptance. He argues that: "Most people don't look at anything. Considering the wasteful speed with which most people move around, this is understandable. The contemporary compulsion of society to save what is known as precious time is responsible in part for nobody having time to see anything. All surfaces of things are known vaguely and more or less by heart, so that contemporary reality is without dimension or truth." However, if we can blame present miseries on a reality created by our faulty vision, we can also change that reality by imposing new conditions on life. Saroyan concludes that "The beginning of the full exploitation of the experience of living . . . is through seeing" and that "it will be impossible for the living to achieve grace or dignity, adulthood or power, effectuality or understanding until they learn to see."[4]

It is this messianic impulse to force mankind to recognize the dangers of its present behavior that stands at the very heart of Saroyan's strategy in *The Time of Your Life*. Saroyan defines theatre as "looking closely and listening carefully and finding out,"[5] and he structures the dramatic experience so that the two and one-half hours of performance serve to awaken the audience not only to the necessity for a new approach to life but also to the absurdly theatrical nature of its own behavior. Saroyan accomplishes his end by inviting the spectators to interpret events in terms of the romantic and heroic conventions so popular in the theatre of his day. These idealistic attitudes are subsequently challenged by intrusions of reality that frustrate expectations and that eventually compel the audience to acknowledge its own failure to see clearly what was before it. This admission prepares the way for a closer examination of the action and for discoveries about the true nature of the world. The audience is not allowed, then, simply to witness the mistakes of the central character Joe; the viewers share Joe's errors in judgment and his disturbing insights about how to live in the time of your life.

At the conclusion of "On Reality," Saroyan observes that "nobody is around with both the perception to see the present reality for what it is and the personal vigor to personally expose it, and to introduce an aspect of what it *might* be."[6] *The Time of Your Life* represents his effort to accomplish these ends. The following discussion explores Saroyan's artistic strategy, focusing first on the main plot and then shifting to the role played by the elements of the setting, the pinball machine, the saloon's inhabitants, and the preface-credo.

Influenced by Bernard Shaw's dramaturgy,[7] Saroyan employs his central plot to draw intentionally, if temporarily, upon the spectators' conventional values to mislead the audience into identification with Joe's idealistic attempt to create a perfect world. Joe's misguided efforts are subsequently challenged, exposed, and supplanted. This process occurs in two movements, the first of which uses the play's initial three acts to convict the audience of too simplistic an assessment of the world and thereby to prepare the ground for a later understanding of the nightmare of contemporary reality.

At the outset the spectators are encouraged to view Joe as an heroic figure and to share in his noble quest "to find out if it's possible to live what I think is a civilized life. I mean a life that can't hurt any other life."[8] Indeed, Joe appears to be extraordinarily successful as he wins longshot wagers on racehorses, heals a prostitute's spiritual brokenness, fulfills his friend's romantic dreams, and generates a nurturing atmosphere throughout the honky-tonk. However, the major action of the first three acts is the growing challenge to Joe's control over events and the simultaneous frustration of the audience's romantic expectations. Again and again reality enters to complicate the Hollywood scenario. Blick's menacing visit, Mary's sudden departure, Kitty's continuous sorrow—all confront the viewer with evidence of a threatening reality against which Joe is powerless. This progression is underscored by a radical change in the central character's behavior which devolves from complete confidence through agitated concern to the confession that "I don't understand things." However, it is Joe's absurd attempt "To correct the errors of the world" through a blatantly romantic fantasy (one in which his friends play out their dream of the beautiful young actress who meets the handsome doctor, falls in love, weds and lives happily ever after) that completes this phase of Saroyan's strategy. This pretense is rudely shattered by the arrival of a sailor who wants to buy the prostitute's services, plunging Kitty into tears of humiliation and thereby exposing the foundation of wishful thinking upon which Joe's idealism is built.

In this first movement, then, the audience learns that dreams, no matter how beautiful or deserving, cannot sustain themselves against reality and that illusion is not a mature response to the world. Moreover, they discover the basic rhythm of contemporary life, a rhythm in which "Man is forever dreaming and life is forever denying."[9] This painful flux is the product of the world's present ethic and consists of perpetual movement between yearning for an ideal existence and experiencing repeated disillusionments. Seen from this perspective, Joe's unfounded optimism is not merely misguided; it is cruel and insensitive. The audience is now prepared to view Joe differently and to study future happenings more critically.

The second movement presents itself in the play's final act where attention shifts onto the causes for mankind's suffering and the need for a more authentic mode of existence. This transition is marked by a significant event: the man who wanted a life that would not hurt anyone sends away his toys and takes up the revolver. The toys look back to the failures of the romantic frame of mind with its childlike belief that illusions can permanently supplant reality; the gun looks toward the upcoming exposure of the heroic ethic with its naive assumption that physical aggression can improve the human condition.

Joe's melodramatic attempt to kill Blick is not successful because the gun does not fire. Realistically, of course, the failure is due to the earlier removal of the bullets; symbolically, however, the malfunction suggests the futility of seeking to correct life's errors by the elimination of one evil man. The significance of this moment is not lost on Joe who "sits down dead to the world" and examines his recent actions. In *Here Comes, There Goes, You Know Who*, Saroyan explains what his central character is discovering: "People hurt people, although things frequently seem to hurt them too, but after you investigate a little you discover that it was the action of people upon the thing that actually did the hurting . . . Joe didn't want to hurt people. He was so determined not to, he sat all the time. But even then he discovered that he hurt them. When he tried to help them he discovered that he hurt them."[10] Joe sees now that it was his actions that brought harm to those he wanted most to help. Kitty has been stripped of her self-esteem and faces her new life accompanied only by poetry books and a boy whom she cannot satisfy. Tom has been sent without a driver's license or union membership into a world that had almost annihilated him three years earlier. His inability to handle Kitty's tears as well as his violence toward the sailor serve as foreboding omens of the doom that awaits this couple. Yet, while Joe accepts his culpability, he does not yet understand how his noble actions could produce such disastrous results.

Ironically, at this very moment, he is surrounded by the evidence that could resolve his bewilderment. The presence of the newsboy, the sounds of "The Missouri Waltz," and the reappearance of the drunkard recall the play's opening and highlight the forms of evasion used by Joe to escape reality. Yet, he fails to see what is before him just as he has previously blinded himself to life's harsher aspects in order to verify the essential beauty of life.

The play's climax occurs when a confused and uncertain Joe tries to flee the bar and is blocked by Kit Carson. Kit is a benevolent "con man" who envisions himself as an exceptional individual and who lives almost totally in an imaginary world of tall tales. He paints himself as a representative of the Old West's self-reliant code in which a hero uses his six-shooter to rectify evils such as an insult to a lady's honor. It is these two aspects of Kit's personality that coalesce in his description of Blick's murder: "(Loudly, bragging, but sombre) I shot a man once. In San Francisco. Shot him twice. In 1939, I think it was. In October. Fellow named Blick or Glick or something like that. Couldn't stand the way he talked to ladies. Went up to my room and got my old pearl-handled revolver and waited for him on Pacific Street. Saw him walking, and let him have it, two times. Had to throw the beautiful revolver into the Bay." His words reveal how thoroughly Kit's consciousness mingles illusion and reality in order to escape reality's harshness, and, thereby, open Joe's eyes to his own flaw. Joe sees himself in Kit and recognizes his own "bluff" with its heroic concepts of honor, nobility, and tragedy. In "A Special Announcement," Saroyan describes the emptiness of this heroic ethic which consists only of "Loud speech, frantic whispers, violent and unreasonable emotions, absurd impulses, and very bad manners" so that "The tragic understood neither themselves nor their neighbors. They dramatized themselves."[11] Joe (as well as the audience) understands now that Blick's murder did not change the world; there is still hunger, impending war, social unrest, and two friends headed for disaster. Events have proven the wisdom of McCarthy's pronouncement that "Only the weak and unsure perform the heroic. They've got to. The more heroes you have, the worse the history of the world becomes." Joe gives his gun to Kit because the weapon belongs to the old man's self-reliant code to which Joe no longer subscribes. For Joe, heroic gestures are now anachronisms that should be thrown into the bay along with Kit's pearl-handled revolver.

Joe experiences what Saroyan calls "the shock of genuine knowing."[12] He sees the nightmare of contemporary reality in which man condemns himself to a form of living death by accepting romantic and heroic values which are little more than theatrical bravado and which block any hope for a meaningful existence. He realizes that mankind must embrace a new ethic in which: "We *endure* tragedy. If it destroys us, we do not destroy others and ourselves. We know every emotion the others knew, but we know more, too. The greatness of man in our time is no less than it has ever been. If anything, it is a greater greatness. It does not destroy itself when exposed to error and waste and inferiority: it extends itself."[13] If Joe is to truly live in the time of his life, he must abandon his effort to change the world and must begin to confront the world on *its* terms. This ethic offers man the only hope for some degree of greatness.

The honky-tonk gains new significance for Joe. He selected the bar for his experiment because it was set apart from the world's ambiguities and offered a limited arena in which life's essential goodness would be verified. Joe understands now that the saloon is built from the patrons' illusions, sustained by alcohol and inhabited by the existentially dead. Knowing he must reject this world, Joe prepares to leave again. This time there is no uncertainty. He confesses his past dedication to illusion by mimicking one of Kit's tales[14] and walks purposefully "to the stairs leading to the street."

Saroyan notes that "Honor is impossible not to love but inevitable to betray. It is when the betrayal does not mortify a man that he may be said to be an adult."[15] Joe's decision to leave the bar represents his emergence from childhood. His early actions were surrounded by symbols of his immaturity—his boyish appearance, his penchant for games, his fascination with toys. Later, he traded the toys for the more serious but equally-immature revolver. When Joe leaves the saloon, he leaves behind his earlier ethic and accepts the challenges of adulthood. Joe becomes, in Saroyan's words, a member of "the true human race, the race which believes at least that if there is no meaning, if there can be none, there can be a way of knowing, and of going, that (however senseless) is at least art."[16]

The play's process alters, therefore, the audience's concept of heroism. Joe appeared initially as a romantic hero who could change the world through his high ideals and determination. By the final curtain, the audience sees the absurdity of this kind of heroism. Such behavior is not noble, but pathetic and self-destructive. The spectators find in the enlightened Joe a more credible hero, one in whom they can recognize their own humanity and through whom they can understand how to live authentically in the modern world. They learn the truth of what Saroyan observes in an early short story: "The finest rebel is the quiet man who knows the end of all things yet is pleased to go on breathing."[17]

Joe's journey from blindness to perception serves as the major catalytic force in the audience's discovery of its own faulty vision of reality. Still, while the main plot is the primary element in Saroyan's strategy, other aspects of his dramaturgy—notably, the setting, the other characters, the pinball machine, and the play's credo—contribute to the dramatic process.

In *Places Where I've Done Time*, Saroyan comments that "from the most primitive to the most worldly, the human finds a place, and it is *inside*, it has limits, and it keeps out the things the human doesn't want or the things he fears."[18] Nick's Pacific Street Saloon appears initially to possess these qualities. It is an anachronism that radiates the nostalgic charm and innocence of the old honky-tonk and, thereby, creates a feeling that it is set apart temporally and spatially from the modern world. Its patrons see it as a refuge from a reality filled with strikes, hunger, war and police brutality. Here, they think, is an uncomplicated realm where man's essential beauty can shine and where happiness can be achieved. The war is treated in a comic monologue; the strike debated over beers; a childhood is resurrected.

This initial assessment is challenged as the play unfolds. There is a gradual increase in the number and the force of reality's intrusions into the bar so that the myth of a protected place dissolves. Wesley and Kit are physically harmed; Kitty is humiliated; the society people are chased away. Even the saloon itself faces extinction, for the murder of Blick removes Nick's defense against the church people and the police: "I don't break any laws. I've got a dive in the lousiest part of town. Five years nobody's been robbed, murdered, or gypped. Your swanky joints uptown make trouble for you every night." The audience is brought to see, therefore, that it overlooked the true nature of this place and to agree with Nick's opinion that his bar is "not out of the world. It's on a street in a city, and people come and go."

Lawrence Langer recalls that in the original production of *The Time of Your Life* "We were in serious difficulty over the last act, however, and each time we discussed the matter with Saroyan he would state that 'the climax of the play is the pinball machine. If you don't have a good pinball machine the play has no climax.' "[19] This recollection emphasizes the vital role that the pinball machine plays in the dramatist's strategy, a role as the central symbol for the destructiveness of the world's ethic. The machine is associated with Willie Faroughli. His battle with the pinball is described in a stage direction which underscores the heroic proportions that this confrontation takes in Willie's mind: "Himself vs. the machine. Willie vs. Destiny. His skill and daring vs. the cunning and trickery of the novelty industry of America, and the whole challenging world." It is impossible not to delight in his enthusiasm and to look forward to his success. His victory speech celebrates a basic American value when he exclaims that "I'm the kind of guy who makes up his mind to do something, and then goes to work and does it. There's no other way a man can be a success at anything." His success is qualified in the spectator's mind, however, by the awareness that for five acts he has been on the periphery pouring nickel after nickel into the machine and now receives back only thirty cents and a cacophony of sounds, lights, and waving flags. Willie has not defeated the world; he has only evaded and bluffed. His heroic self-image has blinded him to his true status as a victim of a system that fosters illusions of victory while it drains the lifeblood. Minutes after his success, he is once again putting money into the machine, a tragedy emphasized by the machine's dramatic malfunction. It is the marble game's "beautiful American routine" that holds the audience's attention as the final curtain falls because it is this symbol of civilization's misguided strivings for success that Saroyan wishes the audience to carry with it from the theatre.

The pinball machine's routine comments upon not only Willie but also the bar's other inhabitants. These men are variations of Willie—each challenging Destiny in an heroic manner, each believing himself the victor, each failing to understand how he was swindled. Dudley views himself as a romantic lover in quest of the perfect woman; this success is limited to one night with her in a cheap hotel before he is ushered off to war. Harry believes that he is a talented comic who needs only the chance to prove that he can make the world laugh; he gets his opportunity from Nick, but there is no salary and the first performance is cancelled. Kit sees himself as a hero of the Old West and seeks to give his life importance by getting strangers to believe his imaginary adventures; he convinces Joe, but his fantasy leads to Blick's murder. These men possess larger-than-life personalities and enormous vitality, attractive qualities which capture the audience's sympathies at the outset. It is only as their various bluffs clash with reality that the spectators see the emptiness of such theatrical behavior and that the earlier admiration turns to pity for these "tragic, unbelievable, confounded people." The audience learns, as Saroyan laments in one of his short stories, that "instead of living by truth, it seemed that man lives by deliberate lies, or by the deliberate withholding of truth, or by the deliberate distortion of it."[20]

The audience feels pity rather than scorn for these characters in part because of Joe's response. He does not attempt to awaken these men to the folly of their actions; he only waves farewell and leaves. There is even a modicum of admiration because he knows that no man is "a fool who is so sick of inferiority in the world and in living"[21] that he strives for a better reality. Still, these men would not understand what Joe discovered about life, for "The masses aren't ready, I'm afraid, for the shock of genuine knowing and not spiritually equipped to face the inward tragedy which occurs with genuine knowing."[22] Joe knows that the majority want "the time of its life carefully mapped out,"[23] and he learns through Kitty that you cannot remove people's illusions without providing a substitute ethic. If we laugh at these men, then, it is not in a disapproving way. Saroyan's comedy is critical not so much of the individual but of the false values that mankind accepts. In "Sleep in Unheavenly Peace," Saroyan describes the kind of laughter that the audience experiences when he observes that "you do not really laugh; it is a feeling you experience, a sadness for man that can only be articulated through laughter."[24]

It is now possible to understand the role that the preface-credo serves in the dramatist's strategy. Discussing this brief statement, Burns Mantle reports that "Mr. Saroyan also planned, with the first production, to have the play's theme announced over a loud speaker before the curtain rose."[25] Far from being the statement of a theme which the play demonstrates, this *desideratum* conveys Joe's initial beliefs, idealisms that will be tested by the play. While these tenets are unquestionably desirable, some place too heavy a burden on reality to be achieved. Joe may believe that no man should be the superior to another, but he himself assumes that attitude toward Tom, a point stressed by Saroyan's describing Joe as "always superior" and by Nick's calling him "Your Highness." Also, the harm that Joe brings to Tom and Kitty exposes an existential truth which qualifies seriously the maxim that "In the time of your life, live—so that in that good time there shall be no ugliness or death for yourself or for any life your life touches." Finally, Joe's abortive effort to kill Blick suggests the futility of the credo's imperative that "if the time comes in the time of your life to kill, kill and have no regrets." No, Saroyan did not set out to declare themes which the play's events would validate. Part of the play's suspense comes from a tension between the preface's platitudes and action's realities. The credo's reading was designed to condition the spectator to view the action in terms of romantic and heroic values and, thereby, to prepare the viewer to experience personally the tragic rhythm resulting from such idealism.

In "Noonday Darkness Enfolding Texas," a short story whose title served as a preliminary title for *The Time of Your Life*, Saroyan explores his ideas about man and reality. While travelling on a train toward El Paso, the story's central character undergoes a metaphysical awakening not unlike the one experienced by Joe. The traveller sees in the desolate, dust-bowl terrain a metaphor for contemporary reality, a metaphor which prompts his examination of such issues as "are we to live, or not? . . . Is our presence here to be something, or nothing?" With these questions in mind, he tours El Paso and concludes that "It was a dead city, it was part of a dead world, a dead age, a universe dying, aching with loneliness, gasping for breath." He sees also that mankind has chosen a way of living that lacks dignity so that "suddenly I began to cry, roaring with laughter, because I knew we were all dead, didn't know it, and therefore couldn't do anything about it."[26] The audience's experience during *The Time of Your Life* is another such journey. The spectators travel through the performance as the story's protagonist journeys through Texas—slowly discovering the truth about the world and about their own careless vision. Their mutual destination is hardly comforting, for it involves a confrontation with the "nightmare of an idiot" and the acceptance of "the tragedy of genuine knowing." The merging of theatre and life is finished. The audience must now leave behind the theatre of illusions for the greater drama of life beyond the auditorium doors and for the challenge of how to live in the time of their lives. What remains after the curtain falls is the audience and the world. Now, according to Saroyan, the real play begins.

Notes

1. William Saroyan, "The Great American Goof" in *Razzle Dazzle* (New York: Harcourt, Brace and Company, 1942), pp 63–64.
2. William Saroyan, *The Time of Your Life* (New York: Harcourt, Brace and Company, 1939), pp 241–246. This essay appears also in *Theatre Arts Monthly*, XXIII (December, 1939), pp. 870–875 under the title "The Coming Reality."
3. Saroyan, *The Time of Your Life*, p. 209.
4. William Saroyan, "How to See," *Theatre Arts*, XXV (March, 1941), pp. 203–205.
5. Saroyan, *The Time of Your Life*, p. 209.
6. Saroyan, *The Time of Your Life*, p. 246.
7. Saroyan declared repeatedly that Bernard Shaw was the greatest influence on him. The similarities between Saroyan's technique for engaging the audience and that used by Shaw in his early works are interesting. As I have argued elsewhere, both men use what Shaw called "the terrible art of sharpshooting at the audience, trapping them, fencing with them, always aiming at the sorest spot in their consciences" to overthrow the audience's narrow values and thus prepare the way for the dramatist's own ideas.
8. Saroyan, *The Time of Your Life*, p. 149. All subsequent references from the play will be from this edition.
9. William Saroyan, "Many Miles Per Hour" in *Little Children* (New York: Harcourt, Brace and Company, 1937) p. 12.
10. William Saroyan, *Here Comes, There Goes, You Know Who* (New York: Simon and Schuster, 1961), p. 42.
11. Sarayan, "A Special Announcement" in *Razzle Dazzle*, p. 180.
12. Saroyan, "Public Speech" in *Three Times Three*, p. 70.
13. Saroyan, "A Special Announcement in *Razzle Dazzle*, p. 181
14. This line appears only in the 1939 edition of the play. It seems to me an essential

line if the audience is to understand Joe's transformation and his subsequent treatment of the bar's inhabitants.

15. Saroyan, *Here Comes, There Goes, You Know Who*, p. 41.

16. Saroyan, *Here Comes, There Goes, You Know Who*, p. 271.

17. Saroyan, "Baby" in *Three Times Three*, p. 109.

18. William Saroyan, *Places Where I've Done Time* (New York: Praeger Publishers, 1972), p. 161.

19. Lawrence Langer, *The Magic Curtain* (New York: E. P. P. Dutton & Company, Inc., 1951), 323.

20. William Saroyan, "The Typewriter" in *The Bicycle Rider in Beverly Hills*, p. 59.

21. Saroyan, "A Special Announcement" in *Razzle Dazzle*, p. 180.

22. Saroyan, "Public Speech" in *Three Times Three*, p. 70.

23. William Saroyan, *Three Plays* (New York: Harcourt, Brace and Company, 1940), p. 6.

24. Saroyan, "Sleep in Unheavenly Peace" in *The Daring Young Man on the Flying Trapeze and Other Stories*, p. 274.

25. Burns Mantle (ed.), *The Best Plays of 1939–40* (New York: Dodd, Mead and Company, 1940), pp. 250–251.

26. William Saroyan, "Noonday Dark Enfolding Texas" in *Peace, It's Wonderful* (New York: Modern Age Books, Inc., 1939), pp. 207–211.

"What. What-not." Absurdity in Saroyan's *The Time of Your Life*

John A. Mills*

In the conclusion of his 1976 article entitled, "Joe as Christ-Type in Saroyan's *The Time of Your Life*," Kenneth W. Rhoads suggested that "other interpretations of Joe may be validly advanced (although so far they seem not to have been)" (242). Seven years of critical silence having followed the issuance of Rhoads's invitation, the time would seem to be ripe for an alternate reading of the character and the play, the more so since Saroyan's recent death is likely to have stirred up fresh interest in his work.

I should like to propose that Joe be viewed as an *"homme absurde,"* as defined by Camus in *The Myth of Sisyphus*, and that the play over which he presides be seen as an embodiment of the absurd sense of life, expressing in its structure and all its parts man's confrontation with nothingness, with "the unreasonable silence of the world" (*Sisyphus*, 21).

To speak of a work by Saroyan in these terms is, in large measure, to fly in the face of received opinion. Saroyan's depiction of the human condition is usually thought of as sunny and positive, bordering on the sentimental. The two obituaries of record, in the New York *Times* and the London *Times*, both voiced the orthodox view. The former spoke of "his message of the disinherited rising above adversity with humor and courage" (19 May 1984, B14) and the latter referred to "Saroyan's indestructible brand of rhapsodic optimism" (19 May 1984, 16).

There is something in that, of course. Saroyan typically shows his characters coping with earthly existence with a light-heartedness which approaches the meretricious. There is an element of sweetness in his work which has no counterpart in the drama and fiction of Camus or Sartre, to say nothing of Dostoevsky or Beckett. But there is no fundamental incompatibility between an absurd view of the human enterprise and the adoption of an optimistic stance in the face of ultimate absurdity, pessimistic as most absurdist literature undoubtedly is. Brian Masters quotes Camus as having once said to an audience of Dominican Friars: "If Christianity is pessimistic as to man, it is optimistic as to human destiny. Well, I can say that,

* Reprinted from *The Midwest Quarterly* 26:2 (Winter 1985), 139–59, by permission of the editors.

pessimistic as to human destiny, I am optimistic as to man" (87). One thinks in this connection of Grand, in *The Plague*, a "little" man who carries on in the face of meaninglessness with a sanguine indomitability which differs from the posture of Saroyan's characters less in kind than in degree. But these are analogies which must be validated by close examination of Saroyan's text.

Before undertaking such an examination, however, it will be useful to establish Saroyan's spiritual kinship with the evangelists of the absurd, by reference to materials other than *The Time of Your Life*. Such a kinship is revealed again and again in Saroyan's first three volumes of personal reminiscence, *The Bicycle Rider in Beverly Hills, Here Comes There Goes You Know Who*, and *Not Dying*. Since all three were written ten to twenty years after *The Time of Your Life* (1939), the observations on life which they contain must be used with some care. But even if one looks only at those statements in which Saroyan records his earliest responses to existence, the absurd sense of life stands clearly revealed. A representative sampling will suffice to make the point.

From *The Bicycle Rider:* "From a very early time in my life I sensed quite accurately the end of life. That is, that it *must* end, that it *could* end any time, that the end did not come to pass by reasonable or meaningful plan, purpose or pattern" (37). "After swimming I remember sitting with my friends on the hot earth of the pasture bordering the ditch, in the wonderful light and heat of the August sun, and being miserable about my own impermanence, insignificance, meaninglessness, and feebleness" (98).

From *Here Comes There Goes:* "I took to writing at an early age to escape from meaninglessness, uselessness, unimportance, insignificance, poverty, enslavement, ill health, despair, madness, and all manner of other unattractive, natural, and inevitable things" (2). "The cat would be gone for a good three or four days, and then it would come back looking like a wreck and sprawl out and start to heal, the writer of Ecclesiastes himself. All vanity. All sorrow and ignorance. For God's sake, where's the meaning of it, and the dish of milk?" (157).

From *Not Dying:*

I'm not sure, but then the thing that I am *about*, the thing I have for the greater part of my life *been* about, is to consider and reconsider, and then to consider and reconsider again, in the expectation of either finding out or of *knowing* it is impossible for me to find out. I don't know. I mean, of course, that I don't know anything, with absolute certainty, with finality, with (if you like) *final* finality (52).

I have always had a sneaking suspicion that work is a kind of excuse for failure, general failure—to know, to understand, to cherish, to love, to believe, and so on. It is a kind of evasion, a kind of escape from the knowledge that one is entirely without grace, that one is altogether ill and mad (191–92).

Such asseverations reveal a mind fully conversant with absurdity, and hence, a mind fully capable of creating a dramatic character imbued with a similar sensibility. That Joe is such a character can be seen in nearly everything he says and does in the course of the action.

One of the most conspicuous features of Joe's character is his immobility. Except for the move to Kitty's hotel room (about which more later) he scarcely stirs. Others come and go—indeed, the play is more than commonly replete with exits and entrances—but not Joe. He remains a still center amid the flux of quotidian activity, relying on the faithful Tom to do such fetching and carrying as he requires. At one point he hints that he is physically incapable of locomotion. "I don't dance," he tells Mary, and then goes on to say, "I can hardly walk." When she asks, "You mean you're tight?," he says "No. I mean *all* the time" (78).

Saroyan comments revealingly on this exchange in *Here Comes There Goes:* "Dance? I could hardly walk. Joe, in this same play I'm talking about, said it for me, precisely in those words. This didn't mean something was the matter with his feet and legs, though. It meant something else" (36). From the context in which this observation occurs it is clear what, for Saroyan, that "something else" is. He has been declaring his admiration for Bojangles and others he has seen who *can* dance and in the process the term is elevated to the metaphoric plane where it takes on the meaning of "to live, to know how to live, to be engaged, to have found a role, a purpose for living." Joe's physical immobilization may thus be seen as the external counterpart of an inner, psychic immobilization. Joe is stalled, incapable of movement, because, having glimpsed the absurd, he is unable to believe in the efficacy of human action, *any* human action.

This state of mind is manifested in many other ways, both explicitly and implicitly. As he can hardly walk, he can also hardly talk, can hardly summon up the will to verbally engage external reality. His typical utterances are terse, laconic, flat and monosyllabic. It is significant that he delivers himself of more than a single, simple declarative sentence almost exclusively on those occasions when he is goaded into explaining his inertia; paradoxically, he talks only to account for his failure to talk (or walk, or act). One such speech occurs when Tom finally musters the courage to ask where Joe gets his money. Joe looks at Tom *"sorrowfully, a little irritated"* and *"speaks clearly, slowly and solemnly"*: "Now don't be a fool, Tom. Listen carefully. If anybody's got any money—to hoard or to throw away—you can be sure he stole it from other people. Not from rich people who can spare it, but from poor people who can't. From their lives and from their dreams. I'm no exception. I *earned* the money I throw away. I stole it like everybody else does. I hurt people to get it. Loafing around this way, I *still* earn money.

The money itself earns more. I still hurt people . . ." (149). This much of the speech, if read in isolation from what follows immediately and in isolation from other materials in the play, might seem to make Joe a social rebel, a man who has withdrawn in protest from the capitalist system, who refuses to be party any longer to the social Darwinism which makes every man a predator of his fellow creatures. Indeed, there is no reason to deny Joe a social conscience. Undoubtedly it was a causative factor in his withdrawal from the world. But it was only a factor, and a relatively minor one. Joe's quarrel is with existence, with the human condition, *sub specie aeternitatis*, and not merely with the institutions of twentieth-century industrial society. This is revealed, in a negative way, in Joe's reluctance to condemn Blick, the play's chief representative of militant fascism, a bully who is "out to change the world from something bad to something worse" (64). "It's not him," Joe tells Nick. "It's everything" (66). And a few lines later: "He may not be so bad, deep down underneath."

Joe has little or no faith in social revolution as a cure for human malaise. When McCarthy, speaking for suffering humanity, tries to get Joe to side with him against Krupp, another fascist-type ("All I do is carry out orders, carry out orders" [84]), Joe remains steadfastly neutral: "Everything's right. . . . I'm with everybody. One at a time" (86).

Even when confronted with ocular proof of Blick's bullying ways, Joe is unable to take decisive action against him. He goes through the motions, points the gun and pulls the trigger, but nothing happens. He blames "dumb Tom" for having bought "a six shooter that won't even shoot once" (189), but, in fact, he had himself removed the cartridges not ten minutes earlier. Whether the attempted assassination of Blick is pure charade or Joe has actually forgotten about the cartridges (his mind dulled by drink?) is impossible to say. But if Saroyan manages the incident rather clumsily, his reason for including it seems nevertheless clear: he stays the hand of his protagonist because he recognizes that decisive action would run counter to the radically uncommitted nature of the character he has been at pains to depict in all that has gone before. Joe does not act because he lacks the necessary conviction, however much he may hide that fact from his own consciousness by conveniently "forgetting" that the weapon is unloaded, or however much he may hide it from others by blaming Tom.

That Joe cannot act, in the social sphere or any other sphere, he explains in the conclusion to his lengthy answer to Tom about the source of his income. "I don't do anything. I don't *want* to do anything any more. There isn't anything I can do that won't make me feel embarrassed. Because I can't do simple, good things. I haven't the patience. And I'm too smart. Money is the guiltiest thing in the world. It stinks. Now, don't ever bother me about it again" (149–50).

Surely such remarks can be interpreted in a way that establishes a family resemblance between Joe and the alienated, disaffected, anti-heroes who people the world of modernist fiction and drama. In Camus's terms, Joe has come to regard all tasks as Sisyphean, as so much meaningless activity, activity which is "embarrassing" because it does not have, cannot have, intrinsic value or ultimate efficacy. Like Dostoevsky's Underground Man, Joe is cursed with "lucidity," that "full-fledged disease" which obviates action; he is "too smart." Like the Underground Man he envies those "spontaneous people and the men of action" who lack lucidity but he knows he can never again be one of them. He cannot "do simple things," cannot, like a Russian peasant, be a contented hewer of wood and drawer of water. Consciousness will not allow it. "Before encountering the absurd," Camus writes, "the everyday man lives with aims, a concern for the future or for justification. . . . He weighs his chances, he counts on 'someday,' his retirement or the labor of his sons" (*Sisyphus*, 42). Joe has been an "everyday man" but can never be again. When Mary asks why he drinks, he replies: "Because I don't like to be gypped. Because I don't like to be dead most of the time and just a little alive every once in a long while. (*Pause*) If I don't drink, I become fascinated by unimportant things—like everybody else. I get busy. Do things. All kinds of little stupid things, for all kinds of little stupid reasons. Proud, selfish, *ordinary* things. I've done them. Now I don't do anything. *I live all the time*. Then I go to sleep" (73). Not yet grasping his point, Mary asks: "What are your plans?" and he answers: "Plans? I haven't got any. I just get up." And then the light dawns. *"Beginning to understand everything,"* she replies: "Oh, yes. Yes, of course." Following this, Joe returns to the question of why he drinks, struggling, as usual, with inarticulateness, but eventually *"working it out."*

> Twenty-four hours. Out of the twenty-four hours at least twenty-three and a half are—my God, I don't know why—dull, dead, boring, empty and murderous. Minutes on the clock, *not time of living*. It doesn't make any difference who you are or what you do, twenty-three and a half hours of the twenty-four are spent *waiting*.
>
> . . . .
>
> That goes on for days and days, and weeks and months and years, and years, and the first thing you know *all* the years are dead. All the minutes are dead. There's nothing to wait for any more. Nothing except *minutes* on the clock. No time of life. Nothing but minutes, and idiocy. (*Pause*) Does that answer your question? (75–76)

This is a view of the human condition which bears a striking resemblance to one put forward by another "immobilized" protagonist, Hamm of *Endgame:* "Moment by moment, pattering down, like the millet grains of (*he hesitates*) . . . that old Greek, and all life long you wait for that to mount up to a life" (70).

Joe's sporadic outbursts of self-analysis provide perhaps the most explicit evidence of his immersion in absurdity, but his state of mind manifests itself in other ways as well. In the play's opening sequence, after Joe has purchased a stack of newspapers, glanced at them and thrown them away in disgust, the Arab picks one up, reads the headline, and *"as if rejecting everything else a man might say about the world,"* intones for the first time a line which is to run through the play like a lyric refrain: "No foundation. All the way down the line" (20). The incident establishes a spiritual nexus between the two characters; the Arab says what Joe thinks; they share a belief in the emptiness of all human endeavor; it has no foundation, no intrinsic value. Repeated and embellished throughout the play, the Arab's judgment upon the world carries the same thematic force as the cryptic pronouncement with which Estragon opens *Waiting for Godot:* "Nothing to be done."

The second time we hear from the Arab he develops his theme, his *sole* theme, at greater length: "No foundation. All the way down the line. What. What-not. Nothing. I go walk and look at sky" (90). Krupp immediately turns to Joe for an explanation: "What? What-not? What's that mean?" It is significant that Krupp fails to comprehend because Krupp is a man who cannot live without absolutes, without direction. He has surrendered his freedom, put on a uniform, and follows orders, bashing heads at the command of his masters, secure in the conviction that they know what is to be done, even if he does not. It is also significant that Joe *does* understand and is ready with an explication, further revealing that he and the Arab are like-minded men, differing only in the beverages they choose as aids to lucidity: "What? What-not? That means this side, that side. Inhale, exhale. What: birth. What-not: death. The inevitable, the astounding, the magnificent seed of growth and decay in all things. Beginning, and end. That man, in his own way, is a prophet. He is one who, with the help of *beer*, is able to reach that state of deep understanding in which what and what-not, the reasonable and the unreasonable, are one" (90). Once again, Saroyan shows himself to be Beckettian *avant la lettre*; that "inhale, exhale" reminds us of the later playwright's thirty-second dramatization of the human condition called *Breath*, and the evocation of "Beginning, and end" expresses the same sense of life as Hamm's "The end is in the beginning and yet you go on" (69).

The Arab thus functions as a kind of choral character, articulating in a quasi-lyric mode that sense of estrangement, of being rudderless in "a universe suddenly divested of illusions and lights" (*Sisyphus*, 5), which colors everything that Joe says and does. The Arab's presence in the play expands its reference, amplifies its resonance, by suggesting that Joe is not to be written off as a special case, an aberration, but is to be viewed as broadly representative. At the end of Act Four, when the Arab plays a solo on the harmonica, Wesley reminds us that the music expresses the age-old pain of earthly existence: "That's deep, deep crying. That's crying a long time ago. That's crying a thousand years ago. Some place five thousand miles away" (142). Much the same might be said of the Arab's verbal laments. Coming just after his declaration that he no longer works ("For what? Nothing"), the Arab's harmonica threnody reinforces his similarity to Joe. Both have been stopped dead by their perception of the absurd. They have fetched up in "those waterless deserts where thought reaches its confines." For such men, Camus continues, "The real effort is to stay there . . . and to examine closely the odd vegetation of those distant regions" (*Sisyphus*, 8). With the aid of champagne and beer, respectively, Joe and the Arab keep the absurd vividly present to consciousness, so as not to be seduced into "bad faith," into the delusion that "little stupid things" are important, into performing tasks which are "for nothing," as though they were "for something."

But stasis is not the only possible posture before the absurd. Camus points out that "on the one hand the absurd teaches that all experiences are unimportant, and on the other it urges toward the greatest quantity of experiences" (*Sisyphus*, 46). This "quantitative ethic," this joyous acceptance and energetic use of freedom is exhibited in the play by Kit Carson ("real" name Murphy), a man who seems to know what Joe and the Arab know but who has gone on from there. Carson seems to know that in the absence of absolutes "everything is permitted," and so he has led a rootless, improvised, richly varied existence, reveling in a multiplicity of sensations in the brief time alloted before all sensation ceases. Of the four human types whom Camus describes as embodying most fully and clearly the quantitiative ethic which absurdity leads to—Don Juan, the creative artist, the actor, and the conqueror—Carson most closely resembles the actor. He has herded cattle on a bicycle, passed himself off as a mining engineer, masqueraded as a woman and changed his name as casually as other men change their shirts. He calls himself Murphy now but Saroyan says *"he looks as if he might have been Kit Carson at one time"* (106), and that is the name the author assigns him throughout. The actor, Camus explains, "abundantly illustrates every month or every day that so suggestive truth that there is no frontier between what a man wants to be and what he is. Always concerned with better representing, he demonstrates to what a degree appearing creates being" (*Sisyphus*, 59). And so it is with Carson as Joe, characteristically, perceives. "Now, son, don't tell me you don't believe me, either?" Carson asks, after recounting some of his adventures. "Of course I believe you," Joe answers. "Living is an art. It's not bookkeeping. It takes a lot of rehearsing for a man to get to be himself" (112).

Joe does not live as Carson lives but he immediately recognizes and approves of the ethic of experience which the latter has embraced. They are brothers in absurdity, fellow outsiders. "You're the first man I've ever met who believes me," says Carson.

That they are both alike and not alike is seen in their responses to the cruelty of Blick. Both deplore it but only Carson is able to turn his moral repugnance into effective action, striking down the oppressor moments after Joe's abortive attempt to do so. Though Carson has, by his own account, repeatedly run away from violence on occasions when only his personal safety was at stake, he feels constrained to stand and fight against the threat to the general good, to universal human nature, which Blick, the totalitarian idealogue, so chillingly embodies. In this, Carson resembles Cherea of Camus's *Caligula*. Though he agrees with Caligula, "to a point," that "all [actions] are on an equal footing," Cherea executes the tyrant, because, as he tells him, "you're pernicious, and you've got to go" (52).

Joe, the Arab, and Kit Carson are perhaps the play's most vividly rendered exemplars of the absurd sensibility but others among the dramatis personae also bear witness in a variety of modes and degrees. Prominent among these secondary characters is Harry the Hoofer. Saroyan introduces him as a man who is *"out of place everywhere, embarrassed and encumbered by the contemporary costume, sick at heart, but determined to fit in somewhere"* (41). In short, he is another character whose life has "no foundation"; he lacks a ground of being but manfully shoulders the task of improvising one, the existential task of "making himself." His primary medium is the dance and he thus embodies a variation on the dance metaphor which we have found Joe using. Harry's restless, ceaseless soft-shoe patterns and variations are the obverse of Joe's immobility; Harry constructs designs to fill the void left by nature, replacing one configuration with another in full awareness of the ultimate emptiness of all of them. "I felt that man must make," Saroyan has written, "that he must make ceaselessly, again and again . . ." (*Bicycle Rider*, 64).

Harry also "makes" in another medium; he is a stand-up comic and his monologues speak always of flux and incoherence, of life's refusal to make sense:

> Now, I'm standing on the corner of Third and Market. I'm looking around. I'm figuring it out. There it is. Right in front of me. The whole city. The whole world. People going by. They're going somewhere. I don't know where, but they're going. I ain't going *anywhere*. Where the hell can you go? I'm figuring it out. All right, I'm a citizen. A fat guy bumps his stomach into the face of an old lady. They were in a hurry. Fat and old. *They bumped*. Boom. I don't know. It may mean war. War. Germany. England. Russia. I don't know for sure. (*Loudly, dramatically*, he salutes, *about faces, presents arms, aims, and fires*) WAAAAAR (43–44).

This, like Harry's other routines, is an absurd work of art in miniature. "The absurd work of art," Camus explains, "illustrates thought's renouncing of its prestige and its resignation to being no more than the intelligence that works up appearances and covers with images what has no reason. If the world were clear, art would not exist" (*Sisyphus*, 73). Small wonder that most of the regulars at Nick's waterfront honky-tonk fail to comprehend Harry's bizarre accounts of day-to-day existence. They represent a "new kind of comedy," a comedy at which it is difficult if not impossible to laugh—black comedy, in short. "Nothing is funnier than unhappiness," says Nell in *Endgame*. "Yes, it's like the funny story we have heard too often, we still find it funny, but we don't laugh anymore" (18–19).

Strong intimations of absurdity appear also in the little episode involving Elsie and Dudley. After a peremptory exchange of greetings with her suitor, Elsie, a nurse, launches a bitter critique of the terms upon which human beings hold their tenure of life: "So many people are sick. Last night a little boy died. I love you, but—" (133). Dudley protests, but she is adamant: "Love is for birds. They have wings to fly away on when it's time for flying. For tigers in the jungle because they don't know their end. We know *our* end. Every night I watch over poor, dying men. I hear them breathing, crying, talking in their sleep. Crying for air and water and love, for mother and field and sunlight. We can never know love or greatness. We *should* know both" (134). The scene is analagous to that crucial confrontation in *The Plague* between Dr. Rieux and Father Paneloux, following the death in agony of the son of M. Othon. "That child, anyhow, was innocent, and you know it as well as I do," says Rieux. "And until my dying day I shall refuse to love a scheme of things in which children are put to torture" (202, 203). Like Ivan Karamazov before him, Rieux refuses to countenance a fabric of human destiny which requires the torture of the innocent. In that "immoral" scheme of things lies one of the great headwaters of the absurd. Elsie's revolt against this irrational evil no doubt strikes us as rather facile, unearned, compared to the hard-won and meticulously articulated perceptions of Rieux and Ivan, but it springs from an identical source.

Another familiar topos of absurdist literature occurs, if only in a radically truncated form, in the behavior of The Lady, a socialite who has come to Nick's with her husband on a "slumming" expedition. When Joe passes cigars around, the Lady blithely takes one, bites the tip off, and accepts a light from Carson, to the distress of her straight-laced spouse: "The mother of five grown men, and she's still looking for *romance*. No. I forbid it" (172). In thus flouting the arbitrary social code which proscribes cigar-smoking for a wife-and-mother, she opens herself up to experience, making a brave, if pathetic, little bid for that freedom which is a consequence of the acceptance of absurdity. Characteristically, Joe defends her against her serious-minded, law-giving husband: "What's the matter with you? Why don't you leave her alone? What are you always pushing your women around for?"

That we are to see the Lady's inchoate rebellion in existential terms is suggested not only by Joe's energetic support of it but also by the context in which it occurs. Joe distributes the cigars immediately after removing from his mouth the enormous wad of gum he has put there in his chewing contest with Tom and Carson. In the mock earnestness with which Joe engages in this competition, he parodies those struggles for achievement which characterize the serious world, the world of "aims," which he has repudiated. The incident has something of the flavor and point, though not the force, of the celebrated passage in Beckett's *Molloy*, where the eponymous hero is made to wrestle for five pages with the logistics involved in transferring sixteen pebbles, one by one, from his pockets to his mouth and back again. The gum-chewing match creates a climate of challenge to orthodox opinion about "allowable" adult behavior into which the "unseemly" conduct of the Lady fits very naturally. The point is underscored by the fact that Joe wraps his gum in a *Liberty* magazine, one of three publications (the others are *Time* and *Life*) which Joe had Tom purchase along with the gum and cigars. *Time* and *Life* echo, of course, the key terms of the play's title (as does Precious Time, one of the horses Joe bets on) and frequent use of such terms serves to remind us of the play's primary thematic thrust: the time of life is short and ends in death and time is therefore precious and must be savoured in the lucid acknowledgment of total liberty.

Yet another image of absurdity appears in Willie's running battle with the saloon's "marble-game," or pin-ball machine. Saroyan points up the symbolic significance of Willie's heroic struggle in a lengthy stage direction: "[Willie] stands straight and pious before the contest. Himself vs. the machine. Willie vs. Destiny. His skill and daring vs. the cunning and trickery of the novelty industry of America, and the whole challenging world. He is the last of the American Pioneers, with nothing more to fight but the machine, with no other reward than lights going on and off, and six nickels for one. Before him is the last champion, the machine. He is the last challenger, the young man with nothing to do in the world . . ." (21). Willie eventually "defeats" the machine, mastering Destiny, he believes, through skill and force of will: "I just don't like the idea of anything getting the best of me. A machine or anything else. Myself, I'm the kind of a guy who makes up his mind to do something, and then goes to work and does it. There's no other way a man can be a success at anything" (160). But his triumph is hollow and short-lived. The next time he attacks his adversary, the machine records a victory by sheer chance, and goes on doing so, unpredictably, arbitrarily. Like the cosmos which it represents, the "machine is out of order." "Something's wrong," Willie ruefully reports (190–91).

The absurd sense of life is expressed not only in the statements and activities of the characters but in the very structure of the work. The play is conspicuously non-linear, palpably static, mirroring in its randomness and clutter that chaos which, in the absurdist view, characterizes life itself. The play lacks plot because life lacks plot. In life, as Camus says, "there is no scenario, but a successive and incoherent illustration" (*Sisyphus*, 32). It is true, of course, that all of Saroyan's work, fiction as well as drama, is slack and disjointed, but the fact remains that on this occasion (whatever may be the case elsewhere) the looseness is thematically functional, operating in close congruence with the elements of thought and character which carry the essential import of the work. The harmony of feeling and form is much of the reason why *The Time of Your Life* is one of Saroyan's most aesthetically satisfying accomplishments. He once confessed that he wished to write "the way snow falls." The metaphor is strikingly apt. In *The Three Sisters*, another work comprised of the "aimless" accumulation of incident, Tusenback, told that life as he has described it does not "make sense," replies: "It's snowing out there. Does that make sense?" (61)

But the play is not absolutely free of consequential action. In the relationship between Tom and Kitty Duval there is a boy-meets-girl plot, of sorts, presided over by Joe and by him propelled forward to a dramatically predictable denouement. Joe's involvement in this romance between a lovable stumblebum and a whore-with-a-heart-of-gold represents his chief departure from non-alignment and, correspondingly, Saroyan's chief concession to conventional storytelling. As such, the whole episode seems out of key with the desultoriness which is otherwise pervasive; it represents an aesthetic lapse which is "given away," as it were, by the theatrically awkward shift of locale to Kitty's apartment in Act Three; the abrupt and short-lived excursion to a different physical world transports us to a different dramatic world, temporarily dissipating the emotional and spiritual ambience emanating from the honky-tonk. It is as though Hamm and Clov have ventured out of the shelter.

Though the Tom-Kitty plot borders on sentimental cliché, Joe functions in it in a way that is not fundamentally alien to his nature as *homme absurde*. Though he succeeds in his match-making partly by providing material assistance to the lovers—a job for Tom, a new wardrobe and domicile for Kitty— his more important contribution is spiritual. Rhoads focuses on this point in developing his case for Joe as Christ-type. Tom becomes Lazarus, brought back from death by Joe prior to the action, and Kitty becomes the woman taken in adultery, treated with compassion by Joe and told to go and sin no more (238–39). These parallels are admittedly quite arresting, more so than some of the other scriptural analogues which Rhoads presents. Joe is indeed a kind of saviour. But if we are to think of him in such terms we would do well to associate him with the Christ of Dostoevsky's "Grand Inquisitor" vignette, rather than with the Messiah described by Matthew, Mark, Luke, and John. For, like Dostoevsky's Christ, Joe has no gospel to preach, no glad tidings to bring, except the gospel of existential freedom. He repeatedly refuses to be dogmatic. When Tom declares, with something like worshipful awe: "You're a different kind of a guy" (117), Joe rebukes him: "Don't be silly. I don't understand things. I'm trying to understand them." Earlier, he has told Nick: "I study things" (106), and when Tom asks him to explain why he has called his three hours in the automobile with him and Kitty "the most delightful, the most somber, and the most beautiful" he has ever known, Joe repeats the self-description with quiet emphasis: "I'm a student. I study all things. All. All. And when my study reveals something of beauty in a place or in a person where by all rights only ugliness or death should be revealed, then I know how full of goodness this life is. And that's a very good thing to know. That's a truth I shall always seek to verify" (148). Hence, the only "word" he has to offer the lovers is that their lives are in their hands, that they are free to make, or remake themselves as they choose. There is no "way" except the way of choice. "You've got to figure out something to do that you won't mind doing very much," he tells Tom. When Tom fails to come up with anything, Joe offers a gentle nudge, couching his suggestion in the same language he has used earlier in speaking of his own work experience: "Tom, would you be embarrassed driving a truck?" (167) Tom eagerly accepts the position offered and in so doing adopts a philosophic stance not unlike Joe's own, the stance of the outsider, keenly aware of life's absurdity: "Joe, that's just the kind of work I *should* do. Just sit there and travel, and look, and smile, and bust out laughing . . ." (168).

Joe's ministry to the "fallen" Kitty also stresses the paramount importance of freely-accepted, self-created values: "I put her in that hotel, so she can have a chance to gather herself together again. She can't do that in the New York Hotel. You saw what happens there. There's nobody anywhere for her to talk to, except you. They all make her talk like a whore. After a while, she'll *believe* them . . ." (166). Understandably, Kitty reacts with fear and trembling to the freedom Joe offers her. Her first, very human, impulse is to assign irresistible power to the social and psychological forces which have cast her in the role of prostitute: "Too many things have happened to me. . . . I can't stand being alone. I'm no good. I tried very hard. . . . Everything *smells* different. I don't know how to feel, or what to think. . . . It's what I've wanted all my life, but it's too late . . ." (178–79). Joe remains nondirective; the choice must be hers: "I don't know what to tell you, Kitty. . . . I can't *tell* you what to do . . ." (179–80).

But Blick precipitates a climax in Kitty's struggle for self-possession and self-determination. By forcing her to perform a strip-tease, he seeks to demonstrate, to her and to the world, that she *is* a slut, essentially and irrevocably. Only then does Joe take a hand. He stops the shameful proceedings and by sending her off across the country with Tom puts her feet, if only tenuously, on the first rung of the ladder of self-realization.

A few moments later, having failed to kill Blick and having learned that someone else has succeeded at that task, Joe says goodbye to the saloon, probably for good:

NICK: Will I see you tomorrow?

JOE: I don't know. I don't think so (193).

Where is he going? "I don't know," he says. "Nowhere." Rhoads finds "the aura of vagueness and mystery" which hangs over this departure appropriate to a Christ-figure, whose "ending, whether it be in death or mere disappearance" should be as obscure as his origins. His "ministry" here is finished, Rhoads concludes; "other Toms and Kittys in other places need him, and a new mission calls" (241).

But Joe's mission has been a mission of self-discovery as much as anything else and it seems as reasonable to conclude that he now changes his base of operations in order to continue his "study"—of himself and the world and his place in it. He has, after all, some new material to work on; he has for the first time tried to act on an old desire: "I always wanted to kill somebody, but I never knew who it should be," he had announced as he took up the unloaded pistol. His action has brought with it both self-exposure and self-confrontation and we can imagine him wanting to withdraw in order to think further on these things. That something of the sort is on his mind is strongly suggested by the event which triggers his leave-taking. "Joe, you wanted to kill that guy," Nick says with surprise and admiration, and offers to buy him a bottle of champagne. Joe immediately goes for his hat and coat. "What's the matter?" Nick asks. "Nothing. Nothing."

Joe might be compared here to Scipio in *Caligula*. Invited by Cherea to join in the assassination of Caligula, Scipio cannot make that choice, though he understands and partly approves of Cherea's motives. Instead, he leaves, determined to "try to discover the meaning of it all."

At virtually every turn then, the dramatic materials which make up *The Time of Your Life* evoke comparisons with that spiritual topography familiar to us in the masterworks of modern existential literature. Saroyan's ability to translate his vision of the absurd into a wholly apposite and powerfully expressive symbolic form no doubt falls below that of his more illustrious forerunners and contemporaries. It is all too easy to read the play as an amiable, if somewhat eccentric slice-of-life, a mere chronicle of the quaint goings-on at a typically American waterfront saloon. On the surface, of course, the play *is* that, and it is as such that it has won an honored place among the classics of American realism. But its surface charm ought not to blind us to the weightier metaphysical import which lies just beneath.

Works Cited

Beckett, Samuel. *Endgame*. New York, 1958.
Camus, Albert. *Caligula and 3 Other Plays*, trans. Stuart Gilbert. New York, 1958.
———. *The Myth of Sisyphus and Other Essays*, trans. Justin O'Brien. New York, 1955.
———. *The Plague*, trans. Stuart Gilbert. New York, 1972.
Chekhov, Anton. *The Three Sisters*, trans. Tyrone Guthrie and Leonard Kipnis. New York, 1965.
Masters, Brian. *Camus: A Study*. London. 1974.

Rhoads, Kenneth W. "Joe as Christ-Type in Saroyan's *The Time of Your Life*," *Essays in Literature*. Macomb, Ill., 1976.
Saroyan, William. *The Bicycle Rider in Beverly Hills*. New York, 1952.
————. *Here Comes There Goes You Know Who*. New York, 1952.
————. *Not Dying*. New York, 1963.
————. *The Time of Your Life*. New York, 1939.

William Saroyan and the Autobiographical Pact: A Look at His Last Published Book, *Obituaries*

Lorne Shirinian*

Although William Saroyan's literary career has had a certain impact on American letters, his work has been the focus of only two book-length critical studies: Howard Floan's *William Saroyan* in 1966 and David Stephen Calonne's *William Saroyan: My Real Work Is Being* in 1983.[1] Seventeen years separate these books, yet one leads naturally into the other. In the preface to his study, Floan divides Saroyan's work at that time into four phases, the fourth being marked by the addition of autobiography. Floan's bibliography of Saroyan's work stops in 1964 with the publication of *One Day in the Afternoon of the World*. Calonne writes, ". . . from 1964 until his death in 1981, Saroyan devoted himself primarily to the explanation of his past through a steady output of autobiographical writings."[2] Some titles in this series which are telling in themselves for what they reveal as to their thematic content are: *I Used to Believe I Had Forever, Now I'm Not Sure*, 1968; *Letters from 74 rue Taitbout*, 1971; *Places Where I've Done Time*, 1972; *Days of Life and Death and Escape to the Moon*, 1973; *Sons Come and Go, Mothers Hang in Forever*, 1976; *Chance Meetings*, 1978; and finally, *Obituaries*, 1979. Saroyan left a massive amount of unpublished material to be administered by the William Saroyan Foundation which he himself created. In the context of his concern for autobiography, this is significant, and I will return to it below.[3]

The object of this study is to show how *Obituaries* works as an autobiography and to demonstrate how the autobiographical pact, that is, the contract, agreement, or understanding between the reader and the author, is created and what importance this has in terms of Saroyan's last published book.

Saroyan has left enough information for one to understand that since his integration into American society was never fully accomplished, writing was for him a means of affirming life. As early as 1962 in *Here Comes There Goes You Know Who*, Saroyan wrote, "The Armenians were considered inferior, they were pushed around, they were hated, and I was Armenian.

*Reprinted from *The Armenian Review* 3 (Autumn 1986), 23–31, by permission of the editors.

I refused to forget it then . . ." (p. 139). Saroyan's family, as all the survivors of the Armenian Genocide, had lost families, homes, and a country. Dispersed from their lands to all over Europe, the Middle East, and North America, Armenians had to wake from the nightmare of what had happened to them, re-establish themselves, and become citizens of new and strange countries. With this background of loss and instability, it would have been important for Saroyan to be accepted into American society, to anchor his life. However, this was denied him, as he tells us, and it marked him deeply. He remained a marginal, albeit at times a well-known marginal.

Another event marked Saroyan deeply—the death of his father in 1911 when Saroyan was three. His son Aram wrote, "Saroyan experienced the deepest trauma of his life. His Armenian immigrant father, Armenak, died of a ruptured appendix in San José, California, and his mother, Takoohi, was forced to put him along with her three older children, into an orphanage for the next five years."[4] After having achieved success as a writer, Saroyan asked himself, "Well, first of all, just where was my home? Was it in Fresno, where I was born? Was it in San José, where my father died? Was it in Oakland, where I spent four very important years? Was it San Francisco, where the whole family had moved . . . Home was in myself, and I wasn't there, that's all. I was far from home."[5]

The first lines of *Here Comes There Goes You Know Who* are, "I am an estranged man . . . estranged from myself, from my family, my fellow man, my country, my world, my time, and my culture" (p. 1). In the same book he wrote that he took to writing at an early age, "to escape from meaninglessness, uselessness, unimportance, insignificance, poverty, enslavement, ill health, despair, madness, and all manner of other unattractive, natural, and inevitable things."[6] Against this background of separation and estrangement, Saroyan's writing and particularly his desire to write autobiographies and memoirs can be seen as an attempt to unify the severed self. Saroyan wrote in *Obituaries*, "My work is writing, but my real work is being" (p. 324). He paraphrases Shakespeare by saying, ". . . if we live in language at all, it is only after we really live, after we live outside language . . ." (p. 102). Life must always come before art, but for Saroyan they are very closely associated, to the point that one cannot be conceived without the other, as we shall see below. Saroyan's writing gave him identity in life. The psychiatrist R. D. Laing has written on the perception of identity which has particular bearing on Saroyan in this context:

Self identity ("I" looking at "me") is constituted not only by our looking at ourselves, but by our looking at others looking at us and our reconstitution of and alteration of these views of others about us . . . even if a view of me is rejected it still becomes incorporated in its rejected form as part of my self-identity. My self-identity becomes my view of me which I recognize as the negation of the other person's view of me. Thus "I" becomes a "me" who is being misperceived by another person. This can become à vital aspect of my view of myself.[7]

One way to gain identity, self-identity, is, then, by allowing oneself to be scrutinized; in Saroyan's case, this was done through his writing. Since autobiography is more or less the opening of one's life, the autobiographical act not only accomplishes what Laing describes by permitting a person to formulate his opinions and organize his life on paper, but also forces one's own identity on oneself through contrast and opposition to others. The "I" Saroyan speaks through on nearly every page of *Obituaries* automatically posits a "you" in the discourse as the person addressed. Emile Benveniste, the French linguist, has shown in his work on utterance that the second person "you" is necessarily designated by the first person "I." This polarity of persons in language is the fundamental condition for communication.[8] Thus the very nature of Saroyan's discourse imposes the structure of identity that Laing outlined above.

Throughout his career, much of what Saroyan wrote was autobiographical in nature and intent: short stories, novels, memoirs, and straight autobiography.[9] In *Obituaries*, he adopts a form that allows him to move freely through the text. Although the generic question is a problem area in autobiographical studies, it poses no stumbling block in this study.

An accepted definition of autobiography describes it as a self-portrait.[10] This could be straight description, a history or development of one's intellectual or emotional self. The writer of the autobiography becomes the center and focus of the text. However, writing about the self can take many forms: the diary, the letter, the journal, the memoir, the first person poem, long or short fiction. Saroyan has used many of these forms for his own purposes. The problem of genre, however, can be avoided precisely because the conditions of autobiography offer a large framework inside of which a wide variety of styles may occur. We can avoid talking about an autobiographical style or form because there is no such generic style or form.[11]

James Olney writes that the most productive approach to autobiography is not in formal or historical considerations which separate it from the writer's life or personality but rather to view autobiography in relation to the vital impulse to order that has always caused man to create, which determines both the nature and form of what he creates. He states that when a writer puts into print something that is confessedly autobiographical, then we should be able to trace the creative impulse that was uniquely his.[12] He carries on, saying, "A man's autobiography is thus like a magnifying lens, focusing and intensifying the same peculiar creative vitality that informs all the volumes of his collected works . . ."[13] This is particularly apt in the case of Saroyan, a large portion of whose work is overtly autobiographical.

Paul de Man writes in "Autobiography as Defacement" that the theory of autobiography has been plagued by a recurrent series of questions that are confining because they take for granted assumptions about autobiographical discourse that are highly problematical. One of these problematical areas that de Man identifies is specifically this attempt to define and to treat autobiography as if it were a literary genre.[14] This leads him to state, "Attempts at generic definition seem to founder in questions that are both pointless and unanswerable."[15] For de Man autobiography isn't a mode or genre but a way of understanding through reading. Through an understanding of the reading process, we can see autobiography in a productive way.

Another contentious area in the study of autobiography that has relevance to *Obituaries* is the line between truth and fiction. As in the previous paragraph, I believe that this question is ultimately pointless; the questions are unanswerable precisely because the difference between truth and fiction in such a text is blurred. Saroyan himself has commented on this in *Obituaries:* "Memory—remembering an event—is artful. . . . The one who remembers makes more of that which happened, or less, as he decides he should" (pp. 6–7). A more profitable way of studying Saroyan's text is to see how one gains access to it. How does the autobiographical intent work to direct the reader to see it as an autobiography?

Taking the autobiography and the subject in an autobiographical text as a linguistic structure offers us the possibility of studying Saroyan's text from the point of view of the reader's response. Wolfgang Iser in *The Act of Reading* writes: "Central to the reading of every literary work is the interaction between its structure and its recipient. This is why the phenomenological theory of art has emphatically drawn attention to the fact that the study of a literary work should concern not only the actual text but also, and in equal measure, the actions involved in responding to that text. The text itself simply offers 'schematized aspects' through which the subject matter of the work can be produced, while the actual production takes place through an act of concretization."[16]

From this position, greater possibilities of understanding the workings of an autobiography exist rather than getting bogged down in discussions of genre or the truth / fiction problem, which is impossible to resolve. If we look at the autobiographical situation, we will see that a writer of an autobiography writes from a specific point of view and at a specific point in time. This is set against the sum total of his past experience and has the effect of interpreting his past and present. Faced with these conditions, how is the reader supposed to understand the autobiography? This situation is far from straightforward, for reading an autobiography means encountering a self as an imaginary being.[17] In fiction, a character is the object of someone else's imagination. In autobiography, the hero, Saroyan, the "I" in *Obituaries*, has identity as the object of his own imagination. In turn he takes on a new life in the reader's imagination. Perhaps the difference is that in understanding fiction, we are after an imaginary grasp of someone else's meaning; in understanding a memoir or autobiography, which is personal history, we are after an imaginative comprehension of someone else's historical identity.[18] Our response to a work is determined partly by the expectation we bring to the work and partly by the signals in the text. A study of the subject in the discourse in *Obituaries* will show how the signals in this text lead the reader to an understanding of how Saroyan's autobiographical text works. This, in turn, will help us understand his necessity in writing such a text.

Literary texts offer a system of perspectives which present the author's vision; these are the narrator, the characters, the plot, and the fictitious reader. One of these may dominate or combine with others to lead the reader into and through the text. In Saroyan's autobiographical text, the two dominant aspects are the narrator and the fictitious reader. They guide and offer the reader points of entry during his actualization. These two perspectives converge and finally meet at a general place called the meaning of the text. A pattern thus forms from these various changing points of view the reader occupies.[19] In *Obituaries*, the primary starting point is the narrator, the "I." The reader sees and knows all only through him. There is no outside world apart from the one created by the narrator. The other main perspective in Saroyan's text is the fictitious reader. Saroyan directly addresses the reader through the fictitious reader much as Fielding and Sterne did. "Will do, will do, will get along to the list of the dead, but hell-fire, man, shucks, friend, shoot, brother, good Lord, enemy, gosh, reader, there is such a thing, is there not, as a preface and preparation?" (p. 9). "[P]ermit me just the same, reader, my enemy if you prefer, permit me please to say to all who are in the saloon . . . reader permit me once again to notice what a thing it is to be alive, and how much more intense and right this thing becomes when death draws near. . . ." (pp. 11–12). The real reader is brought into the text, pulled by the narrator's address to him through the fictitious reader, creating a circular movement:

$$\text{Narrator} = \text{Fictitious Reader} = \text{Real Reader}$$

In this way, the reader is continually invited to continue through the text. Saroyan implicates the reader in the theme of the text while appealing directly to him, "Reader, it's worth it, it's a fight and you lose every day and you need time to try again in the morning, but yes, it is worth it . . ." (p. 153). The book becomes a way of affirming Saroyan's life as well as exhorting the reader as to life's joys in general. "Christ man, it's fun, it's fun, having the sun, having the seasons, having the whole damn thing all around and in depth . . . having it all, all, all of it going on all the time . . ." (p. 173).

In an autobiographical text, the narrator and the main character are bound together most often, as in the case in *Obituaries*, in the use of the first person singular, what Gérard Genette calls *la narration autodiégétique*.[20] For Genette this occurs when the narrator is the hero of his own story. The autobiographical nature of *Obituaries* works in this manner, which can be illustrated by a series of equations:

> Author = Narrator
> Author = Main Character
> Narrator = Main Character

This fulfills the criteria for what Philippe Lejeune calls the classical autobiography; that is, first person narration when the narrator and the main character are the same.[21] The question remains, however: who is the "I" in the text? This question is resolved when the subject in the discourse allows his identification to be known inside the discourse itself. It is in the proper name that person and discourse come together. In the name on the book cover, the entire existence of the author comes into being, and the meaning of the equations becomes clear. In fact, this is the only mark in the text, that is related to a context outside of the text itself. This mark refers to a real person who takes the responsibility for having written the whole text.[22] *Obituaries* works as an autobiography because the name Saroyan on the front cover is the same as the narrator's and the main character's. This is the autobiographical pact. What defines the autobiography for the reader is this contract of identity sealed by the proper name.[23] In contrast to fiction, autobiography is a referential text which claims to bring information about a reality outside the text which is verifiable. Whether or not the information is true is a problematical area, as we have seen; however, what such texts do is seem to be true. This creates another pact, the referential pact which defines the reality in the text as a truth given by the author, which the reader accepts at the same time as he accepts the autobiographical pact.[24]

Saroyan begins *Obituaries* with the solemn observation, "People die" (p. 1). When someone else dies, and we note it, "We live a little, too, and that's the reason the obituary page of the paper is so popular" (p. 4). The premise for this book is Saroyan's going through the alphabetical list in *Variety* of those who died in 1976. This seemingly ordered structure gives way to free association in Saroyan's mind as names of those he knows and even those of strangers trigger responses due to some resonance associated with the name, reminding him of others. The result is a free flowing stream of consciousness narrative. He begins with the first name on the list in chapter eight and then quickly moves to the last name in chapter nine. In chapter ten he goes back to the beginning of the list and ends up through association in London in 1944. "And now as long as I am in London, in 1944, I want to remember Noel Coward" (p. 26). Of course, how he got to Noel Coward is quite a trip in itself. This is an example of the text as pretext for his own fancy. Yet the play is never gratuitous. The lines are never thrown away; they always manage to wind around the central theme of the text, Saroyan's remembrances and the fact of death. Another device reinforces the internal monologue nature of the narrative. In a description of one of the dead he is remembering he writes, ". . . and Armenians everywhere heard the man's name (which I will remember in a moment) and rejoiced in the man's talent and growing fame . . . and then all of a sudden the shocking news reached Fresno that Haig Yaghjian (that's it), not yet even 40 years old, had died . . ." (p. 77). The reader, like Saroyan, is without the name; then suddenly in the middle of the discourse as Saroyan remembers it, the reader too becomes party to it, caught in the flow of the monologue. In this way the reader and Saroyan move along together. As the reader reads, he becomes a witness to and an accomplice of Saroyan's mental processes in the creation of the autobiography.

In *Obituaries*, Saroyan reiterates one of the major themes of his life, the necessity of writing. When asked in an interview in 1975, "Do you think that you will stop writing altogether one day?" he replied, "I don't think so. I shall write up to my death, if possible."[25] In the same interview he stated that he will never forget he is a writer: "You will forget that you are alive."[26] In *Obituaries* he wrote, "Why do I write? Why am I writing this book? To save my life, to keep from dying, of course" (p. 132). This necessity to write can be seen as a way of resolving his particular dilemma: how to reconcile himself with his past and how to hold back the inevitable. Losing his father at the age of three had a profound effect upon him, as we have seen. Aram Saroyan writes that Armenak [William Saroyan's father] had left several notebooks of his own writing, including poetry in Armenian, none of it ever published.[27] In *Obituaries*, Saroyan offers a clue that in his own way as a writer he could connect with his father: "And I talk to myself, which is the poorest possible way of saying that I talk to my father . . . the father dead before I was three is unknown to me . . ." (p. 27).

In explaining the motives behind his writing—that is, the fight against death—he created his own form of notebooks as his father had done.

The other pole of the dilemma was his desire to ensure his survival even after death. In order that his work would endure, Saroyan set up the William Saroyan Foundation and at his will signing in 1980 left all his papers and collections to the Foundation to be used for educational purposes. All royalties were to be used to maintain the properties, offices, and officials of the Foundation. Money left over would go to provide scholarships for writers, particularly Armenian-American writers.[28] In 1984 an inventory of Saroyan's property ran over three hundred pages and listed millions of words of unpublished works. He had written, "I will be discovered again and again."[29] These attempts give Saroyan's words, "My work is writing, but my real work is living" (p. 324), added meaning. He said, "My business is to live. Writing is living and there comes a time when writing and living, art and reality, come very close and I want them close in my life."[30] Life and art, then, become united in the man.

He knew he was dying of cancer, and as the end approached, he phoned the San Francisco office of the Associated Press in April 1981 to dictate his last words, part of his own obituary, not to be revealed until after his death. "Everybody has got to die, but I have always believed an exception would be made in my case. Now what?"[31] As the poet and novelist David Kherdian has written, "In book after book Saroyan salvaged his life, and in the end with no book to write he phoned in his story and died."[32]

Notes

1. In stories like "The Daring Young Man on the Flying Trapeze" and "Baby," Saroyan broke new ground that was later picked up by the Beat Generation, Jack Kerouac in particular. See David Calonne, *William Saroyan: My Real Work Is Being*, p. 33, and Aram Saroyan, *William Saroyan*, pp. 89–90. Barry Gifford and Lawrence Lee have written in their book, *Jack's Book* (New York: St. Martin's Press, 1978), "By his [Kerouac's] own word the stories he had written on the rented Underwood mimicked Hemingway, Saroyan, and Wolfe" (p. 29). From Ann Charter's book, *Kerouac: A Biography* (San Francisco: Straight Arrow Books, 1973), "He'd [Kerouac] learned from Burroughs and Ginsberg, but his instinctive response had been to model his writing on Wolfe, Hemingway and Saroyan" (p. 64).

2. David Stephen Callone, *William Saroyan: My Real Work Is Being* (Chapel Hill: The University of North Carolina Press, 1983), p. 12.

3. Aram Saroyan, *William Saroyan* (New York: Harcourt Brace Jovanovich, 1983), pp. 141–143.

4. *Ibid.*, p. 4.

5. William Saroyan, *Here Comes There Goes You Know Who*, pp. 89–90.

6. *Ibid.*, p. 2.

7. Quoted in Elizabeth Bruss, *Autobiographical Acts: The Changing Situation of the Literary Genre* (Baltimore: The Johns Hopkins University Press, 1976), p. 13.

8. Emile Benveniste, *Problems de linguistique générale* (Paris: Gallimard, 1966), tome 1, pp. 228, 232, 260.

9. David Calonne, p. 9.

10. William L. Howarth, "Some Principles of Autobiography," *New Literary History* (Winter 1974): p. 364.

11. J. Starobinski, "The Style of Autobiography," *Literary Style: A Symposium* (London: Oxford University Press, 1971): p. 285.

12. James Olney, *Metaphors of Self: The Meaning of Autobiography* (Princeton: Princeton University Press, 1972), p. 3.

13. *Ibid.*, pp. 3–4.

14. Paul de Man, "Autobiography as Defacement," MLN 94 (1979): p. 919.

15. *Ibid.*, p. 919.

16. Wolfgang Iser, *The Act of Reading: A Theory of Aesthetic Response* (Baltimore: The Johns Hopkins University Press, 1978), pp. 20–21.

17. Patricia M. Spacks, *Imagining a Self: Autobiography and Novel in Eighteenth Century England* (Cambridge: Harvard University Press, 1976), p. 19.

18. Francis R. Hart, "Notes for an Anatomy of Modern Autobiography," *New Literary History* (Spring 1970): p. 458.

19. Wolfgang Iser, p. 35.

20. Gérard Genette, *Figures III* (Paris: Editions du Seuil, 1972), p. 253.

21. Philippe Lejeune, *Le pacte autobiographique* (Paris: Editions du Seuil, 1975), p. 18.

22. *Ibid.*, pp. 22–26.

23. *Ibid.*, p. 33.

24. *Ibid.*, p. 36.

25. Garig Basmadjian, "Candid Conversation: An Interview," *Ararat* (Special Issue on William Saroyan, Spring 1984): p. 38.

26. *Ibid.*, p. 41.

27. Aram Saroyan, p. 20.

28. *Ibid.*, p. 143.

29. Lawrence Lee and Barry Gifford, *Saroyan: A Biography* (New York: Harper & Row, 1984), p. 310.

30. Garig Basmadjian, p. 38.

31. Lawrence Lee and Barry Gifford, p. 307.

32. David Kherdian, "The End of an Era,"*Ararat* (Special Issue on William Saroyan, Spring 1984): p. 62.

[Saroyan and the Armenian Past]

Harold Aram Veeser*

> I'm hemmed here. The Allies like sump
> in the harbor. If I could shake one British
> Admiral, he'd not believe this tale—
> a hundred miles from his bow. Here, a poet's
> words, "Armenia is a scarlet herb, a walking
> shadow."
>
> — Peter Balakian
> "In the Turkish Ward"

"Once you like a place, you always like it," William Saroyan told Michael Arlen as they drove through the night rain to a Fresno graveyard. But *amor loci* tends, for these expatriates, to resist easy consummation. When beloved places close their borders, only the foolhardy return. Most resign themselves to exile: home remains a dead zone, beyond their grasp.

Although Saroyan spent a lifetime evading Armenian history, he walked in its "scarlet . . . shadow." During the last ten years of his life he faced the past squarely—in that final decade he wrote the three plays now edited by Dickran Kouymjian and published as *An Armenian Trilogy*. If the same obsessive concerns dominate all three, he nonetheless wrote each for a different occasion and considered each an independent production, not part of a single project. By calling this selection a trilogy, the editor implies more coherence than the author intended. Yet in boldly juxtaposing these plays, Kouymjian links their connecting filaments and thus illuminates a matter that increasingly preoccupies younger Armenian writers and intellectuals: Saroyan's relationship to Armenian culture.

As a literary precursor with whom subsequent Armenian writers must grapple, Saroyan seems destined to act the part either of a Charon who ferries them to the hellish past or of a professed "crazy Armenian" who defines their present realities. Wherever such writers begin, Saroyan precedes them. In a crucial chapter of his *Passage to Ararat*—the section that recounts his own pilgrimage to see Saroyan in Fresno—Michael J. Arlen affirms that "it

*Reprinted from *The Journal of Armenian Studies* 1 (Winter/Spring 1990–91), 95–108, by permission of the editors.

was a strange, deep feeling, as if we had known each other all along."[1] Once he has secured Saroyan's blessing—"I'm glad," the older man pronounces, that "you decided to find out about Armenians"—Arlen may proceed with his own *Passage to Ararat*. The troubled Armenian past now includes Saroyan himself, a giant that Arlen, Peter Balakian, and Armenian intellectuals in general have to pass on their way to literary maturity.

An Armenian Trilogy relocates Saroyan in a broadly European tradition of surrealism and modernism that includes Beckett, Ionesco, Joyce, and Brecht. Thickened with the chronic ache of homelessness, displacement, and *mal du pays*, the three plays—entitled *Armenians*, *Bitlis*, and *Haratch*—also link Saroyan to post-colonial literatures marked by an overpowering sense of exile from origin, home culture, and tradition. With his Dickensian childhood—five sobering years in Oakland's Fred Finch Orphanage, expulsion from school, peripatetic jobs as a newsboy and a bicycle telegraph-messenger—Saroyan remained a chronic outsider. Although he sought to connect himself to others, intimacy eluded him. Both his marriages to the same woman disintegrated, and he had at the end only a nodding acquaintance with Aram, his son, and Lucy, his daughter. Waiters, editors, and cab-drivers were often his closest friends; restaurants and racetracks the nearest things to home.

Recent scholarship has suggested already that Saroyan repeatedly turned for his sense of identity to the Armenian intelligentsia gathered around the *Hairenik* periodicals published in Boston. These writers and intellectuals were his sustaining culture; in the deepest sense, his family. What the *Trilogy* now makes clear is that Armenian literary culture enabled him to survive the distorted responses and misreadings of American critics. In adolescence he met, at his famous Uncle Aram's law office, such influential Armenian intellectuals as Reuben Darbinian, the editor of *Hairenik Weekly*, whose personal and professional importance to Saroyan is fully established in James Tashjian's study.[2] Whereas fame often destroys less well-grounded American heroes, Saroyan seemed unawed by reputation, declined to accept the Pulitzer Prize, and wrote almost obsessively right to the end. Those who disparage the "ethnophilic Armenians" whose "unqualified veneration . . . did [Saroyan] little good, either personally or professionally"[3] have surely overlooked the sturdy affiliations that held the author's life and art together.

An Armenian Trilogy traces an epic process: a disoriented mass of refugees progressively articulates its identity, its politics, its cosmopolitan complexion. The process itself is archetypal: first, a vision of loss or crises, raising the question of survival; second, a reductive answer to that question; third, a better answer, though with a continuing awareness of loss. It is not precisely an Armeniad, however: no ultimate homecoming or new imperium rewards the battered searchers. *Armenians*, the first play, recreates the author's native Fresno circa 1921. In that year Lloyd George and Woodrow Wilson refused to assume the Armenian protectorate that, when it served their interests, they had reassuringly proposed. Turkish General Kaizim Karabekir, bearing down on Alexandropol, promised to conclude the ultimate solution that had already claimed one-and-one-half million Armenian lives. The two-year-old, crippled Armenian Republic fell to the Red Army for the second and definitive time. Saroyan raises the curtain on three priests, a sexton, an old woman, and a skeptical, Harvard-educated physician. Although these people have been in California for some time, they have just begun to sense the price they have paid to assimilate. Charges and countercharges fly—"each of you lost that little part of yourselves which was entirely Armenian"—and obsessive memories haunt everyone: "They were all killed. . . . I lost them all."

After a brief scene in the church office, the professional men adjourn to the Patriotic Club for coffee and cards. There, Armenian Immigrants, cocooned in private angers and griefs, crowd around the table, demanding revenge and a wholesome military assault on the Russians. "What does a pompous little Protestant preacher know about Armenia?" fumes the man from Bitlis. An appeal to Christ draws another angry riposte: "You keep Him out of this. He's done enough damage to the Armenian nation." Homelessness, *angst*, radical doubt—the leitmotifs belong to literary modernism. One character's speech recalls Gayev in Chekhov's *The Cherry Orchard:* "Again we have failed. We cannot even talk together about the same thing. Our minds wander. Well, all the same, I say long live Armenia." As in Chekhov, dilatory speech dwindles from strong assertions to empty phrases. The stock character of the good physician (a hoary tradition demolished by Ibsen in *Ghosts* and *The Wild Duck*) also comes in for a modernist critique: the physician "Jivvy" Jivlekian fails to resolve provincial rivalries. Just as he makes a final lunge to wrap up loose ends, a new character pops in to assert his own regional claims: "Just a minute. Let me put in my two cents worth. I am from Giligia." Armenians offers little sense of closure. Saroyan intends that his audience remembers this fragmentation, ever present in Armenian community life.

In *Armenians* all characters but one endure a psychic immobility that matches their claustrophobic surroundings. That one character—the Reverend Knadjian, modeled on the minister who gave books to the young Saroyan—confesses a rather peculiar habit. "I write history. Well, at any rate I write what I have felt, and of course I also invent out of these things a kind of truth which I feel is greater than factual truth . . . Armenian truth." Knadjian alone uses his imaginative resources to graft the New World to the Old. The rest, revolutionaries all, clamor for a military solution while they languish and give the Patriotic Club—actually the Fresno offices of the nationalist paper *Asbarez* (Arena)—the thick, idle timelessness common to airports, bus depots, and the bar in which Saroyan set *The Time of Your Life*. In the act of writing, Knadjian attempts to transcend useless reverie. It remains for the later plays, and especially *Haratch*, finally to dissolve the barrier dividing politics from imaginative action.

It is worth pausing briefly to notice that the poet Peter Balakian follows Knadjian's program quite faithfully. When Balakian recreates the long-dead figures of his grandfather and Siamanto (the Armenian poet killed in 1915 on orders of the Turkish government), he is fashioning a kind of truth—a richly textured kind that enables the reader to "smell Turkish boots in the hall" and see "the Allies like sump / In the harbor."[4] Through Knadjian the current vogue for New Historicism in poetry proleptically enters Saroyan's drama of 1971.

In the succeeding play, *Bitlis*, Saroyan reconstructs his own 1964 trip to that city, which Saroyan family lore had enshrined, a place where the author had long dreamt that he might really feel at home. The play faithfully records the way his fond hopes unraveled.

Early in *Bitlis* we learn that "history is inferior behavior on behalf of support to a program of profit"—a piece of Rochefoucauldian cynicism that *Bitlis* goes far to justify. The Turks and Kurds "watch us, for they think we have come to dig up the buried gold of our fathers," and the sole resident Armenian wishes to go "home" to Beirut, where he can die among his fellow displaced compatriots. Here in "Armenia," Kurdish youths bait and rough up the octogenarian. Saroyan's ancestral stone houses have vanished, and when the ingratiating Turkish mayor leads "Bill" to the site of his grand-mother's home, nothing but a tumble-down cooking hearth remains, desolate and exposed. As if this were not emblem enough, Armenian headstones pave the streets. "Bill's" friend Ara from Istanbul observes that "every now and then if you look down you will see a piece of a gravestone in the street and on it you will see Armenian words and names: Sarkis Da-and the rest is broken away." The Armenian past lies asunder, fractured and ruined. Instead of really going home at last, as he had hoped, "Bill" finds himself *pied à pied* with the facts that have destroyed that home forever.

With his Bitlis a virtual Hades, an ominous rune that discloses hatred and violence, "Bill" has to reconsider his quest. This time it is the character named Ara who holds out the golden bough. Much as Knadjian looks beyond hard facts, Ara looks beyond real estate. "We do not need the childish support of a geographical country," he intones, "to enjoy being who we are." But can Armenians survive without Armenia? Editor Kouymjian has his doubts, for he contends that Ara merely rationalizes the loss of Armenian territory. But he misses Saroyan's point. "Rationalization" implies shameful evasions or comforting nostrums. In fact, Ara formulates the intellectual breakthrough that propels the Trilogy forward. By renouncing the *idée fixe* of geographical homecoming, Bill is able to perceive that "any place can instantly be home . . . because there are Armenians there." The final play (its title, *Haratch*, actually means "forward") throws a challenge: to re-conceive "Armenia" *un*geographically.

Readers of Edward Said will recognize this strategy. According to Said, dispossessed Palestinians can afford to demand full territorial repatriation no longer. "To affirm a prior belonging, a long historical *patriation*, has involved for us a prolonged denial of what we have now become, disinherited outsiders." Much to the dismay of the Palestinian nationalists, Said understands dispossession itself to be the basis for Palestinian identity and survival. Thus he supports a sort of willed homelessness: "How does one rise beyond the limiting circumstances, beyond negatively, into a positive affirmation of what we are and want? But this is not just a matter of will, it is also a matter of finding the right modality, the right mixtures of forces to harness, the right rhetoric and concepts by which to mobilize our people and our friends, the right goal to affirm, the right past to drop away from, the right future to fight for."[5] Saroyan's Ara also proposes that a people wronged and slaughtered—the Armenians in his case—drop their territorial ambitions. Does he represent the author's own position? That is far from clear. The Saroyan figure in the play challenges Ara's opinion. Yet it may be that Ara is the wiser party, and in *Haratch* his anti-nationalism wins out.

Armenians recollects a community riven by nostalgic dreams, *Bitlis* attempts to realize a long-anticipated homecoming, and *Haratch* builds a truly Armenian new world. Saroyan endeavors here to complete much the same imaginative project that Said has proposed for the Palestinians: "to give national shape to a life now dissolving into many unrelated particles."[6] To simplify, Said is arguing that the experience of eviction and exile has forged a new sense of Palestinian solidarity. The *Trilogy* suggests, as we have seen, that as late as 1921 provincial loyalties precluded an overarching Armenian identification. The Fresno Armenians of that play all lived in proximity but remained sharply divided. *Haratch* diametrically reverses the pattern. Scattered to the earth's four corners—Paris, Fresno, New York, Massachusetts, Yerevan—and radically split on political issues, they feel united. Clearly, collective identity has superseded limited, private self-interest. "We are not the only human family, but we are the family that we are, and all of our talk here is out of that condition of being a family," remarks a perceptive character. The myth of return makes a modest reappearance, it is true. "Saroyan," again a central character, betrays his own confusion: "It is a very difficult thing to make sense of loss, and absence, and displacement, and destruction—but whoever is alive in a place, he is the owner of the place, that is the law of history, and Bitlis is gone, and I wish I knew how it might be brought back to us." Yet Khachig's knee-jerk rejoinder— "Only by fighting for it!"—gains no ground. "Spoken like a Dashnak, a revolutionary, but of the year 1895," scoffs Hrachia, the Soviet Armenian who refuses easy nationalist sentiment. When Khachig needles him, saying. "And what about our sheep, are they happy?" Hrachia simply laughs that "It's better than being shishkebab." It is telling that the Dashnak-Marxist debate is reduced to a humorous sub-plot: the Armenian intellectual community has left behind the narrow terms of that debate. Instead, all these people have flocked into intellectual vocations—they are professors, poets, editors, writers of memoirs. Whereas other people can cherish unthinkingly the centripetal comforts of being at home, Armenians need self-discipline to embrace the centrifugal and disseminative powers of writing.

Just as Saroyan's early fiction exudes a warmth that life itself denied him, these late plays form a communal identity that nationalism manifestly failed to provide. A strenuous, hard-won internationalism connects the contributors to such "places" as *Haratch* and *Hairenik Weekly*. Apropos of the cosmopolitan setting, the new Armenian polity sweeps away the racial basis for identity: "Now and then we do see a trace of Asia in an Armenian face," "many Turks have Armenian eyes," and though Zohrab comes from Moush, "if we were to find him in Cairo among Egyptians we might instantly believe he was one of them, or in London, among cockneys, we might believe he was one of them." This intellectual polity unites even the social classes. Both the professor of literature at Wesleyan and the rough-hewn peasant with his memoirs can place their work in *Haratch*. Literature seems to dissolve national and linguistic boundaries. By writing in English, notes Zulal, Saroyan writes also "in French and Italian and Spanish and Russian and German. English is translated ten times to one time in Armenian. He has said, hasn't he, that he is an Armenian writer . . . and always will be?" So dispersed and uprooted a nation as the Armenians must uncircle the wagons, open the collective fist. Dissemination—what Jacques Derrida has called the movement of writing itself—has to replace the enfolding comforts of filial ties and involuted culture. Armenians have mastered the paradox that Said urges upon Palestinians—the paradox of making a home out of homelessness itself, finding unity in the diaspora.

Saroyan creates the perfect figure to represent the new, affiliative Armenian "family." Arpik is the thirty-year editor-in-chief of the international daily, *Haratch*, a woman who, childless and urban, inverts all the traditional iconography of Maia, the earth mother. She undisguisedly replaces the ties of nature with the bond of writing. "It doesn't take any woman very long to sound like the mother of all kids if she has none of her own. . . . Every issue of this paper *Haratch* is a new child, I suppose." She says she loves equally each issue of the newspaper she produces, just as a mother loves all her children alike. The word "issue" completes an associative circuit, equating periodical literature and biological progeny.

The densely material quality of writing in *Haratch* should make the reader distrust critics who impute to these plays a transcendental or Platonic-idealistic intention. Granted, *Haratch* recalls other great philosophical dialogues—More's *Utopia*, Diderot's *Rameau's Nephew*, Wilde's *The Critic as Artist*. Kouymjian notes that *Haratch* and Plato's *Symposium* follow parallel tracks, with "being Armenian" substituted for "love" as the subject, Paris for Athens, and whiskey for wine. But Plato would surely have balked at Saroyan's love for things of this earth, writing chief among them. Socrates abjures writing as the shadow of a shadow, a deceiving simulacrum of reality that blocks access to the higher world of invisible Ideas, a reproducible medium that destroys the human capacity to remember distant origins, obviates two-way exchange, and thus kills the philosophical dialectic. For Saroyan, precisely this solidity and reproducibility make writing the *sina qua non* for Armenians to recollect who they were and can be again.

Reviewers have belittled Saroyan's supposed sentimental idealism, but that charge merits scrutiny. North American reviewers have called Saroyan "the heir of a tradition which, among Americans of a more reflective or mystical temperament, has included Jefferson's ideal of human perfectibility, Emerson's Oversoul, Whitman's multitudinous Self,"[7] and "the tradition of American transcendentalism."[8] But such critics have mistaken Saroyan's purpose, at least on the late evidence these plays provide. When William Saroyan crashed the gates of ethnocentrism and taught American readers what "Armenian" meant, reviewers called him "Ethnic Naive." They judged the Aram stories, set in Fresno, as a sort of Grape Leaves of Wrath. Literary tastemakers condescended to a Saroyan who "had written so charmingly of his immigrant forebearers" in prose "smeared over with sticky sweetness." Because Saroyan wore the Armenian colors proudly, he fell easy prey to the syndrome that Edward Said has named "Orientalism": a cluster of atavistic labels that include sloth, mental weakness, irrationality, and emotional excess.

Some reviewers stuffed Saroyan into an American Transcendentalist raiment and snickered at the ill fit. James Agee wrote in *Time* magazine of Saroyan's "brassy, self-pitying, arty mawkishness" and dismissed him as a "schmalz-artist." Edmund Wilson bemoaned the "self-befuddling and self-protective fantasy" of his later works that were "surely some of the silliest nonsense ever published by a good writer." Thus colonized and shoved to the margins, Saroyan's work has evoked fewer critical studies than that of any American writer of comparable stature. Moreover, since Saroyan rapidly came to stand for all Armenians, the Orientalist cliches he attracted have shaped the experience of an entire people. How instructive, then, to observe that other-worldly, sentimental, aestheticized writing has its advocate: Zulal reveres Keats and the Armenian poet Harout Gostanian, who withdrew from the world, and forcefully demands an Armenian literature beyond the reach of politics. "What are we talking about? Is it poetry? Or is it politics?" he fumes, seeing high fences between two realms where there are, in fact, broad causeways. Again, asking "what is it that has real meaning for each of us?" Zulal sprints to his own conclusion: "Isn't it what we keep deepest inside, unconditionally ours, and not what gets itself forever entangled in politics, geography, history, race, religion, language, and back again to politics?" Yet the play finally endorses just the opposite sort of writing, a sort not only embedded in communal affairs—in the writer's "family, his race, his tribe, his history, his geography, his religion" and in "the language by means of which we find out, each of us, his reality, both natural and artful"—

but indeed a writing that has enough torque to repair nature's defects, to supply artificial limbs as good as those that history has lopped off.

Saroyan always held writing to be the most down-to-earth of activities. He remained in school just long enough to learn to type, and his first jobs as a wandering newsboy and as a telegraph messenger brought him an early enthusiasm for codes and the material production of words. At the beginning of his career, forty years earlier, Saroyan had written a stirring paean to a printing press: "It was a beautiful sight. I thought I hadn't seen anything more beautiful. Wordlessly I begged life to let me have some relation to the press. It was something man had made, something out of his own mind and restlessness, something apart from nature, and in its way greater than it. The press was black and massive and it made a noise that suggested events, the articulating of history."[9] Forty years after writing this hymn, Saroyan still reveres hot type. Printed language and the web of the text suggest themselves to him as ligatures that—emanating from restless minds—can operate "apart from nature, and in its way greater than it" to restore human connections that deportation and genocide have torn away. Throughout *Haratch* the characters contend that Armenians have a particular genius for cultural achievements and that these attainments make them—in sharp contrast to the Turks—a world historical people.

The *Trilogy* thus is not above making its own brief foray into Orientalist racism. We have been prodigal contributors to the arts and sciences, remarks the character Saroyan, while the Turks produce nothing. Inert, unproductive, intellectually dead, the Turks come perilously close to the Semitic stereotype that Western scholars have long propounded. "Saroyan" stuns the other characters by pitying the Turk and blessing the massacres. Indeed, he quite seriously proposes that the Turks suffered the greatest loss in the massacres; for as he explains, the disease of unconfessed guilt has rendered them cultur-ally impotent. Yet this brief lapse is Saroyan's only descent into mindless polemic: the reader is spared the sort of hysterical screed that most writers about genocide find it hard to suppress.

Whereas the Romantic and Armenian Transcendalist writers enshrined nature and—as Wordsworth put it—"the soul's inviolable retirement," Saroyan celebrates a Blakean forge, loud with the clatter of typewriters, the clamor of dialogue, and the clash of contending forces. Beneath the characters' poignant awareness that they remain only visitors, that their fortuitous, temporary, fragile *hunjook* (or *khnjoyk*, party) will soon end, they confidently assert the power of their own writing to last out the *longue durée*. The final moments serve as a fitting denouement, when Zulal observes, "the truth is that we are really only enjoying being at home, in a sense, for Armenians are never so at home as when they are in an editorial office and near printing presses. Whenever I am confused about who I am I go in the back and look at the four different black printing presses. I just look at them. What great faces and bodies they have, and what glorious work they are able to do."

When huge machines inspire tender emotion, we are bound to feel that love has undergone a weird metamorphosis. Yet the unearthly history that Armenians have survived justifies and explains such transmutations. How firmly these characters embrace casual companions, even like-minded strangers, as adequate substitutes for the natural genealogies of blood and soil.

In constructing a community "apart from nature and in a way greater than it, forged out of restlessness and mind," the *Armenian Trilogy* completes a life-long project and solves certain puzzles. Critics have wondered, for example, at the lapse in verisimilitude when, in *The Human Comedy*, "a wounded buddy of the dead soldier—fortuitously an orphan without ties—appears on the scene and quite literally takes the brother's place in the household as if nothing had happened."[10] The Trilogy enables us to see that this is more than a weak-minded "miracle," as critic William J. Fisher suggests.[11] Non-filial relationships often constitute an Armenian's most vital mode of being. One observes the same pattern in the story "Seventy Thousand Assyrians," where the "fragility of his national ties has freed the humble Assyrian barber to join the race of man, 'the part that massacre does not destroy,' " notes Margaret Bedrosian.[12] Frequently Saroyan's writing reconnects broken genealogies, restores the hacked limbs, revives "the screaming infants lit like candles"—though such a phrase (Balakian's) never came from Saroyan's pen. The progression is Vico's: first, the body, huge and uncontrolled; next, the poetic speech that restrains gigantic fears; finally, a society, wherein arts may flourish. Saroyan compresses this entire Vichean sequence into an early memoir on bicycling: "Moving the legs evenly and steadily soon brings to the rider a valuable knowledge of pace and rhythm. . . . The physical action compels action of another order—action of mind, memory, imagination, dream, hope, order. . . . I learned [my style] from things on which I moved, and as writing is a thing that moves I think I was lucky to learn as I did."[13] Physical action "compels" imaginative action, of which the final form is writing. And yet the further stage is the founding of a whole society. For as Saroyan remarks. "There is probably no Armenian in the world who cannot write. Armenian . . . is a language, in fact, evolved solely to hold its people together as a family."[14] Just as poetic language allows Vico's giants to reduce their fears and themselves to human form, language alone capably reduces the horrors of 1895 and 1915.

Although Saroyan founds no Rome and recovers no Ithaca, he returns at last to the greatest problems that every Armenian must face: What price assimilation, intermarriage, unlearning the Armenian language? Will the Soviet Armenian Republic sustain our culture or demolish it? Saroyan's genius for dialogue brings these questions to life. Such questions engage him deeply. An impassioned and nearly embarrassing honesty marks his ongoing dialogue, for example, with and against Michael J. Arlen. The oddest sort of tangled interchange occurs between them. Young enough to be Saroyan's son (Saroyan was indeed a friend of his father's), Arlen nonetheless published his narrative of return to Armenia before Saroyan completed his own. He shows the senior writer considerable deference. "Nobody could write to a person (me) the way that William Saroyan wrote," he remarks in an early chapter of *Passage to Ararat*. There Arlen represents Saroyan as a true literary progenitor: "It made one think with a kind of pleasure that J. D. Salinger must have heard that voice, and Richard Brautigan, and Jack Kerouac, and all those writers of the personal sound, the flower-writers, the writers of our modern Era of Feeling." This homage goes beyond professional respect: Arlen actually flies across the country to see the old writer. "I felt something surprisingly paternal in his voice," confides Arlen, recalling his pilgrimage to Fresno; "I could feel his rough cheek scrape against mine. His rough, robust cheek."[15]

As Freud and Nietzsche insist, however, parricidal impulses usually follow hard upon paternal worship. While the chapter devoted to Saroyan gives Arlen the strength to complete his book—the older man's blessing operates as a sort of fairy-tale talisman—the interlude also allows Arlen to put the old man aside once and for all. (Arlen is hardly the true heir of flower-writers from the Era of Feeling, but rather a polished analyst of popular culture, the television critic for so glossy a magazine as *The New Yorker*, and author of such trade books as *The Camera Age and Thirty Seconds*.) Literary critic Harold Bloom's theories about the "anxiety of influence" might help to illuminate Arlen's motives for putting Saroyan near the front of his book, a book as "focused as the uneasy bond between a father and a son" (as the jacket copy announces). A new work of literature can take shape only, remarks Bloom, when "an intolerable presence (the precursor's poem [or novel or play]) has been voided."[16] By depicting Saroyan in his own way Arlen neutralizes the overpowering influence or removes what Bloom calls the Covering Cherub who blocks Arlen's path to literary self-realization. Arlen chooses to conclude the encounter with a peculiarly subterranean scene. Having just completed a nocturnal jog among the rain-soaked Armenian tombstones in the Fresno cemetery, Arlen leaves for Yerevan and self discovery. Saroyan remains behind, little more at this point than a graveyard ghost. The symbolism will escape no one. Arlen has exorcised his paternal specter.

But patriarchal shades in literature rarely lie quiet for long. *Bitlis* and *Haratch* revive the paternal demand to "Remember me!" If Saroyan's plays represent the older man's resistance to Arlen, that fact at least clears up the major question that has troubled critics and editors: Why did Saroyan wait eleven years before writing his 1964 Armenian journey? "Had Saroyan's usually sharp memory faltered?" wonders Kouymjian, "or was the experience so unsettling he repressed it?" It seems likely that Saroyan's plays respond to Arlen's implicit challenge.

The dates reveal much. Arlen's *Passage to Ararat* appeared as a three-part "Profile" in the *New Yorker* in February 1975. Saroyan read the piece intently (Kouymjian has written that he was "struck" by the work) and in

March, the next month, he wrote *Bitlis*. Although Kouymjian has studied Saroyan's reaction and quotes from a letter in which the senior writer praises Arlen's book somewhat ambiguously—"these things need luck," Saroyan concludes—the editor seems reluctant to explore the agonistic competition that engaged these two writers. In *Haratch* Saroyan offers a critical and somewhat reductive account of Arlen's book, suggesting that Saroyan's own play is in part an answer to Arlen—an alternative pilgrimage that seeks to revise Arlen's impressions. In *Haratch* Saroyan remarks, "We [the Armenians] lost all our wars, and according to Michael J. Arlen in *Passage to Ararat* the truth has given us a terrible inferiority complex, and he also put forward the theory that we refuse to forget the crime of genocide inflicted upon us by Turkey because we have profound self-hatred, and don't know what else to do to somehow deliver ourselves from this destructive condition. We are losers and hate ourselves for not being winners." This headlong diatribe exaggerates Arlen's rather innocuous story of self-discovery. A literary father is responding with some violence to the son who has dared both to inherit and to usurp. But strong poets protect themselves by misreading their precursors, and the peculiar chronology that placed Arlen's book before the master's undoubtedly explains the involuted response.

Kouymjian's minor lapses aside, the volume reflects Saroyan's regard for the printed word. Carefully proofread and supported by excellent scholarly documentation, the volume offers such unexpected dividends as an Armenian-to-English glossary and fifty-five black-and-white plates depicting Saroyan's Armenian journeys, friends, pen-and-ink sketches, and holograph papers. The plays are brilliantly situated by Kouymjian's thirty-eight page introduction. The edition heralds, in short, a new maturity in Saroyan studies. The care lavished on this text bodes well for the many still unpublished Saroyan works housed at California State University at Fresno. Whereas the *Trilogy* brings forward an author long obscured by patronizing, uncomprehending, and ethnocentric North American critics, the cogent analysis of writing and homelessness that emerges here also demonstrates how Saroyan's worldly and secular vision ties his work to that of a younger generation of Armenian-American writers as well as to Palestinian and other third-world intellectuals. The present volume constitutes a mandate to reevaluate Saroyan's earlier writings. In giving us this surprisingly politicized portrait, the *Trilogy* allows Saroyan to remain somehow ineffably himself, open as ever to every experience. Consider his pilgrimage. A perusal of Said's *Orientalism* makes it evident that such sojourns are the classic way in which Westerners have approached the East, for in this mode the sovereign ego of narrator moves through proliferating wonders and exotic details only to emerge all the more completely in control. When Arlen reached Yerevan, he followed the Napoleonic Orientalists' pattern. Steeped in the literature, knowing the culture, he looked; and seeing only himself, Arlen stayed in his Yerevan hotel room, studying the Armenian history books he had brought along and avoiding his Armenian guide, Sarkis. Saroyan drove into Bitlis, perspiring freely, heart pounding, then walked through Tsapergor shouting "Bitlis, Bitlis, Bitlis." He clowned with a performing bear, hugged the villagers, and vowed to write a commemorating play—less a pilgrim than an exile, hemmed by scarlet shades, and yet in that shadow of shadows, in his Armenian writings, definitively at home.

Notes

1. Michael J. Arlen, *Passage to Ararat* (New York: Farrar, Straus & Giroux, 1975), 48.

2. *William Saroyan: My Name is Saroyan*, edited with a Commentary by James H. Tashjian (New York: Coward-McCann, 1983), 13–36.

3. Aram Saroyan, *William Saroyan* (New York: Harcourt Brace Jovanovich, 1983), 108.

4. Peter Balakian. "In the Turkish Ward," *Sad Days of Light* (New York: Sheep Meadow Press, 1983), 23–26.

5. Edward Said, *The Question of Palestine* (New York: Vintage, 1980), 174.

6. Idem, "Permission to Narrate," *London Review of Books* (February 16–29, 1984): 16.

7. William J. Fisher. "What Ever Happened to Saroyan?" *College English* (March 1985): 340, 336.

8. D. Keith Mano, "Gnomic Naive," *National Review* (May 12, 1968): 600.

9. *Hairenik Daily*, Dec. 12, 1933, quoted in *My Name is Saroyan*, 66.

10. Fisher, 338.

11. Ibid.

12. Margaret Bedrosian, "William Saroyan and the Family Matter," MELUS, (The Society for the Study of Multi-Ethnic Literature of the United States) 9:4 (Winter 1982): 13–14.

13. *The Bicycle Rider of Beverly Hills* (London: Faber & Faber, Ltd., 1953), 19–20.

14. *My Name is Saroyan*, 300.

15. *Passage to Ararat*, 47, 48, 64.

16. Harold Bloom, *A Map of Misreading* (New York: Oxford University Press, 1975), 71.

The Unforgettable and the Ordinary in Saroyan's Last "Voyald"

Walter Cummins*

Despite William Saroyan's claim that he is "profoundly realistic," for Peter Sourian "the best of Saroyan's . . . writing keeps the real world out and thus maintains the fabulous integrity of the Saroyan world—with everything larger than life."[1] Leo Hamalian considers Saroyan a religious writer because of "his talent for transforming and illuminating by his own special inner radiance anything that is drawn into the sacred circle of his imagination."[2]

Nevertheless, in his 1956 collection *The Whole Voyald and Other Stories* (the last collection published in his lifetime),[3] rather than excluding or transforming "the real world," Saroyan's characters confront their reality with gratuitous challenges. Their goal is not a spiritual transcendence. Instead, they seek to demonstrate superiority to the ordinary, to make themselves meaningful by proving that their existence is special. The rare people who are truly worthy take pains to demonstrate that they are "unforgettable" and "famous."

In the story "Love for London," the narrator, a newspaper vendor, announces to a friend and customer that he intends to walk into the new Liberty Theatre to a see a film called *While London Sleeps* on its opening night without paying the admission fee. The year is 1918 and the narrator has netted a dollar and a quarter profit for the day. "I could well afford to pay the ten-cent admission" (32), he tells the reader.

The rest of the story is a description of the process of getting in, the narrator "keeping an eye on the girl in the ticket booth," lingering at exit doors for an opportunity to slip inside, eluding the usher, and finally finding a seat. Not only does he see "the whole show—on Opening Day, just as I had planned—free"; the very next night he invites a friend to sneak in with him all over again. The story's final sentence offers a facetious explanation of his conduct: "I was always crazy about London, I guess" (38).

Of course, the real reason for the narrator's behavior is the challenge itself, proving that he can outsmart the system and the dullards of authority.

---

*This essay was written specifically for this volume and is published here for the first time by permission of the author.

The usher, a man in uniform, becomes the antagonist, driven by his duty to chase the rule breaker, seizing him by the elbow and expelling him in his first attempt, demanding his ticket stub in his second, only to have the narrator "break away from his grip and run," leaving the usher blocked and helpless behind a group of patrons.

The issue of this story is neither the need of a penniless young man to strike out against an unfeeling society, nor the conflict of art versus material deprivation. Instead, this narrator wants to prove the bravado of his public announcement. He is a smart aleck, a rogue, a version of the *picaro*, though, unlike the traditional *picaro*, he is not a victim battling the forces of oppression but rather the one who casts the usher as an oppressor, creating an arbitrary confrontation. It's not a matter of achieving justice, but rather of outwitting the system and proving—to himself and others—an ability to control the circumstances of his world.

The narrator's arrogance would tend to alienate most people. He opposes authority, breaks rules, lives according to a standard that violates the norm. From most perspectives, he doesn't deserve to succeed because he threatens assumptions that the rest of us are supposed to respect. But Saroyan— through tone and attitude—makes him a winner. Because this figure masters life, he affirms a new set of values: the person who gets away with acts of rebellion, whose behavior mocks the mundane, matters more than those who accept and follow the rules.

Variations of this newspaper vendor appear frequently in the stories that make up *The Whole Voyald*, either as protagonists or as admired people who demonstrate assertive independence. Not every story has an usher, a foil, to play off against the rogue; but the majority assume that the rebel is superior to the mass of mankind.

This distinction seems contrary to the popular notion of Saroyan as affirming all humanity, embracing the down-and-out, a writer who skirts the edges of sentimentality by considering nothing human as alien to him. For Nona Balakian, "Saroyan's people seem to exist for the purpose of establishing the fraternity of man."[4] William J. Fisher takes a similar stance, celebrating the "concept of restored individuality [that] governed Saroyan's principal attitudes, his impulsive iconoclasm as well as his lyrical optimism,"[5] even while finding this perspective limiting simplifying. But the treatment of the usher is hardly an affirmation of human fraternity; if it helps the narrator exhibit his individuality, that exhibition comes at the cost of another's. Saroyan appears to be selective in forging a brotherhood, finding some people much more worthy of admission than others.

The integrity of the nonconformist is glorified at the expense of those who confirm to the bland guidelines of the norm. To judge the values behind this antagonism is to raise a fundamental question about how to respond to a Saroyan story. Because these fictions are so often essayistically autobiographical,[6] most critics have found it difficult to separate the fiction from the man. But what does that man represent? Philip Rahv, in an early review of *The Daring Young Man on the Flying Trapeze,* calls Saroyan "prolix, naive and egocentric."[7] But Frederick I. Carpenter turns the terms of Rahv's negative assessment into virtues by designating Saroyan an American transcendentalist: "Like Whitman, he celebrates himself and his America, but above all the America of his dreams. Not only his personality and his method suggest the good gray poet, but most of all his philosophy and his moral values are those of Whitman, Emerson, and the American transcendental tradition [. . .] Perhaps Saroyan's combination of egotism, originality, and integrity may best be described by the old phrase 'self-reliance.' "[8] Nevertheless, Saroyan's egotism in *The Whole Voyald* differs from Whitman's collective celebration of humankind through the "Song of Myself" ("In all people I see myself, none more and not one a barley-corn less, / And the good or bad I say of myself I say of them.") The stance taken by Saroyan's characters is much more defensive. While Whitman identifies himself with others, the characters in these stories use others to verify themselves. In some cases, they defeat adversaries to demonstrate their superiority; in others, they elevate those who populate their worlds as a means of elevating themselves.

Of all the stories in *The Whole Voyald,* "The Home of the Human Race," which follows the introductory essay, is quintessential Saroyan in technique, tone, and attitude. The story is more essay than narrative, a thesis demonstrated through a compilation of dramatic character sketches that reveal how the author discovered the human race in Fresno: "What was the human race I discovered in Fresno? It was my family, my neighbors, my friends, the teachers at school, the classmates, the strangers in the streets, and myself: most of all myself, and the strangers who were not strangers, who could not be strangers because I saw them, recognized them, knew them" (15). He tells of his mother's cousin, Hovagim Saroyan, one of his first heroes, who lost a wife to death and two sons who went to live with her family, and yet "No one was so fiercely devoted to kindness and to truth as this lonely man" (17). Scrawny old Mr. Huff, with a forbidding black eye patch, another lonely man, became a friend of the ten-year-old Saroyan, "a good man, a helpless one, an earnest one, my neighbor, my friend, my contemporary" (20). He adds a barefoot boy in his school and others worthy of meaning.

Beyond getting to know people, he learned that human meaning is achieved through the inventions or discoveries of art. He wanted to believe that these "strangers" were not truly hopeless. Through art he could overcome hopelessness. Nevertheless, his reason for dignifying them in his writing is less to affirm their dignity than to assure his own value: "If *they* were hopeless, then of course so was I, and I didn't want to be hopeless" (16).

The goal of all this compassion, then, is ultimately personal and egotistical. The value found in the lives of others is actually a verification of his own value. The challenge of the artist is to create meaning, and in doing so to control experience by giving it a point. Perhaps the Saroyan who violated the rules of the well-made story was setting up a deliberate challenge by handicapping himself with an apparent randomness, only to triumph by making it all cohere in the end. It's like breaking into a movie theatre when you have more than enough money to buy a ticket and could have followed the crowd through the normal entry route.

Saroyan says as much in the essay that serves as an introduction to the collection, "A Writer's Declaration," in which he boasts of his unwillingness to accept editors' requests for revisions, of his huge debt in back taxes, of his gambling losses, of his refusal to write for money despite all that he owes. He scorns financial security and is offended by the compulsion to hoard money. He regrets not one word he has written in the first twenty years of his career. He announces that he set out to revolutionize American writing and that his main contribution to writing in general is freedom. He will not live according to anyone else's standards: "The writer is a spiritual anarchist, as in the depth of his soul every man is. He is discontented with everything and everybody. The writer is everybody's best friend and only true enemy—the good and great enemy. He neither walks with the multitude nor cheers with them. The writer who is a writer is a rebel who never stops. He does not conform for the simple reason that there is nothing yet worth conforming to" (14). This romantic vision of the artist differs from Shelley's "unacknowledged legislators of the Universe," "the wisest, the happiest, and the best" of men, whose poetry "strips the veil of familiarity from the world, and lays bare the naked and sleeping beauty, which is the spirit of its forms."[9] In contrast to Shelley's artist, who finds universal truths by delving within, Saroyan's artist uses external truths as a path to discover the essence of self. "I think [artistic creation] is an obsession to get to the probable truth about man, nature, and arts, straight through everything to the very core of *one's own* being" (12).

In this introductory essay Saroyan reveals himself as a foe of the ordinary, denying the average. But he also sends a contradictory message. Defending himself against critics who accuse his writing of being "unrealistic and sentimental," he asserts that he considers his writing to be "profoundly realistic" and not sentimental, "although it is a very sentimental thing to be a human being" (8). At the heart of the contradiction lies the evidence of the stories in which the only lives worthy of sentimental regard are those that pass a test of rebellion and noble suffering. Money hoarders and ushers are not sentimental things, nor are teachers and principals.

In "The Failure of Friends," the latter get little sympathy. The story tells of an episode at Longfellow Junior High School when the eleven-year-old Saroyan was a student in Miss Shenstone's ancient history class. This teacher, though a drab forty, has the reputation for being fast—smoking, laughing, engaging in horseplay. Saroyan challenges her the very first day of class, asking how she knows that Stonehenge is 20,000 years old. She reacts with outrage, and he runs from the room directly to the principal, Mr. Monsoon, to explain his case. The principal tells him, "Nobody but an Armenian would have asked a question like that." Instead of being praised for his brilliance, as he had expected, the boy is threatened with a thrashing. He bolts from the school building and runs home to tell his story to Uncle Alecksander, a law student. The uncle negotiates a settlement with teacher and principal. The teacher will seek an answer to the Stonehenge question, and William will ask future questions with more respect.

"I felt sure," Saroyan tells us, "the principal and the teacher would one day remember how handsomely I had behaved in this unfortunate affair, but as I've said, they didn't, and so I have *had* to" (30). In fact, the teacher disappears from the school after another four days, and the principal left after a month. Saroyan himself transferred to Tech High to learn how to type.

Both Miss Shenstone and Mr. Monsoon are like the usher, authority figures defeated by the challenge of the rogue and, in this case, his shrewd uncle. Together they beat the system, here institutionalized education, which accepts the assertions of textbooks and doesn't think to question. However, Longfellow High is far from Dickens' Dotheboys Hall. It's not sadistically abusive, only unimaginative. The teacher began as a lively woman, the principal as a man resigned to an unpleasant duty. Yet the encounter with Saroyan as a boy defeats them, and the narrator treats their fate with wry detachment rather than sentimentality, implying that they got what they deserved for being so limited.

"The Failure of Friends" deals with a time many years before the author became William Saroyan, the public figure. That notion leads to a brief consideration in the third paragraph of all the other William Saroyans' including a distant cousin nicknamed Bill, whose real name, Hoosik, means Hopeless: "He is not the dashing, attractive fellow I am, carries a briefcase, wears glasses, and moves about on flat feet. He has been to the university, though, and appears to have cut quite a figure among politicians and procurement officers. I do not mind the man's imposture and say to him, 'Better luck next time' " (24). This passage exemplifies the double-edged approach, mingling superiority and sentimentality, that allows Saroyan to get away with this stance. Here he is both self-deprecating and smug at the same time. The effect is that of an Escher drawing; close one eye and it is one thing, close the other and it is something else. Saroyan appears to be laughing at himself. Yet Hoosik, with his briefcase, shares a similar status with school teachers and principals, those drab agents of officialdom.

The people with whom Saroyan admires and sympathizes are those who live at the edge of a social system they can't beat and yet gain insights into the heart of things. In addition to "The Home of the Human Race," Saroyan presents such characters in the day laborers of "The Winter Vineyard Workers." The fifteen-year-old narrator, now expelled from Fresno High, joins with Señor Tapia, two younger Mexicans, and a Japanese man named Ito, who constantly describes himself as *baggarro*, sorrowful, because thirty years before he had killed and buried a man after a quarrel over a card game. The group discusses guilt, wealth, and the "poverty, pain, sorrow, hunger, and anger" in the art of Orozco that Saroyan found reproduced in a magazine. Señor Tapia identifies the universal rage of a man in one of the water colors with Ito's *baggarro*. This story illustrates Saroyan's conviction that art can get to "the probable truth" (12), and does it though the insight and essential dignity of people society would reject as losers. The concluding sentence sums up the value of these people: "In the common language of workers many things were said during that month, a few of them unforgettable" (66).

For Saroyan, those who say or do something unforgettable are people of true worth, and the only ones capable of such remarkable achievements are the outcasts, rogues, and rebels, those who transcend the rules of the commonplace. In many of the stories of *The Whole Voyald*, the victory of the eccentric comes at the expense of people who uphold the ordinary. But in others, unconventionality flourishes without the foil of an antagonist. The unusual behavior contrasts not with a single person but with the norm, the expected way of doing things.

"The Idea in the Back of My Brother's Head" tells of how Henry, the sixteen-year-old brother of the thirteen-year-old narrator, has his own notions of unique achievement. He decides to improve the functioning of the family's Model-T Ford. It turns out that he is learning about automobile mechanics by disassembling this engine. When the car is running again, he will drive his younger brother to San Francisco and spend the thirty dollars he has saved. Yet the reassembled engine will not start, and the brothers turn to Shag Kluckjian, already a legendary mechanic at age nineteen, to correct Henry's many mistakes. Henry offers to pay him the thirty dollars, but Kluck returns the money and the brothers head off on their adventure, the narrator "excited about the great idea I had in the back of my head about getting out there in the great world and doing something unforgettable" (58).

This story, like "The Failure of Friends," is specifically antieducation in its antiestablishment manner. Experience is the only true teacher, whether it's Henry's idea of taking apart the engine or the narrator wish to experience the great world. While Henry works on the car, a peacock belonging to the multimillionaire who owns the square block across the street comes out to the street and screams. When an uncle asks Henry why the bird screams, Henry explains, "He's *got* to." That necessity motivates both brothers. They have got to do something unforgettable (the same word applied to the laborers' conversations in "The Winter Vineyard Workers"). And in the story they succeed: the car ends up functioning; the boys set off into the great world; Kluck extracts no price. Rewards come without cost to those who are unique and true to themselves.

This concern for doing something unforgettable is echoed in the word "famous" in "A Visitor in the Piano Warehouse," a whimsical story in which a narrator named Ashland Clewpor takes a job working in a piano warehouse for Oliver Morgan Spezzafly, the sixty-nine-year-old scion of the family that founded the Sligo, Baylie music store. The names of the characters alone make it clear that Saroyan is writing a fable here, a version of a fairy-tale test. According to the girl in personnel, despite the promise of an five dollar raise after every month of employment, no one can work with Mr. Spezzafly. Ashland turns out to have no duties, just to sit at a desk and await Mr. Spezzafly's bidding. Because Ashland has no expectations, they get on famously, and Ashland proposes to the girl in personnel, but she is married. He visits her once a week, and each time she offers him another more normal job with the firm that he turns down. It turns out that Mr. Spezzafly's singlemost goal is to have a visitor in the warehouse, and finally a Miss Stella Mayhew appears. Ashland falls in love with her immediately, and Mr. Spezzafly approves of the union. At the end, Ashland, married and a father, still works in the warehouse and still turns down opportunities for standard employment. Spezzafly, the man with the reputation of a ogre, turns out to be a sweetheart for the person who understands how to interact with him.

The characters exist in a small and limited world, but Ashland calls them all "famous," explaining to the girl in personnel, "Now, being famous the way famous people are famous is not *really* being famous, but being famous the way Mr. Spezzafly's famous, that's being really famous. And a few others I know" (118). Frothy as this story is, it's consistent with the principle that relates all the stories in the collection. The truly worthy person follows a unique personal standard that defies the ordinary way of doing things, whether that uniqueness come from sneaking into a movie, disassembling an engine, or challenging a teacher. The people Saroyan makes famous in his fiction are too special to be appreciated by the mundane world; only those who understand true worth will realize their value. Their fame is apparent only to the exceptional few who are equally deserving.

The story that concludes this collection, "The Whole Voyald and Heaven Itself," opens with a boy up in a tree looking down at the world spread out below him as his father climbs their secret path and tells him they are moving on. The boy must part from his new and only friend, Greg Alakhalkhala. He broods a bit but resumes the spirit of comradeship in adventure he feels with his father. They have left mother and sister for a life on the road in an old Ford Ranch wagon in which they sleep, getting by on minimal cash, with just twenty dollars left at the time of the story. They rarely stay in one place more than a month. As the father tells him, "We live everywhere." And at the end of the story the boy, having caught fish for that night's dinner, agrees that their new location *"was* Heaven": "I was glad my father had come and got me out of the tree in San Francisco and brought me here to the beach at Morro Bay.

And I was glad that we lived in a Ranch Wagon and the whole voyald, instead of in a house stuck in the mud somewhere" (242–43).

Though not the extreme fairy tale of "A Visitor in the Piano Warehouse," this story too has the atmosphere of a wish fulfillment, the small boy's fantasy of perpetual adventure with his father, one step beyond the trip into the great world that concludes "The Idea in the Back of My Brother's Head." Father and son, with their fish and trees and secret paths, are doing something unforgettable. They have abandoned the trap of living in the same world as ushers and teachers. Like the narrator who walked into a movie just because he felt like it, they do what they want to do when they want to do it, and they pay no price. They live in a world where they make the rules and no authority figures can inhibit the freedom of their whims.

Even though no one else is aware of their activities, this father and son are "famous" in their own realm. Like the protagonists of the other stories in *The Whole Voyald and Other Stories*, they prove their superiority to the mundane majority. For Saroyan in this collection the truly unforgettable are those who violate the tedious norms of society and flaunt their eccentricities.

Notes

1.   Peter Sourian, "The Armenian Buffalo Bill" in Leo Hamalian, ed. *William Saroyan: The Man and the Writer Remembered* (Rutherford: FDU Press, 1987), 59.

2.   Hamalian, "Preface," in *William Saroyan: The Man and Writer Remembered*, ed. Leo Hamalian (Rutherford: FDU Press, 1987), 14.

3.   *The Whole Voyald and Other Stories*. (Boston and Toronto: Little, Brown / Atlantic Monthly, 1956). All pages references are to this work.

4.   Nona Balakian, in *Edward Halsey Foster, William Saroyan: A Study of the Short Fiction* (New York: Twayne Publishers, 1991), 142.

5.   William J. Fisher, in Foster, 145.

6.   Foster, 68–69.

7.   Philip Rahv, in Foster, 117.

8.   Frederick I. Carpenter, in Foster, 120.

9.   Percy Bysshe Shelley, "A Defense of Poetry" in Charles Kaplan, ed. *Criticism: The Major Statements*. Second edition. (New York: St.Martin's Press, 1986), 332–35.

Not Dying: Theme in Saroyan's Memoirs

Walter Shear*

Five days before his death, William Saroyan called the Associated Press with this statement: "Everybody has got to die, but I have always believed an exception would be made in my case. Now what?" Much of Saroyan is here—the monstrous ego, simultaneously outrageous and self-mocking, the keen awareness of the media's importance in contemporary culture, and the totally personal response to what most would regard as simply universal fate.

What is perhaps most peculiar is the manner in which the remark fits into an 18-year project conducted in a series of memoirs whose culmination, *Obituaries*, forms an apology (in the traditional sense of defense) conducted in a postmodern mode. In its initial phase, the series is so casual as to belie both the intensity of interest Saroyan will display in developing his theme and the long, buried background which will surface periodically in reminiscences evidencing a lifelong preoccupation. The third volume opens with this exchange:

INTERVIEWER: To what do you attribute your old age?

SAROYAN: Not dying.[1]

Even in 1963 this was an old joke and Saroyan probably did not consider himself to have reached "old age" at the time. (He was 55.) But, ever the instinctive writer, Saroyan with his exchange has uncovered his final obsession, and it is with a growing awareness of death's power that he begins to flesh out his life in the volumes that would follow.

Random statements in his fiction and drama suggest that death had been a recurrent theme throughout his career, perhaps stemming from the trauma of his father's death when Saroyan was three and his being placing subsequently, with his brothers and sisters, in an orphanage. Biographers Lee and Gifford note that "at first Willie could not be convinced that Takoohi [his mother] might not vanish as completely as [his father] had done."[2] Another biographer, his son Aram, has argued that "death without a name proved to be the most powerful and fundamental experience of Saroyan's

*This essay was written specifically for this volume and is published here for the first time by permission of the author.

life."³ Saroyan's most extensive academic critic, David Stephen Calonne, observed that in his last works Saroyan seemed "quite literally fighting off death itself."⁴

Only in the memoirs does the theme of not dying emerge as a direct, vital creative impulse, the phrase itself capable of multiple meanings—an excuse, a strategy for holding off the world, a rationale for working, a program and justification for a kind of living, a glimpse of finality that becomes a meditation upon life. It was in the second volume of memoirs, *Here Comes There Goes You Know Who*, that a happy egotistic younger author declared, almost with a flourish, "the purpose of my life is to put off dying as long as possible."⁵ In the volumes that followed Saroyan worked to accomplish this purpose in seemingly rational, discursive prose, trying on a cognitive level, utilizing language as simply and deliberately an articulation of the psyche, to clarify his own confusions about himself and his world. At this time in his life, the 1960s through the 1970s, Saroyan was going through a series of personal crises involving the breakdown of family relationships, the disappearance of his creative talent for fiction, and his gradual fading as a literary figure.

Not Dying, the significant title of the third memoir, ultimately suggests its opposite, that at a deeper level Saroyan as a writer is dying and he knows it. On a structural level the scattering of interviews throughout the book demonstrates his concern at the time (1963) with his popularity as a writer, his public image and his audience. This concern would not become explicit until *Obituaries*, the last volume of the series, where he notes that if you fail to get publicity for "two or three years people tend to believe you have died."⁶ But already in *Not Dying* the prospect of failure seems to inexorably generate a sense of what Saroyan elsewhere called the ultimate failure, death. In *Not Dying*, rejection functions as an ultimate category, with Saroyan imagining death as the audience which he must trick "into letting me stay a little longer" (14–15). He claims he must "demonstrate . . . how I . . . can do something that is likely to be fascinating, or at any rate appealing, to death itself," perhaps feeling that the personification functions as much to hold anxiety at bay as it does to express his situation.

The basic metaphor for the entire series of memoirs becomes the struggle against nothing less than obliteration, an obsession that grows more familiar without losing its compelling power. By *Obituaries* the potency of death as ultimate rejection has grown into "total effacement of memory, of the vast stored 'life' experienced, dreamed, imagined, wished, witnessed in reality. . . . Death takes on that instant totality which nothing else ever takes on" (7). "Death is everything, man; death is not just a little part of everything, it is the whole thing, but of course what we mean is that life and death are together" (9). And it is the violence of this force to which Saroyan as writer feels twice exposed: "The dying of the man, the breaking down of the machine that produces the art . . . is the lesser of the two dyings that are in store for everybody who goes out to compete . . . to accept rivals and to run with them in the short races and in the long races" (346). The implication of the competitive metaphor is that this has always been the case, that the act of, the doing of, writing is not dying and further that from the beginning not dying is for the literary man writing. This also involves one consistent perception: that writing as this kind of activity must court and forever face the fact of dying.

Although Saroyan rather consistently upholds the value of skepticism—"All people who believe something or other to the exclusion of doubt about all things have got to be lousy writers"—he reminds both himself and the reader that a writer's faith in himself is crucial (*Not Dying*, 83). Early in the series, he uses the example of a failed writer, Owen Francis, to draw a moral for himself: "the thing that killed the man . . . was the fact that he didn't believe in his writing, *couldn't* believe in it" (12). Saroyan seems constantly aware that to be successful, to be involved wholeheartedly in the process of not dying, he must convince himself that "it is lucky to be a writer," that "there is something to say," and he must "fight off every day's impulse to find this theory false."[7] Inevitably, Saroyan found himself both articulating his despair and vowing to overcome it.

In the course of proving his capability, warding off total rejection, Saroyan conducts a public investigation of the spiritual pain and essential health within himself. The sheer number of books in the memoir series—eight—is, of course, evidence that he could be optimistic, periodically envisioning for himself a "scheme of procedure by which [he found] himself acceptable and therefore capable of a life of enjoyment" (50). In this stage of Whitmanesque exuberance he could regard even death as "a great personal triumph . . . and all forms of *failure* sources of great power, wisdom, and meaning" (51). In these moods, acting as the inspired memoirist, he would imagine a point from which his "past [might] be found useful to him, to have been useful to him, so that now he is on the threshold of an order of himself which must find human reality a very simple unavoidable majesty and joy . . ." (51). Most of the time, however, he merely argued with himself for a modicum of contentment: "A writer has a right to be pleased that he has found his work and is able to do it" (39).

His dark nights of the soul were extremely black and more and more persistent. The failure of his marriage, his feeling that his children had turned against him, the fading of his dream of family life exacerbated his sense of a writer's loneliness: "In a sense I suppose the thing I don't believe is that I am alive at all. . . . the fact is everything of an external kind that I expected I got, such as fame and money, but it always turned out to be only for myself, and that had never really been the idea" (26–27). One memoir, *Letters from 74 Rue Taitbout*, dredges up a variety of characters who are lost, lonely, and / or in a "state of spiritual shock." They encourage Saroyan to look at himself as a person suddenly "without home, continuity, and meaning. I was without myself, my own ghost. I was cut down. I was in fact dead. But I *seemed* to be alive. . . ."[8] In this mood he is haunted by visions of death-in-life. In one instance, seeing one of his former witty old school friends operating an elevator, Saroyan imagines asking him, "What killed you, old pal?" (68).

Saroyan's more prosaic reasons for writing fit into a vision of the world and the self in flux, humankind always "arriving and departing." Thus there was a value simply in recording facts, thoughts, and events: "a man knows all too little about what happened, for having left it all to the accidents of memory" (*Days*, 49, 46). His definition of the journal writer—one who "is obsessed by the wish to know what happened . . . the only way he can ever hope to know is to have the written daily account to consult at his convenience"—seems to demonstrate uncertainty, the reaching for some anchor (23).

Significantly, however, only one of his memoirs, *Days of Life and Death*, takes the form of a journal. To "know what happened" was the problem, not the solution. At this stage of his life Saroyan was becoming extremely anxious about placing himself for posterity. Aware of this anxiety, he tried to harness its energy for the purposes of art. His stylistic gifts had always included the ability to dramatize the movement of his mind, and in the crises that are the memoirs he consciously revolts against the constraints of rhetorical form with contradictions, abrupt shifts of thought, digressions, repeated confessions of uncertainty—all seemingly part of a desperate hope that improvised thought would uncover hidden truths. As a result, the movement toward defining significance, coming to conclusions, even accepting the value of the self, seems never ending. Writing, thinking, evaluating—all undoubtedly forms of not dying—become pure process.

Versions of the self appear and disappear. At one time Saroyan is convinced the individual alone knows the significance of his own life and even if he were to write it down, it might be only "personal, private, useless," (though "fascinating") to other people (111, 112). The idea that some basic meaning can never be communicated is a fearful suspicion for a memoir writer, but what makes the concept particularly frustrating is the fact that earlier in the same book Saroyan had seemingly solved this problem, by concluding that all human experience had a common root in its relationship to mortality. The latter notion in fact seems the key empowering assumption in the series. But not until *Obituaries* does he begin to put such ideas together: "We are all one another, but we don't like the idea . . ." (75–76).

Throughout the series Saroyan's shifting and sorting of such ideas and his changes of mood create abrupt twists in development, emphasis, and conclusion. The best of Saroyan's other work suggests that life is essentially serendipitous and that it is only our mule-headedness that insists otherwise, but the memoirs go further in this direction by focusing on randomness. It is writing that both articulates and dramatizes the arbitrary. In *Not Dying* he talks about the writer he used to be, one who expected to change the world because it was not right: "[The world] is chaos . . . and a kid can't cherish chaos. He wants order. He wants balance. He wants rightness" (194). In abandoning this project in his maturity, Saroyan began to notice similarities between writing and one of his favorite pastimes, gambling: "You can never predict what the stuff is going to be; you work and wait for it" (35, 45). Now he concludes that even memory is arbitrary: "it works its own wheel, and stops where it will, entirely without reference to the last stop, and with no connection with the next" (9). From its inception, life has been a gamble: that family we encounter at birth and are bound to for life—these folks, he argues, are "not the people any of us, had we indeed had a choice, might be likely to have chosen. These meetings are chance meetings" (1).

He further notes that an element of chance is generated simply by volume of work: "writing every day you couldn't possibly not say something at least once a year" (*Days*, 22). And he wonders about the power of "careless words," which often "have more meaning than the writer could ever have known when he wrote them (*Days*, 46, 47). He concludes that we are all relatively ignorant of the basic facts of personal existence: "We don't know anything accurate about any given day or hour of mortality, of being somebody, each of us, ever . . ." (*Obituaries*, 120). And Saroyan himself grows more detached from basic values. In *Days of Life and Death* he awakens "to remember the world, I am not in love with it, and I am not in love with the human race . . . I'm just there in the morning" (69). Finally he is content not to push material into shape: "Any writer . . . getting along in years and feeling it enough to know he can't do what he used to do . . . [should] take it slow and easy," like taking "a walk without a purpose or destination, free, spontaneous, and therefore satisfying" (38).

Saroyan recognizes the value of "remembering systematically by time and place" for a record, a formal memoir, autobiography, or history, but he objects that this "kind of sensible order does not exist in nature, is not permitted to exist in nature" (*Chance*, 124). In the world of Saroyan's memoirs "anybody connects almost instantly with everybody," and anything with everything (*Obituaries*, 92). By choice or chance, the titles of many of the books themselves suggest connections and frameworks for connections: places, days, letters, chance meetings, even, as he regards them, obituaries. In *Letters from 74 Rue Taitbout*, Saroyan addresses a variety of people, most of whom he knew only vaguely, generating in these monologues some oblique meditations on the value of any human contact.

Days of Life and Death uses the journal form to meditate on time. In it Saroyan envisions significance as a frustratingly gradual unfolding: "I have always been determined to know what happened. This instant is too swift to be understood. Tomorrow it will begin to have its proportion and meaning, but a year from tomorrow its real meaning will begin to be clear, and ten years from now it will be a useful part of a still unfolding form whose design will continue to the end" (137). Man's plight is thus to understand the deeper significance of the events of his life only as these events recede with time.

Obituaries, the culmination of this group, looks at death as the basic arbitrary fact of life, "a strange order of event," and responds to it with an extremely arbitrary form of writing. The book has no paragraphs and is organized in 135 chapters of nearly equal length, eighty lines of ten words each, the length of the typing sheets which were cut for him. The sequential pattern for this organization is provided by *Variety*'s alphabetical listing of the show business dead for 1976. Such a mechanical organization not only emphatically rejects a narrative sense of history, it oddly creates the kind of open form of which Saroyan was always fond: "it is a demonstration of life to write about just about everything that is there or comes along—for that is the way we live, the way we stay alive, from minute to minute" (181). Nonetheless, it is a procedure which, in its very arbitrariness, creates a responsibility: "it is my work to notice and remember everybody on the list whom I know, and to say whatever I must say about everybody else . . ." (96). As a source of inspiration, the name of the person on the list is regarded as "a magic if mysterious symbol . . . of something for which there is really no adequate word: a life going on, a life ceased" (45), as if the dead could provide the mysterious shock for awakening themselves or alternately, confirm the kind of finality death signifies.

Getting this close and this attentive to death inspires in Saroyan a naked honesty, for "there is no protection for anybody in the human family, and indeed in any animal family—from death, that is" (320). But the book is both a confrontation of and evasion of death. In this text death is social rather than physical, an event that paradoxically intensifies a relationship between people. Though God may control biological life and death, existence itself is a mysterious interaction of individuals and societies. In this context the flatness of the mechanical arrangement of Saroyan's essay may be intended ultimately as the exorcism of those glamorous cultural demons that tormented Saroyan's existence with their sporadically winking temptations and indifferent glances.

Saroyan is frequently an indirect presence in the text. Early in the book he argues that an awareness of death is a strong motivation to do something, to adopt a "program of work" which will "compel astonishment and admiration," to achieve, in short, fame or notoriety (2). Like many of his other assumptions, this idea applies most readily to his own case, but it comes to have wider implications. No man alive, Saroyan declares, is not "the darling of himself," so any attention is gratifying. But it is fame as a kind of measurement which goads his imagination—and the *Variety* list with its famous, once famous, and obscurely famous people affords him perfect raw material—to conduct an investigation of the value and uselessness of the self.

Sounding like Steinbeck's Jim Casy, Saroyan claims that part of the self, the ego, finds humanity simply a source of tension: "We are all one another, but we don't really like the idea—it offends us—each of us has a piece of natural procedure born into us which both permits and compels us to believe that we are unique, and so we don't like [the] notion that we are all one large (and should I say, should I dare to say, foolish) entity of some kind . . ." (75–76). One person's thought, for Saroyan, is thus everyone's thought—"anybody who says anything is each of us speaking, is he not?"— and each is merely a "precise tiny part of the immeasurable entirety of human life" (93, 103, 76). This assumption provides one basis for the arbitrary nature of social life and death where "anybody connects almost instantly with everybody," and "whoever we know . . . must seem to us, when put out . . . the very prop and support of our own presence in life, our own reality in sequence, our own known movement to the same end, with all of its indecisiveness, all of its indecorum, all of its absurdity, all of its almost totally silent and unnoticed meaninglessness" (92, 102). Saroyan envisions the discovery of the true self occurring amidst such connections in the sense that you can only make authentic choices in life "after you have come to see that you are more the other person than you are yourself, you are more the human race than one member of it, you are everybody from the beginning" (249).

To work with these ideas, Saroyan becomes a performer, a man of a myriad roles and moods. On a basic level he is a conventional essayist making observations about his subject, death. He begins almost reverently. "People die. It is a strange event, a strange order of event. . . . Nobody really knows what death is" (1). But as he conceives of death as an inclusive rather than an exclusive topic, he reaches for a more sincere informality: "Death is everything, man; death is not just a little part . . . it is the whole thing . . ." (9). In this memoir, death, as the "dead center of life," is the source for all meaning, and thus the writer is obliged to know death, be constantly aware of it, and even to love and cherish it (12, 13). It becomes a peculiar kind of certification for life. The obituaries Saroyan loves are, from this perspective, paradigmatic forms: "Death concludes every man's story and permits it to be summed up. Everybody who dies is instantly fascinating. He did it, she did it, they did it, by God and this is what happened on their way to the doing of it" (316). In this respect, death, with its finality, is paradoxically the necessary movement to a total significance.

Nevertheless, the irony of fame for the dead, implied throughout the *Variety* dead list, emphasizes the fact that the world Saroyan invokes is the past—the world a much younger Saroyan was so much a glamorous part of but which is now vanished, leaving as its only sign of vitality the agitated voice of the writer. More than any of the memoirs, *Obituaries* seems to evoke the last of Eric Erickson's eight stages of inner conflict—ego integrity versus despair. Here "the acceptance of one's one and only life cycle as something that had to be and that, by necessity, permitted no substitutions" is opposed by despair, "the feeling that the time is now . . . too short for the attempt to start another life. . . . [It is a state in which] Disgust hides despair."[10] In Saroyan's final memoir the struggle is a dialectic between life and death in which the writer runs through moods of self-abasement, self-aggrandizement, and self-justification.

Most often the narrative is an uninhibited outpouring of rage, frustration, reminiscence, resignation, and justification. In many respects Saroyan seems a casualty of the world he is trying to characterize, his tones are those of one who knows his achievements and abilities but wonders who else is aware of them, who in the course of his life has heard too many promises, been told of too many big deals. Various subjects are briefly blasted: supermarkets, the army, London hospitals, other writers, journalists, waste, the Academy Awards ceremony, university critics, Woodstock people, *Time*, and others. But his special hatred is for the entrepreneurs of culture: producers, agents, bankers, publishers. At times his anger comes and goes quickly: "Imagine a writer like William Faulkner needing to feel grateful to Random House for sending him a $250 advance against a new book. Good God Almighty, Bennett Cerf was a multimillionaire at the time, but forget it, forget it" (*Obituaries*, 332).

His mentioning of Jerry Giesler, the lawyer who handled divorce proceedings against him, ignites a long and vitriolic torrent of abuse: "The sons of bitches very nearly murdered me; why shouldn't I rejoice that death murdered them? . . . The bastards that do me, that seek to do me in, that plague my soul, that rob my purse as they say, that belittle my name, that very nearly drive me mad, I am proud to say I loathe, despise, hate and . . . am only reminded for a flash of profound gloating when I hear that death has done them in, the dirty little mothers" (36). His rage, almost a cry against life itself, reflects the pressures of twentieth-century public life. On the one hand he seeks to remind the world, and his audience, of its injustices, but perhaps more fundamentally, in his remarks about murder, he seems on the verge of saying that life has always been in complicity with death. Even his own mother is not immune from his critical ire. Speaking perhaps from his own unconscious sense of having failed as a parent, he accuses her of perverting her role, of approaching him not as an affectionate parent but as a potential lover.

Digging deep into the painful areas of his life, he presents not only his vulgarities, but episodes of humiliation such as the choking of his wife, his sexual frustration with Barbara Nichols and the apparent social disgrace that followed, his drunken boorishness at a party. In an extended episode that recounts his being cheated by his agents, he stresses that he is the one who refuses to read contracts, thus appearing as much the victim of himself as others.

Part of Saroyan wants to be the insider, even the cruel insider, rather than the innocent. At times his tone is deliberately heartless: "And so we come to another stiff of 1976" (150). He remarks with a show business knowingness: "Everybody wants to do good on a wholesale scale after he has played Las Vegas and made movies and talked on television and been to the White House to do five minutes and sometimes even been presented to the Queen—of England itself, and lived to be inoffensive about it" (116).

Since movement is the essential pattern of this work, his tone often abruptly alters as he goes through moods. Chapter 35 ends with his comments to Harry R. Burke, one of the dead he does not know: "I am willing to presume you did something in the general vicinity of entertainment. I hope you did it well, but I am sorry I doubt it. It isn't that you might not have done it excellently, it is just that really nobody does anything well, so why should you be the exception? But enjoy your death, you earned it, and earning takes time and doing. Enjoy the mud in your mouth." The next chapter opens: "How sad it is not to know the dead, for we shall soon enough join them, and then how shall we answer the questions of their eyes, or even of their mouths: what is it with you? what took you so long? how did it ever happen that you misunderstood everything so desperately?" (92).

Even as he indulges himself stylistically, Saroyan also seeks relief from the burdens of his ego. As the book progresses, he increasingly comes to create and respond to an imaginary reader. Early on, the technique seems a comic deployment of the old "dear reader" convention: "Reader, old pal, or dear lady, or gentleman in the penitentiary, or girl in the hospital . . . or anybody, and if it happens to be so, nobody: this is what I have to tell you . . ." (84). Eventually his sense of his audience is strong enough for him to create a short comic dialogue:

READER: You mean that's all you're going to say about Benjamin Britten?
WRITER: Yes, it is, and I'll tell you why, too. . . . (90)

As the technique illustrates, his sense of the reader did clarify his questions about why and how he was writing particular sections of his text. But at times the reader also represents doubts about his performance: "Christ Almighty, perhaps you are thinking, Christ Almighty when is this egomaniac going to stop telling me about how wonderful he is? Well, you have a right to be annoyed, if you are, and I have no excuse at all" (200–1).

Often he feels an identification with his reader, wondering whether the details of his experience might in some way match those of his reader. Toward the end of his book, when he decides that he is writing about "life, not death" (though really "about everything and anything and nothing"), he concludes by saying his text is about a writer and reader (347). The last sentences are addressed to the reader, claiming that his (the reader's) meaning is "fascinating"—though not as fascinating perhaps as that of the writer—and urging the reader to do his best as Saroyan has done in writing the book. Yet the most dramatic deployment of the reader is the totally unexpected cry from the heart that opens chapter 106. "Reader, take my advice, don't die, just don't die, that's all, it doesn't pay, people aren't that sincere, you know, they will pretend to be sorry but really they don't care, they think it is perfectly all right that you died, and it isn't so so don't do it, don't die, figure out how, and stay put . . ." (276). For all its comic impossibility, with which Saroyan's phrases play, there is a serious tone here as well, struck most strongly with the mention of the indifference of others. It is as if Saroyan, sensing in himself a forgotten writer, is still able to use his bond to the "reader" to defy the impossible circumstances confronting him and all human beings—death's omnipresence being the ultimate impossibility.

Like the other memoirs, *Obituaries* employs a familiar question and answer form—"Why am I writing this book? To save my life, to keep from dying . . ."—but the more obvious answer now is process itself, writing as the record of the movement of the writer's mind (132). He notes that both writer and reader need "movement, the cessation of which is in some respects not unlike several things that are painful to experience or even behold: a fall in ballet . . ., dropping dead . . . during a . . . speech . . . or leading the field . . . only to disappear into a deep pit that nobody had known was there" (80).

Thus Saroyan is petulantly explicit about refusing to correct his potential mistakes. Instead of changing the erroneous spelling of a name or a wrong first name, he goes on to present the right form later, as it occurs to him (if it does). He mistakes Lanny Ross for Dennis Day (the singer on the Jack Benny radio show), has John Garfield instead of William Holden in the movie *Golden Boy*, and invents an elaborate career as an actor for director Fritz Lang (310, 137, 245). Beyond illuminating his attitude toward facts, Saroyan seems here to enjoy being pugnaciously defensive about this part of his procedure: "if I've spelled it wrong, let no busy son of a bitch correct it"; "Why don't I just look it up? Because I don't look up. I am not a writer of popular history" (106, 70–71).

The offensive defensiveness about error signals a deeper level of uncertainty—about the writing of this particular book, about his other writing, and about his own life, himself. He tries to steel himself, "I am prepared to find out at the end of [this work] that I have been a fool again" (192). He cannot help sharing with the reader his worry that "no publisher is going to publish this book," that what he is doing just can't compete with what other writers are putting out (219, 253). His doubts expand into question after question: "Why don't I acknowledge to myself that I can't write, that

I am some kind of real weird zombie, a stupid egomaniac who can't write about anybody except himself and can't even do that effectively; an incompetent, a slambang and haphazard, gambling writer, a fool . . .?" (253).

Through it all, the momentum of writing itself becomes the way out, although it necessitates some peculiar turns. In chapter 132 he reacts against a belittling notice of his work—a note attacking its "spurious rapture"—with convincing agony: "it hurts," "it is no fun," and he goes on to claim that this is one reason writers kill themselves: "Dirty words . . . do murder writers" (345). Yet as he moves on, he reverses himself about denigrating criticism, declaring, "I am all for it." "If we can't take it," he asks, "who can?" (345). For a writer, he theorizes, there are two deaths, the critical and the physical one. At least he is still physically alive, but he notes, "It is a lucky thing for most dead writers that they probably can't be watching their terrible dying after they have died" (345). He ends the chapter with this bravado: "Rapture, yes. Spurious, yes. Great nevertheless, bet your ass" (346). Beyond a commentary on the amorality of criticism, this chapter might be regarded as the obituary of Saroyan the writer, as composed by himself.

Saroyan's greatest hope in the book is, perhaps oddly, to regard life as a celebration ("if we are honest in our hearts about it our whole lives . . . are celebrations") and the most simply honest statement in the book may be "I like being" (235, 324). But he has demonstrated convincingly his struggles with despair, discontent, and death. Ultimately, Saroyan's immersion in the world of vanished fame aims at a proof of survival. His improvisatory performance demonstrates that "Memory makes friends of enemies" (287). Here a cultural legend rejects that version of himself and tries to make peace with the world and himself. What the text conveys may be summed up in Saroyan's Armenian-American phrase, "This is how we do"—this is the artistry, the intensely competitive ambition, and the instinct for survival of a twentieth-century life.

To remain completely alive and completely Saroyan, such an existence must be opinionated but supple, both determined and lively, inclusive, and defensively tough:

> permit me furthermore to suggest that if it is your intention to remind me of all of the incredible writers in America alone, all of them well under forty years of age, and this old slob of a young writer already nearly come to four-score-and-ten—is this the slogan I want?—hell, no, but forget it: who's got time for the Gettysburg Address at a time like this?—here I am a year and a half from seventy, and just as stupid and cocky as ever. Reader, if you've got some writing of your own to do . . . drop this idle reading and go to that writing, and good luck to you, but I have got to pass along this dull message of fucking joy: you never know how unspeakably right being alive is until you have gone through a good piece of unspeakably wrong time hanging onto it, and fending off the opposite of it or death . . . (12).

Notes

1. *Not Dying* (New York: Harcourt, Brace & World, 1963), 3.

2. Lawrence Ross and Barry Gifford, *Saroyan: A Biography* (New York: Harper & Row, 1984), 179.

3. Aram Saroyan, *William Saroyan* (New York: Harcourt, Brace Jovanovich, 1983), 14.

4. David Stephen Calonne, *William Saroyan: My Real Work is Being* (Chapel Hill, N C: University of North Carolina Press, 1983), 145.

5. *Here Comes There Goes You Know Who* (New York: Simon & Schuster, 1961), 1.

6. *Obituaries* (Berkeley, C A: Creative Arts, 1979), 250.

7. *Days of Life and Death and Escape to the Moon* (New York: Dial, 1970), 101.

8. *Letters From 74 Rue Taitbout, or Don't Go But if You Must Say Hello to Everybody* (New York: World, 1969), 28.

9. *Chance Meetings* (New York: Norton, 1978), 124.

10. Erick H. Erickson, *Childhood and Society*, 2nd ed. (New York: Norton, 1963), 268, 269.

Index